NAMES FOR THINGS

⌐⌐ Bradford Books

Edward C. T. Walker, Editor. *Explorations in THE BIOLOGY OF LAN-GUAGE.* 1979. The M.I.T. Work Group in the Biology of Language: Noam Chomsky, Salvador Luria, *et alia.*

Daniel C. Dennett. *BRAINSTORMS: Philosophical Essays on Mind and Psychology.* 1979.

Charles E. Marks. *COMMISSUROTOMY, CONSCIOUSNESS AND UNITY OF MIND.* 1980.

John Haugeland, Editor. *MIND DESIGN.* 1981.

Fred I. Dretske. *KNOWLEDGE AND THE FLOW OF INFORMATION.* 1981.

Jerry A. Fodor. *REPRESENTATIONS: Philosophical Essays on the Founda-tions of Cognitive Science.* 1981.

Ned Block, Editor. *IMAGERY.* 1981.

Roger N. Shepard and Lynn A. Cooper. *MENTAL IMAGES AND THEIR TRANSFORMATIONS.* 1982.

Hubert L. Dreyfus, Editor in Collaboration with Harrison Hall. *HUSSERL, INTENTIONALITY AND COGNITIVE SCIENCE.* 1982.

John Macnamara. *NAMES FOR THINGS: A Study of Human Learning.* 1982.

Names for Things

A Study of Human Learning

John Macnamara

A Bradford Book

The MIT Press
Cambridge, Massachusetts
and London, England

Library of Congress Cataloging in Publication Data

*Macnamara, John Theodore.
    Names for things.*

    "A Bradford book."
    *1. Names—Psychological aspects.   2. Psycho-
linguistics.   3. Learning, Psychology of.
4. Onomasiology.   I. Title.*
BF455.M235   153.6   81-18583
ISBN 0-262-13169-2   AACR2

*Typographic design by David Horne
Composition by Horne Associates, Inc.,
Hanover, New Hampshire.
This book was printed and bound
in the United States of America.*

Dom mhac agus dom mhúinteoir
Ciarán

Preface

The learning of names for things is regarded as the simplest part of language learning or indeed of any human learning, yet here is a book about it with thirteen chapters. The truth is that whether or not name learning deserves its ranking, it is a surprisingly complicated matter. And much of the complexity has eluded the abundant literature on language learning. Complexity is as much a nuisance as gout, but sometimes just as real and inevitable. Like gout one avoids introducing it to the system, but confronted with it one has no reasonable alternative but to deal with it. So far psychologists have failed to deal with what strikes me as the very real complexities of name learning.

The aspects that seem most neglected may be surprising when just listed: reference, meaning, hierarchical relations among meanings, the grammatical category to which names belong (noun) and its subdivision, proper and common names. One can point to chapters in books or even whole books in psychology that purpose to deal with reference and meaning. Compare them, however, with the classical writings on the philosophy of language since the time of Gottlob Frege and one must be struck by the difference in depth of analysis. Now either the philosophers have been weaving futile webs (or trying to save us from futile ones) or psychologists have missed something important. After examining the issues I come down on the side of the philosophers, though webs are hardly conspicuous by their absence in the philosophical literature.

On the other hand when they speak of learning, the voice of logicians and philosophers sounds distant. That is pardonable granted the complexity of that which is learned. However, the time has come when we might reasonably hope to give an account of name learning that comes to grips with names as they really are and function. This might be the justification for another book on child language—the ambition to integrate the insights of the philosophy of language with the psychology of language learning, thus enriching psychology and, perhaps, providing a somewhat different perspective on the philosophical issues. The reason for qualifying the philosophical ambition is not merely modesty, but the presence of Wittgenstein in the wings. At any rate I entertain the hope that the logical analysis of names and empirical observations of how they are learned can be mutually improving.

There is surprisingly little literature on how the child learns which words go in which grammatical categories and subcategories. Thus an attempt to throw light on the matter needs no apology.

The book is subtitled *an essay on learning* partly because that is what it is, but partly to suggest that it has a broader relevance in psychology than the psychology of language alone. Its relevance to the theory of learning is obvious. In addition, reference is the contact language makes with the environment; it is the device that enables us to talk about the things we see and touch. Meaning is in some degree the sense we make of that environment; it is to some degree what we have to say about it. Thus the psychology of names relates directly to the conceptual system and to the perceptual one. That is pretty well the core of cognitive psychology.

In fact names relate to so many things that I have had to exclude several topics. I have limited the book to what seem the simplest issues; that is to names for things you could bump into.

After the introductory chapter come four that describe empirical observations aimed at exploring how a child copes with the fact that many different name-like words can be applied to a single object: e.g., *Harry* (the child himself), *you* (a pronoun), *boy* (specific) and *person* (generic).

The second major section of the book (Chapters 6-10) deals with topics that are broadly linguistic. I was guided in my choice not only by the fundamental nature of the topic, but also by whether or not I could find interesting empirical investigations in the area. Chapter 6, on phonology, was included to parry the conclusion, too readily reached by philosophers of quite diverse schools, that the age-old problem of how to categorize objects is solved for the child by the names he hears them called. Other chapters in the second section can be seen to fit in naturally: the learning of grammatical categories (Chapters 7 and 8), the definite and indefinite articles (Chapter 9), and the plural (Chapter 10).

Truth to tell, even in the linguistic section there is a greater emphasis on semantics than this description suggests. That gives the book a coherence that it might not at first seem to have, since the issues of reference and meaning run through all chapters. Those issues occupy the third section entirely. They have been so placed because they were the most difficult to write and will, I fear, be the most difficult to read. Because of the complexity of the issues, the unfamiliarity to many psychologists of the style of analysis, and the controversial nature of many of my conclusions, I placed them towards the end. The pusillanimous may leave them there and skip to Chapter 13. The daring (and the reckless) will, I hope, find them rewarding, even if they do not always agree. All who read them must recognize that I am not being complex, subtle, or obtuse out of wantonness. The complexities forced themselves on me, and would not go away.

The last chapter is a series of reflections on the implications of the book for developmental psychology. If the book is even vaguely right, there is something radically wrong with the current orthodoxies in child development.

The number of chapters is thirteen but that does not equal the number of years I have worked on them. It has been the most interesting project I have undertaken, and while it has at times been tantalizing, and even downright frustrating, it will, I hope, reveal the vitality and color of cognitive psychology broadly conceived. It brought me into continued contact with the most interesting thing there is, the mind of the growing child.

Several friends read the first draft and made valuable suggestions: Andy Baker, Susan Carey, Michael Corballis, Ray Jackendoff, Terri Nash, David Ostry, Eric Wanner, Rose-Marie Weber, and Steven and Judy Zucker. Sandra Trehub helped with the chapter on phonology, Jeremy Anglin with Chapter 4 on hierarchically related nouns, Janet Strayer with the chapter on personal pronouns, and Michael Maratsos with the one on the articles. Jeremy Walker and Anil Gupta worked through the issues in reference and meaning with me. Bill Blackburn helped with problems in reference.

Susan Carey and Steve Pinker read the all but final version and suggested many detailed improvements. My publisher, Harry Stanton, is responsible for the present arrangement of chapters.

Nancy Wargny, my student, and I worked for many years on the experimental work.

I owe a very great debt to Jerry Fodor. He read the entire second and third drafts, covering them with searing comments. The book in its present form is, to a great extent, an answer to those comments. Several of the examples, otherwise unacknowledged, are his.

Without these people, to whom I am deeply grateful, the book would either not be or would be quite different. They must, therefore, no matter their views, share the responsibility for it.

An earlier and less complete version of Chapter 2 appeared in *Child Development* by Katz, Baker, and Macnamara (1974). Parts of that version are reproduced here with kind permission of the journal and of the authors. The use of Strayer (1977) in Chapter 3 is by permission of the author. Parts of Chapter 5 are taken from Nancy Wargny's (1976) doctoral thesis, with her generous permission. A much earlier version of Chapters 7 and 8 appeared in Sankoff (1978). Chapter 11 was read as the annual Terry Anders address at Dalhousie University in 1979. And an earlier version of Chapter 12 will appear in a book that is being edited by Palermo and Weimer.

Contents

1.

Names

*So from the soil Yahweh God fashioned all the wild
beasts and all the birds of Heaven. These he brought
to the man to see what he would call them; each
one was to bear the name the man would give it. The
man gave names to all the cattle, all the birds of
heaven and all the wild beasts.*
   —Genesis 2:19–20

Though the author of Genesis was no philosopher of language, he
surely encouraged that breed of philosophers by the importance
he attached to names. Just how much importance can be seen if
we compare the above text to one that comes a little before it.
There are, in fact, two accounts of creation in Genesis, and the
two texts come from these different accounts. The first has God
say: "Let us make man in our own image, in the likeness of ourselves, and let them be masters of the fish of the sea, the birds of
heaven, the cattle, all the wild beasts and all the reptiles that crawl
upon the earth." The second account, cited above, does not explicitly say that man is made in the image of his Creator, for the
likeness is implicit in man's ability to name. And his very naming
of the animals marks his dominion over them.

  Genesis does not say what sorts of names Adam gave the animals,
but presumably they were specific names, like *dog, cow,* and *eagle.*
The creation story itself, however, makes use of generic names in
telling us what Adam did; it says that he named the "cattle," the
"birds," and the "wild beasts." In chapter three we find the last
explicit reference to Adam's naming: "he named his wife 'Eve'."
In our attempts to describe children's name learning we shall be

very much concerned with these three sorts of names: proper names, like *Eve,* specific names, like *eagle,* and generic ones, like *bird.* Of course there are many species of eagle of which *eagle* is the generic name. We shall not be much concerned with the niceties of taxonomy, however—anymore than were the young children whose vocabularies we shall be studying. To describe these vocabularies we shall need to talk about three types of names, and I believe that the use of the terms *proper, specific,* and *generic* will cause the reader little inconvenience.

There is a difficulty about what to call these three sorts of words. The Jerusalem translation of the Bible calls them all *names;* though some writers would reserve that word for proper names, like *Eve.* I prefer to avoid *noun,* because nouns are specified with regard to the syntactic structure of a sentence. To call a word a noun suggests the role it plays in grammar, and since young children do not speak in anything recognizable as sentences, I will at this stage sidestep the issue of what parts of speech their words belong to. To call them simply *words* would be too imprecise. Logicians use *term;* but while this has the attraction of established usage, it has the disadvantage of being at once too technical and too comprehensive. *Term* is too technical in that it embraces purely logical expressions, such as general symbols for functions and variables; it is too comprehensive in that it embraces such complex structures as *father of Mary.* Besides, *term* seems to lack some of the force that *name* has of denoting objects, or drawing attention to and designating them. For this reason I will press *name* into extended service. There is nothing in principle against doing so, though we should note that frequently common nouns are not used as names. In *Mary is a girl, girl* does not name anything, whereas *Mary* names Mary. The point will come up again; for the moment just accept that common nouns are not always names: proper names always are. By way of comfort for the uneasy, my decision to call proper and common nouns by the single word *name* has the backing of Plato in *The Sophist;* of Aristotle in the *De interpretatione,* though he later changed his views; and of such redoubtable modern logicians as Geach (1962, 1972) and Kripke (1972).

Technical details aside, however, what are we to make of the Bible's reverence for naming? Is it merely a residue of primitive awe at the first attempts at systematic classification? Whatever the risk of being thought primitive, those of us who have spent years in studying how children learn names are more inclined than most to take the texts at face value. In order to name things intelligently the child must know a lot about them, and in addition he must know their names. The power of so naming presupposes the power of distinguishing among objects, recognizing them when encountered again, and assigning them to their classes. To call something a *dog*, with normal understanding, is to claim true of it those characteristics that mark it a dog. How anyone learns to do that has puzzled men from Plato to our own day. In addition, being able, intelligently, to call a creature a *doggie* often implies in some measure the ability to deal with it. The child who knows what dogs are knows that they bark, run, eat, and sometimes bite. He knows what to expect of them. Similarly, when he knows what chairs are, he knows that they do none of the things a dog does, but you can usually sit on one without fear that it will collapse.

Imagine how you would feel if you were sick and went to see the doctor, and the doctor was unable to say what was wrong with you. In Ireland sick people sometimes bewail the doctor's inability "to put a name" on their complaint. It is most disturbing; it signifies to the patient that the doctor has failed to make sense of his symptoms and, consequently, does not know how to treat him. The patient is obviously justified in regarding disease naming as something far beyond linguistic expertise.

Ideal Science of Name Learning

Before embarking on the search for a theory of name learning, it is wise to ask what a good one would be like if we found it. Obviously it should have three major components. It should state what names are and how they function in the language that is being learned; it should specify those properties of mind that are relevant to name learning, those that enable a child to learn names; and it should explain how a child with the specified properties learns names. Let us look briefly at each component, for in doing so we not only shall have a preliminary look at the problems, but also shall outline the scope of the book. Since it is a preliminary look, however, the language will be less precise than it needs to be later.

A. NAMES

The sorts of names we have discussed are distinguished by their semantic functions. Proper names are the paradigm examples of words that refer. They reach out, as it were, to objects and designate them for comment. It is less clear that common nouns also refer, though an interesting case can be made that they do. What common nouns certainly do is describe. If I say *Tom is a cat, Tom* refers to a particular creature; *cat* describes him. Descriptions can be either true or false of the object to which they are ascribed.

Do proper names also describe? At first they might appear only to refer, not to describe. Yet if a proper name is to be applied on different occasions and if it is to perform its task of referring, a single proper name must refer to the same object on all occasions on which it is used. (For the moment forget that there can be several men called John Smith.) What is needed to ensure such constancy? To forestall later discussion, it seems that the name must be associated with a principle of identity, and that is best supplied by some such common noun as *cat. Tom* will continue to perform its function properly if it continually picks out *the same cat.* It seems, then, that proper names tacitly involve certain sorts of common nouns and, thus, certain sorts of descriptions.

If this is right, common and proper nouns can refer and describe. Nevertheless the two sorts of word are semantically distinct. We shall have to explore how they differ.

Specific and generic nouns also differ, mainly in the range of objects to which they can be suitably applied. While all roses are flowers, not all flowers are roses. At the same time a single object can be a flower and a rose. The child has to cope with all this. The family pet may be called *Spot, the dog,* and *the animal.* What sense is the child to make of this proliferation of names used of a single creature? What are the implications for theories of reference and meaning that all three types of word can be employed of a single creature?

Personal pronouns are another sort of word which can be used to refer. Their reference is not so stable as that of proper names. Whom they refer to depends on the speaker, the person being addressed, and what the speaker is talking about on a particular occasion. There can be little doubt that the pronouns refer, and a good case can be made that they also bear meaning. The child must master all this, while distinguishing the semantic force of pronouns from that of proper names and from that of common names.

All the foregoing comes, broadly, under the rubric of semantics. There are also linguistic aspects of name learning. Each name consists in speech sounds. Each language has its own set of speech sounds. The child, if he is to perceive names correctly, must learn to identify patterns of such sounds, and learn, too, what modifications of sounds the language permits. In addition, he must learn to articulate those sounds in recognizable form.

Names belong in grammatical categories, as do all the words of the language. Grammatical categories vary from language to language. The child must learn what ones his language employs and which words belong in which categories. This is a great problem that has not received a fair share of attention in the literature on child language, and in particular in the literature on name learning. Yet the learning of grammatical categories is the fundamental issue in the learning of syntax; since syntactic rules are defined over the grammatical categories.

A subset of common names have plural as well as singular forms. The same subset can also take *a* as well as *the*. This grammatical variation is accompanied for the most part by semantic variation that is not too complicated. Since the grammatical variation may provide the child with useful clues to the subcategories of names, I have included chapters on number and the definite article. I admit, however, that the decision to include those topics and exclude others is to a great extent arbitrary. My choice was to some extent motivated by the availability of interesting empirical work.

B. RELEVANT PROPERTIES OF MIND

What does the child bring to the task of name learning that is useful? That obviously depends on what names are and how they function. The foregoing remarks do not really answer those questions; they merely reveal the scope of the question. Before we can be at all specific about what the child brings to the task, we need fairly explicit theories of reference and of how the language does the work of referring. We also need a fairly explicit theory of meaning for names. In addition we need a theory of phonology and theories of the other grammatical aspects of names that we choose to tackle.

The grammatical aspects of names and their functioning will cause us fewer problems than the semantic ones. Nevertheless we cannot expect more than a sketch of what each involves and of what the child brings to the learning of each. This book will serve its purpose if it provides a sketch that has some chance of being right. Further progress must wait upon theoretical advances and on empirical observation.

The same can be said of the semantic aspects, but here the position is worse. There is little problem in picking out the nouns in an English sentence; there is little in specifying which sounds contrast with which at the phonological level for a particular dialect of English. There is great difficulty in deciding which words refer. And there is enormous difficulty in specifying what reference and meaning are. Still nothing is to be gained by fighting shy of the difficult problems. What I have done is proposed the very best theories of reference and meaning that I could, fully aware how uncertain the ground is on which they are constructed. In connection with each I propose a psychology indicating what the child would need to bring to the task of learning, if the theory of reference is correct. If anyone can improve on the theories, he will, in doing so, have means for improving the psychology. Equally, if anyone can improve on the psychology, he will have means for improving the semantic theories. For there must be a match between the two.

Because of the complexity of the issues, the unfamiliarity to many psychologists of some of the analysis and the controversial nature of the conclusions, I have placed the theoretical chapters on reference and meaning towards the end of the book, as chapters 11 and 12. While some of the issues in the earlier chapters have not been so closely discussed in the psychological literature before, the type of evidence and argument will be familiar to psychologists.

C. LEARNING

How does the child learn names? A satisfactory answer presupposes answers to the questions raised in sections *a* and *b*. For the question is, how does a child as described in *b* learn names as described in *a*?

So sketchy have our answers been that there is little to gain at this point from a direct attack on learning. Let us adopt an indirect one. Some psychologists may consider that psychological learning theory, in principle, provides an answer. It is not, however, the answer given in this book. Indeed there is scarcely any discussion of that theory elsewhere in the book, and courtesy demands an explanation. Besides, in looking at learning theoretic approaches, we will deepen our understanding of the issues already raised.

First, some remarks about animals and language. It does not help our understanding of children to be told that a dog can learn simple commands, such as *bring the ball*. It could be that he senses the master's intention or, as conditioning theory would have it, that he has a gratifying series of associations between hearing the sound, bringing the ball, the master's throwing it, and the excitement of the chase. Unfortunately we do not know what the command conveys to the dog; and naturally all attempts to explain how the dog interprets depend on what his interpretation is. The same is true of the remarkable work done by Gardner and Gardner (1971), Premack (1976), and others in teaching chimpanzees various sign languages. If chimpanzees can learn names for things, they pose us the same problem as children. How do any of them do it?

The most common approaches to the meaning of a word in psychology come one way or another under the heading of associations. Associations are a theoretical construct of great simplicity: an association is a relation between two psychological events, A and B, such that when an event of type A occurs, an event of type B tends to occur also. A and B can be a sensation and a memory, e.g., A can be the sensation of a knife and B the memory of a fork. More to the point, A can be the auditory sensation of a name and B the visual perception of an object, e.g., the name *knife* and the object, knife, respectively. There surely is something of value in this approach, because if children did not simultaneously experience objects and their names, they could hardly learn their mother tongue.

Associations between auditory and visual events were B. F. Skinner's (1957) main theoretical device to explain the learning of names. The word *association* does not figure prominently in Skinner's book, but since his treatment depends crucially on a reinforced connection between visual stimuli and a verbal operant (response), the connection is an association. One problem for the approach is to explain how the child sets up the appropriate equivalence classes. That is, how does he know that several different sounds are all tokens of, say, the word *dog*? The differences among the tokens are likely to be every bit as marked as those between the objects that are called dogs. Chapter six below deals with the variations in sound. The other arm of the same problem is how does he know which objects are appropriately called *dog*? That is the problem which Plato spent his whole life pondering (see White, 1976), and there is as yet no solution. It follows that difficulty in solving it does not distinguish Skinner's theory from any other. Notice that in Skinner's account *meaning* plays no part outside of an association. Perhaps it is best to regard his work as strictly a theory of how the child learns something, rather than a theory of what he learns. Even

then he has a problem accounting for how the child learns names
for imaginary creatures like Hobbits and leprechauns, such abstract
entities as the number seven, and indeed such theoretical constructs
as electricity and heat.

Traditional accounts of language make great play with the word
meaning and it was surely the absence of the word in other accounts
that prompted Osgood (1953, pp. 695 ff.) to propose an associationist theory that allowed for "mediating processes" between
words and overt responses. Together with him can be placed philosophers like Morris (1946) and Stevenson (1944) who saw meaning as a "disposition to respond."

The basic idea in these approaches is that what a person learns is
an association between a word and a response. However, words do
not always elicit observable responses, so an observable response is
frequently replaced by an internal, unobservable one. A child, for
example, may feel some excitement at seeing a dog and attempt to
grab him. In the course of time he may associate just the excitement with the word *dog*. The excitement, then, is the meaning
even if no further reponse ensues. That is Osgood's theory, and it
is close enough to a response disposition to be coupled with it.

The attraction of the position is its ability to explain the fact
that words often have an emotional feel to them. *Christmas* may
still evoke a warm familial glow in some breasts, in others a feeling
of exhaustion and snappy humor. Associations seem admirably
suited to handle such phenomena. However, Osgood's theory has
the same problems as Skinner's in explaining how the learner sets
up the equivalences across variations in speech sound on the one
hand and objects on the other. It also has problems explaining
how a word like *triangle* can have a meaning, even if we experience no feeling or disposition to respond in connection with it.
Finally, *Christmas* does not mean any such thing as warm familial
glow; it means a certain Christian feast, even for persons who are
not Christians.

There is very little chance of either of these theories being an
adequate foundation on which to construct a theory of meaning.
We may ask, however, if associationism is a viable approach to
reference. The answer is no, for two principle reasons. It does not
give an adequate explanation of the principle of identity, the
principle that attaches a name to the same object over time and
over local movement. The associations envisaged are between
perceptual experience and a name. It would be natural for associ-
ationists to appeal to memory and recognition as the foundation

for the principle. But while memory and recognition play a part in the application of the principle, they are not the heart of the matter. For my friend, John Smith, is the same person, even if the ravages of time since I last saw him prevent me from recognizing him. It is the identity that stands when all prods to memory and recognition fail that escapes the associationist.

The second inadequacy of associationism is its assumption that the essence of a proper name is its one-to-one relation with an object. If that were right, there should be no distinguishing a proper name from any other expression that is used exclusively of one individual. Now, often when I meet my son I say, *Hello, handsome!* (which must be short for some such expressions as *Hello! You handsome boy*) and, as far as I am aware, I say it to no one else. Yet it is not his name. It follows that a one-to-one relation between an expression and an individual is not all there is to reference. I am not sure that this is an inescapable argument against all possible associationist approaches to reference, but it is certainly an inauspicious start, and I prefer to look elsewhere for a satisfactory theory.

Associationism meets great difficulties in attempting to deal with names as nouns. As far as I know, no such attempt has been made since the early 1960s. The reason is that nouns are not marked as such in the sensory array. There is, then, nothing that an associationist would recognize in a child's experience that might become associated with a proper name to mark it a noun. This looks like an insuperable difficulty.

More recent work on child language does not use the word *association,* but the general notion of an associative link is, I believe, implicit in the theories. These links are no longer between words and objects or between words and covert responses, but between words and semantic markers (sometimes called "semantic features") and also among the semantic markers themselves.

Eve Clark (1973, 1974, 1977) argues that associated with each common name like *dog* is a set of semantic markers. These constitute the word's meaning. In addition, those that have been abstracted from the sensory array serve as "conditions of application" (Clark, 1977, p. 151) for the word: i.e., they serve in sensory tests of category membership. For example, the markers that go with *dog* might include fourleggedness, a certain posture, a head of a certain shape, and so forth. It is possible, in the psychological tradition, to see the relation between such markers and objects as an association. Hearing the word elicits the markers. And it is possible to see the relations among the markers as associations. They are associated because they have been experienced together.

Katherine Nelson (1974, 1977) constructs a theory in which sensory attributes seem to play a less central role. She denies that initially children analyze objects into sensory components that serve to classify the objects. Instead, they treat objects as wholes and classify them by the functions they serve. However, the contrast with Clark's theory is less than one might imagine. Nelson believes that subsequently children do establish semantic markers that have been abstracted from the sensory array. And Clark does allow semantic features that are based on functions and characteristic activities. The difference between the two theories, then, is mainly one of emphasis.

An important question about a semantic feature that represents a function is, how does the mind form it? Does it abstract the function feature itself on the basis of sensory attributes of an action? If the answer is affirmative, the theory is empiricist; if it is negative, the theory is not.

Vygotsky (1962) has a theory that can be taken as a variant of those just discussed. The essential modification is slight because he retains all the central concepts that we have seen. He relaxes the rule that an object must show some definite set of features or functions in order to fall under the concept. It is enough to pass some subset of tests or even just one of them.

An even more interesting modification in the same spirit is proposed by Bowerman (1978a). Besides sensory features and functions, she claims that similarities in "subjective experience" can sometimes be the basis for using certain words. She instances the use of *heavy* by her two children, for whom the clue seemed to be "physical effort expended on an object." However, like Vygotsky she claimed that certain words were used of objects that satisfied only some subset of the feature tests. In Bowerman (1978b) she gives this example taken from her daughter Eva's speech over the period of 15 to 23 months of age. Eva first learned the name for the moon; then she went on to call by the same name a half grapefruit, a lemon section, the circular chrome dial on the dishwasher, a shiny leaf, a ball of spinach, a crescent-shaped piece of paper, a hangnail, and so on. A truly remarkable list, but by no means unique! It is a matter for surmise whether Eva thought all those objects were moons, so that *moon* could be used of them in the same sense, or whether she used the word metaphorically of them all except the "real" moon. Just for the record, my son, Kieran, at that age frequently used the words *like a*. For example he sometimes described the wheeling searchlights on top of Montreal's Place Ville Marie as "like a helicopter." This strengthens the feeling that many such expressions as those of Eva Bowerman are really metaphorical.

Eva's use of *moon* is a good example of what Bowerman (1978b) calls the organization of a word meaning around a basic object or prototype. She is appealing to the work of Eleanor Rosch (1977) and her associates, who have studied "typicality" in adults. The idea is that adults can easily and consistently rank a set of objects for typicality under some descriptor. Take *bird:* they agree that a robin is a more typical bird than a chicken, and a chicken more typical than a penguin. Rosch argues that in learning the meaning of many words, we establish a basic object for the category which we represent either in the form of an image or of a sensory feature list. This works, Rosch claims, only for categories of which people can easily form images, like robin and bird; it does not work for animal. It is easy to see how Eva Bowerman's use of *moon* can be interpreted in that framework. Some of the objects she called *moon* were shiny like the moon, others were shaped like the moon in one of its phases.

In all varieties of semantic-feature theories there is a strong link between features and tests for category membership. The feeling is strong that meaning provides the means for recognizing members of a category. This aspect of the theories puts one in mind of the early days of logical positivism when Carnap (1932) could write: "the meaning of a word is determined by its criterion of application"; and again (Carnap, 1933): "a sentence says no more than is testable about it." Since those days, logical positivism has faded into philosophy. The reason is a growing doubt that meaning, or any part of it, is abstracted from the sensory array. If it isn't, then meaning does not constitute our means for recognizing category members. The issue is discussed at length in Chapter 12, below, but in the meantime here is an illustration of how doubt invades the logical positivist position.

Imagine a child rummaging through the drawers of a sideboard. In it he might find glasses, decanters, cutlery, place mats, and chopsticks. Let us suppose that he has never seen chopsticks before and doesn't know what they are. He asks his mother what they are and she answers "chopsticks." He now knows their name, and he can distinguish them reliably from everything else, but he does not know what they are for. He might think, perhaps, that they were for use in some game. On the assumption that what chopsticks are for is the principle key to the meaning of the word *chopstick*, we now have it that the child can recognize chopsticks without knowing the meaning of the word. If this is right, one sees how meaning and recognizing category members might be distinct.

Of course, reputable philosophers, Goodman (1951) among them, have argued against the whole notion of meaning. They claim that no useful account of meaning is possible. They fear that talk of meaning will snare us into a belief in strange entities, the most dreaded among them being universals. Why not be content, they ask, with real dogs and sensory tests for them? Why leave the door open to such vague intentional entities as concepts that are constructs of mind or, worse still, to Platonic ideas that exist independent of minds and of physical objects? Meaning is the wedge that keeps the door open.

If we could throw out meaning, as Goodman does, we would simplify psychology. We would not have to explain how it is learned and how it functions. If we keep it, as I believe we must, our psychology becomes complicated. The most we can hope for is to eliminate some initially attractive but unsound theories and through sketching conditions on a satisfactory theory obtain an idea of what a satisfactory theory would be like. Even that is going to be a demanding task and will lead us to explore the network of relationships between words, meanings, concepts, truth value, and sensory tests for category membership.

Psychology of Cognitive Development

Since we shall be studying what the child masters in learning names for things, and since we shall be attempting to specify what he brings to the task, it will be impossible to resist the temptation to speculate about the nature of cognitive development. The crucial question is whether the structure and logic of the child's mind develops as he acquires information about the world and about language.

By "mental structure" I mean the formal systems that the mind employs. The list would include a propositional calculus, a calculus of classes, a basic number system, and a system for finding out causal explanations of phenomena, together with specifications of what will serve as an explanation. (More precisely, I mean the mental representations of those systems, but for the present ignore such niceties.) A bold claim that all the mental structures available to an educated adult are innate is simply false. The adult may know calculus, which is a mental system for handling data, whereas a child almost certainly does not. The interesting form of the question just posed is whether the child has, innately, a sufficiently rich number system from which to deduce the theorems of calculus.

Jean Piaget and his followers believe that all mental structures are the result of mental development (see Macnamara, 1976). The doctrine, that there is no such development, has on its side the null hypothesis of most work in developmental psychology.

That hypothesis is precisely that there is no development of mental structure. It is easy to refute the corresponding hypothesis in developmental anatomy. At one stage the embryo has no hands and later it has. It is easy to refute a similar hypothesis in the domain of information. The adult knows things the child does not. To refute the null hypothesis about mental structure in the sense just indicated is far from simple, and so far as I know has never been done. If that is right, sound thinking bids us stand by it.

The more interesting aspect of the problem for us will be to study the extent of the mental structure that the child must have if he is to learn names for things. We will not obtain a definitive answer to the question of mental development, but we will learn that the child must have rather more mental structure than Piagetians suppose. Chapter 13 is largely devoted to reflections on the issue.

PART I

MATTERS MAINLY PSYCHOLOGICAL

2.
Individuals
(Proper/Common Names)

"Mr. Alacaddaka's long strange name
Always filled his heart with shame."
—*Walter De La Mare*

Most linguistic universals are proposed tongue in cheek, the proposer ready to flee; but there is one that can be made with one's head in the air. In every language there are words that are used to refer to individuals primarily as individuals: *Tom, Dick,* and *Harry.* Of course there is more than one Tom, but in any discourse in which Tom is used the speaker is referring to an individual as individual and he expects his listeners to know who. There are all sorts of other ways of referring to individuals. "The man in the iron mask" refers to a famous individual whose identity is not known. "The author of Waverly" refers to an individual whose identity was for a time unknown, but in the end turned out to be Sir Walter Scott. Neither "the man in the iron mask" nor "the author of Waverly," however, is a proper name, like *Walter Scott.* Sometimes one refers to a person whose identity is known to the company by a descriptive phrase. It is even related that when Scott's Edinburgh friends had discovered that he was the author of Waverly, they agreed not to bring it out in the open, and in his presence they would toast "the author of Waverly." That is probably how certain proper names began, as descriptions that were accepted as unique. So the Irish name Sullivan once meant "the one-eyed."

Then the name crystallized and became a new lexical item, a proper name.

The linguistic universal we are considering is really quite a limited one. In English, proper names are usually not preceded by the article (*a* or *the*) or by any quantifier, such as *one, two,* or *some.* Other modifiers are permitted as distinguishers: *Red Hugh, Little John.* Proper names in the plural always leave something to be understood. *We have two Marys in our family* means we have two women who are called Mary. Common count nouns on the other hand freely take the article, quantifiers and the plural: *a book, the book, some books.* In Irish things are slightly different because there is a definite article *(an)* but no indefinite one. In classical Latin things are still more different, because there is neither a definite nor an indefinite article. The rules for quantifiers and plural do distinguish between common and proper nouns.

As always in linguistics, the regularities are elusive. Gleason (1965, p. 134) points out that we find both *Connecticut* and *The Connecticut,* one referring to a state, the other to a river. We also have *Hartford,* a city, and *The Hartford,* an insurance company. There are linguistic complications connected with the distinction between the use of words as count nouns and mass nouns. The article *a,* quantifiers, and plurals are not permitted when a word is used as a mass noun: e.g. *milk, porridge, gravel.* When the words are used as count nouns—that is, when reference is made to a characteristic form—those restrictions are relaxed. Thus, linguistically, mass nouns resemble proper nouns. For all that, we need to distinguish semantically between proper nouns and all other sorts of nouns, and there are certain linguistic rules, leaky no doubt, that accompany the semantic difference.

In this chapter we will study mainly proper nouns in their semantic function and ask how children learn that certain words are proper nouns. How do they find out that *Freddie* refers to a particular pet and not to other canines? Freddie can also be called *dog,* but so can the neighbor's pet. We will study how the child coordinates the cognitive and the linguistic in this connection. The case I wish to make will depend largely on some empirical data that were collected by Nancy Wargny (1976) and myself.

A First Experiment [1]

Only those objects that are particularly important to us as individuals receive proper names, whereas all objects that we talk about are called by common names. Objects then fall into two classes from this point of view: special ones that are referred to by proper names (though when appropriate they can also be referred to by common names) and objects that are referred to only by common names. The specialness of individuals in the first class endures for long periods of time. Objects in the second class can often be special for a short time. It may be very important to a child which is his plate or his spoon, but at the next meal he may not have the same ones. Plates and spoons do not receive a proper name. Of course there are things like his shoes that remain his for a long time, and yet do not receive proper names. It seems that in the child's world the objects that have proper names are all living or surrogates for living objects, like dolls and Yogi the bear. Adults sometimes call their cars and boats by proper names, and they call houses, streets, and towns by proper names, too. But young children seem to have little notion what is meant by a town or a street (see Piaget, 1964), and they do not often refer to their home or the family car by a proper name.

This line of thought gave us an idea for an experiment. We decided to introduce pairs of objects to children and refer to only one of them by a name. Some of the children heard a proper name, some a common name. Some children were shown a pair of dolls, some a pair of blocks. After the objects had been introduced, the child was asked for the named one; we wanted to see whether he gave the named one or seemed equally disposed to give either. This enabled us to examine the effect of varying objects (dolls and blocks) and that of varying syntax (proper or common name). The results of the experiment are most unexpected, and the matter is of central importance to our general theme, so I will report the experimental work in detail.

Materials and Procedure

The tests were carried out with a pair of small plastic dolls and a pair of plastic blocks. The dolls differed only in hair color, one being blonde and the other brunette. The two dolls wore dresses of the same color, shape, and material and, hair color apart, were identical in appearance. One block was red and one yellow, but they were the same in shape, size, and texture. To make them more comparable to the dolls in perceptual complexity, around each block was tied a green and purple ribbon.

Dolls were chosen because they represent people, and we hoped that the children would treat them as surrogates for people. In ways it would have been better if we could have had two real people. However, if a tester and two other people invaded a home, they would probably bewilder a child, and possibly his mother, too. Moreover, in the course of testing we asked the child to do certain things with the objects. It would have been very difficult for them to do anything appropriate with a person. Taking one thing with another, we believed that dolls were better, and certainly less expensive. We expected that the children would be disposed to accept a proper name for a doll more than for a block.

Each child was tested in only one condition, with either dolls or blocks. In the test one of the objects was named with a nonsense syllable; the other object was not named. The nonsense syllable was to make sure that the name was new to all the children. For half the children the name was syntactically marked as a common name; for the other half it was marked as a proper name. For example, the first words to a child who was tested in the common-noun condition were: *Look what I've brought you. This is a Zav.* In subsequent conversation the named object was called *the Zav.* In the proper-noun condition the article was omitted—in the example the named object was simply called *Zav* throughout.

There were four conditions: dolls with common nouns, dolls with proper nouns, blocks with common nouns, and blocks with proper nouns. The particular doll or block named was counterbalanced across children, to make sure that there was nothing especially attractive about the named object. The following nonsense syllables were used, more or less randomly: *zav, mef, roz, kiv, pex, jop. wug, zon, tiv, vit, neg, cak.* Each syllable was employed an equal number of times with blocks and dolls. Any particular child, of course, learned only one nonsense syllable.

Each of the pair of objects was drawn to a child's attention at least five times. During this learning period the named object was always called by its name. The other object was called "the other one" or "this one." Then testing began. Both objects were placed on the floor within equal reach of the child and he was asked to perform some action with the named one. If the objects were blocks, he was asked to take the named block, to give it to the tester, to show it to his mother, to put it on a pencil, to put it in a house, and the like. The important datum was whether the child performed the operation on the named object. Whether he did or not, questions were repeated several times, but in various sequences. Since flexibility is important in dealing with a child, a tightly fixed schedule of testing was not followed. The session was terminated when the child indicated lack of interest or weariness, but nearly every child was tested at least seven times and some were tested ten, twelve, or even fifteen times. Since the main interest was the proportion of times a child chose the named object, care was taken neither to lead him to choose it nor to avoid it. The named object was not placed nearer. When instructing the child, the tester (Mrs. Erica Baker) looked at neither object. She did not signal that she was more pleased with one choice than another.

The children: Thirty girls whose average age was just under 22 months and 25 boys whose average age was just over 24 months were tested. They all came from middle-class English-speaking homes in the west end of the Island of Montreal. Each was tested at home. Each mother was asked whether she had taught her child names for dolls. Only eight said yes, and they were randomly distributed over the various conditions. It is unlikely, then, that the results have been affected by training in giving names to dolls and not blocks.

Results: Tables 2.1 and 2.2 show the mean results for girls and boys respectively. The data from which means were computed were the percentage of "correct" responses for individual children. If the children chose one of the pair at random, they would choose the named one 50 percent of the time. Thus with one exception the response pattern in each condition of the two tables is roughly a random one.

Table 2.1   Mean Percentage of Correct Responses Given by Girls in Experiment 1

	Common Noun	N	Proper Noun	N
Dolls	48 (.10)	10	75 (.13)	10
Blocks	44 (.17)	5	48 (.14)	5

Note—Standard deviations in parentheses.

However, girls who were tested with dolls tended to choose the named doll provided it was called by a proper name. To explore the finding further, a one-way analysis of variance was carried out on the data in each table. The reason for a one-way analysis was that we wished to see if one cell for girls differed significantly from the other three. The more usual two-way analysis would treat the effect observed in that cell as partly the effect of Object, partly of Syntax, and partly as interaction. So one-way analysis seemed more appropriate. The effect proved highly significant, $F (3.26) = 44.57$, $p < .01$.

Table 2.2   Mean Percentage of Correct Responses Given by Boys in Experiment 1

	Common Noun	N	Proper Noun	N
Dolls	47 (.14)	5	51 (.22)	10
Blocks	42 (.15)	5	55 (.13)	5

Note—Standard deviations in parentheses.

On the other hand, boys showed no significant departures from random responding: F (3.21) = 0.71, $p > .05$. These results for boys led us to suspect that the trouble was the dolls. Boys are seldom given dolls or encouraged to play with them. The dolls we used were female figures. Nor did it seem simply that the boys made progress more slowly than the girls. In a pilot study 12 boys whose average age was 28 months (4 months older than those in the main experiment) were tested with a pair of dolls in the manner just described. They chose the named doll only 60 percent of the time, though it was given a proper name. This is somewhat better than 50 percent. But it is still not as good as the girls, and it would be odd if boys lagged behind girls by more than four months at the age of two years. So to investigate this finding further, we carried out other experiments, which are reported below.

We were not surprised by the girls' responses in the proper-name condition for dolls. In a pilot study which involved only that condition, we tested 16 girls whose average age was 29 months. They chose the named doll 76 percent of the time. We feel, then, fairly confident of the significant result in the main experiment. It seems to arise from the fact that little girls see dolls as surrogates for people; and just as people need proper names, so do dolls.

What was surprising was that the presence or absence of the article should have made a difference to girls (*Zav* or *a Zav*). We had not anticipated that. Indeed we varied the presence or absence of the article only because of a certain scruple built into psychologists to vary possible factors systematically. This time it paid off. Note that the girls' responses varied only with the change from common to proper name when the objects were dolls, not blocks. Already by 22 months of age girls were beginning to take account of the fact that some objects are treated both as individuals and as members of a class. We carried out a second experiment with girls to examine the steps by which they had arrived at where our first experiment found them.

Second Experiment with Girls

Pilot study: Our thinking at this stage continued to be guided by the view that girls had used their knowledge of objects in the environment to discover the semantic force of the presence or absence of the article before a noun. We believed that we could find a stage where a name for a doll would be treated as a proper name irrespective of the article. For this purpose we selected five girls whose mean age was 15 months and five whose mean age was 18 months. They were similar in all other respects to the children tested in the first experiment, and the same method was employed. However, because the work was merely exploratory, we confined ourselves to working with dolls to which a proper name was given. The intention was, if successful, to fill in the other conditions of the design employed in the first experiment.

The results were disappointing. The 15-month-old girls chose the named object only 43 percent of the time, while the 18-month-olds did so 59 percent of the time. This meant that the older of the two groups was merely intermediate between the younger group and the still older group of the earlier experiment. It did not seem likely that much was to be gained with these materials by reducing age.

In passing, note that 18-month-old girls performed at the same level as 27-month-old boys. If we wished to argue that boys were merely retarded relative to girls this would give us an indication of how much. It would suggest that boys of 27 months are 9 months later than girls in learning proper names. We know from several studies (see McCarthy, 1954) that boys tend to develop a little slower, but all that we know should make us suspicious of so large a delay. And indeed we do explore other explanations below.

After our disappointment with the pilot study, a new idea struck us. What if we increased the perceptual distinctiveness of the visual stimuli and again tested to see if the younger girls would accept a name for a doll as a proper name whether or not it was preceded by the article?

Procedure and materials in second experiment. We used the same dolls as previously, but we put new dresses of different colors on them. The dolls now differed in color of dress and in hair color, but were otherwise similar. We chose blocks which differed in shape as well as color. The procedure was the same as that of the first experiment. All the same precautions were taken to avoid leading the children to give spurious responses. Twenty-five girls similar to those of the first experiment were tested in their homes. Of these, 10 were of average age 17 months and 15 were of average age 22 months. The younger girls were tested with dolls only, five girls in each linguistic condition (with or without the article before the name). Ten of the older girls were also tested with dolls, five of them in each linguistic condition. The remaining five older girls were tested with blocks, one of which was given a proper name. It is quite a problem to locate young girls of a given age and visit them in their homes, so we made what economies we could in the design of the experiment. The design just described is "incomplete" but it reveals the main effects of the important factors: (1) the effect of using or not using the article on both the younger and older girls who were tested with dolls of greater perceptual distinctiveness than in the first experiment; (2) the effect upon the older girls of increased perceptual distinctiveness in blocks.

Results: The results are set out in Table 2.3. Analysis of variance (one way) again revealed significant differences among means, F $(4, 20) = 2.87$, $p < .05$. Clearly this is due to the high level of responses from both groups of girls who were tested with dolls when one doll was given a proper name. In the other three conditions responses seem random; the children seemed equally disposed to choose either of the pair.

This is strong confirmation of the results of the first experiment. The level of "correct" responses rises only when the girls were discriminating between dolls, and then only when one of them had been called by a proper noun. The 17-month-olds performed quite as well as the older ones, and seem to have taken just as much account of the presence of the article. This argues that the linguistic competence discovered in the earlier experiment is to be found at the age of 17 months. On the other hand, increasing the perceptual distinctiveness of the blocks appears to have had no effect on responses.

Table 2.3   Mean Percentage of Correct Responses in Experiment 2–5 Girls per Cell

	Age	Common Noun	Proper Noun
Dolls	17	42 (.12)	76 (.17)
	22	53 (.19)	72 (.12)
Blocks	22	–	51 (.15)

Note—Standard deviations in parentheses.

Second Experiment with Boys

Puzzled by the boys' poor responding relative to the girls', we hypothesized that boys were less interested in dolls and less accustomed to them than girls. We thought that boys might respond better if we used male figures instead. We bought two toy construction workers with adjustable arms and legs. They were distinctly male figures and they differed in color.

With these we tested 20 boys in the Montreal region, all from middle-class English-speaking homes. Each was tested in his own home by Reesa Benderoff. The average age was 27 months and the range 24–31 months. There were only two conditions: men with proper names (nonsense syllables) and men with common names. The plan was that if we found differences between these conditions, we would extend the experiment to blocks.

Results: We did not continue because the differences associated with conditions—see Table 2.4—were not significant. The *t*-value associated with the mean difference between conditions was less than one. And neither mean departed significantly from a random pattern of responding; each of the *t*-values computed to assess these effects was less than one.

From this we can conclude that our attempt to improve boys' responses by using male figures did not prove successful.

Table 2.4   Means and Standard Deviations for Boys Tested with Male Figures. Computations Based on Percentage of Correct Responses Given by Individual Children

	Name	
	Proper	*Common*
N	10	10
X̄	57.2	58.6
SD	9.8	9.4

Third Experiment with Boys

If the figures we employed do not explain the difference between boys and girls' responses, and if we are unwilling to accept that the difference could have been due to the sex factor, what could the explanation be? We suspected that boys simply paid less attention than girls to the test. In the course of some other testing we tried out seven boys with the original dolls, but this time, in the midst of introducing the objects, we asked the child, *What did I call this one?* pointing to the named doll; and pointing to the other one we asked, *What did I call this one?* We repeated these questions three times about each object in the course of introducing them. We found that after such a procedure nearly all boys chose the named doll all the time. For the first time we managed to improve boys' responses, but we were not happy with the procedure. We feared that after drawing so much attention to the names, a boy would probably give the named object whether it was a doll or a block. We then devised the following experiment.

Procedures and subjects. The design was in most respects like that of the other experiments. Each child was shown a pair of dolls differing in color and shape. One of the pair, randomly chosen, was introduced to the child with a nonsense syllable (chosen from the list given in describing the first experiment) as a proper name, e.g. *Zav;* or it was introduced with a common name, e.g. *a Zav.* Each object was introduced five times. In this experiment after the objects had been introduced twice each, the child was asked about each in turn, *What did I call this one?* He was not told whether he was right or not, and the introductions proceeded as in the previous experiments. After the testing, which followed the pattern of the earlier experiments, each child was asked of each object in turn first, *What is this?* and then, *What did I call it?*

There were three conditions: (1) dolls with a proper name; (2) dolls with a common name; (3) blocks with a proper name. Five boys were tested in each condition. The boys, who were similar to those tested in the earlier experiments, were tested in their homes by Reesa Benderoff. Their average age was 28 months; the range was from 24 to 30 months.

Results. The results are set out in Table 2.5. The data on which those means and *SD*s are based are the proportion of times a boy chose the named object. Each boy, with few exceptions, was tested seven times.

Table 2.5   Mean Proportions (in percentages) of Correct Responses Given by Boys in Three Conditions. N = 5 in each condition

| | Name | |
	Common	Proper
Dolls	58.4	79.8
	SD = 12.5	SD = 19.3
Blocks	—	54.4
		SD = 27.4

One-way analysis of variance yielded $F(2.12) = 2.19; p > .05$, which is not significant at the 5 percent level of probability. Though the differences among means are as large as those of other experiments that yielded significant results, the variability in this one was large, especially in the condition with blocks. However, we may ask another question of the means: does any one of them depart significantly from 50, the expected level of correct responses by chance alone? To test this hypothesis we use the mean square of the analysis variance in a t-test. The value computed for the condition, dolls with a proper name, is $t (12) = 3.24; p < .01$. Both values computed for the two other conditions are less than unity.

These boys were four months older than the boys of the first experiment. Yet their level of correct responding when tested with dolls, one of which had been given a proper name, was considerably higher than that of girls in the first experiment. Of course we must not make too much of that point because the experimental procedure was different. But the new results suggest that the relevant difference was that boys paid less attention than girls when they were being tested. Boys needed to have their attention focused more. That we did by merely asking them once in the course of introducing the objects what we had called them. The important point is that boys now show themselves as acting on the same rules. verbal and nonverbal, as girls. They notice the presence or absence of the articles, *a* and *the,* before a name when the object is a doll, not when it is a block.

The children's answer to the questions were not revealing. None of the 15 was able to say what the tester had called either object after two introductions to each. Presumably after they had been asked, they paid more attention to names in the remaining three introductions. The questions asked after testing were *What is this?* and *What did I call it?* Nine children gave no answer to either as asked of the named or unnamed object. Three gave the nonsense syllable in reply to all questions; two of those children were in the dolls with a proper name condition and the other in the dolls with a common name condition. One boy tested with dolls and a proper name got the names wrong. He called the unnamed object by the nonsense syllable and the named object "dolly." One boy tested with blocks said of each that it was "a kiv." As I said, these responses are not nearly as revealing as the choice of object.

Diary Data

This series of investigations lends support to the theory that inspired them. It seems that when children come to learn names for objects, they already know some of them as highly important individuals and some as relatively interchangeable with others of the same kind. But they also seemed to notice the presence or absence of the articles, and that was unexpected. The evidence before us is that children as young as 17 months paid equal attention to both factors, the semantic and the linguistic. Nothing in it reveals the direction of learning; did the semantic precede the linguistic and guide it; was it the other way about; or were the two independent? To answer, I turn to a diary I kept of my son Kieran's speech almost from the time he began to speak.

Kieran, like all children, early learned proper names for people and common names for people and objects. Among his very earliest words were *Mammy, Daddy,* and *Freddie* (the dog); his earliest common names were: *baby, cracker, eye, puppy,* and *squirrel.* When he was 14:14 (months: days) I noted that he had begun to mix up *Mammy* and *Daddy,* but never *Freddie.* He never called any dog except Freddie, *Freddie;* he called other dogs various versions of *dog.* On the other hand he never called any individuals apart from my wife and myself *Mammy* and *Daddy.* The reason he mixed us up seems to have been that when we had first taught him *Mammy* and *Daddy* we relaxed and, of course, referred to each other as *John* and *Joyce.* As we were not modeling the use of *Mammy* and *Daddy* for him he became confused after a time. But he never mixed up either name with *Freddie.* For the rest it was uncanny how accurately he used proper names for particular individuals. His only mistakes were mistakes of identity owing to similarity of appearance.

For a time he seemed to assume that proper names were uniquely paired with individuals. The reason for believing so is that when he met his first "doppelgänger" he refused to accept the name. He was at the time 16:13 and had met a cousin of his, Lisa. He was then introduced to a girl of about the same age as Lisa also called *Lisa.* They played for half an hour, yet, most unusual for him, he refused to say her name, no matter how often anyone said it or urged him. Shortly after that he met three girls all named Aimée and he accepted the name for all three.

At no time did he show any hesitation about applying a common name to new objects. *Boot* as soon as he learned the word at 15:11 meant any article of footwear, real or pictured, no matter whom it belonged to. Items of food followed one another, and without hesitation he called each new one by the appropriate name, if he knew it.

How did he distinguish between the two types of name? I cannot help concluding that the main distinguisher was semantic. Till 18:18 every proper name was the name of a person or dog to whom he had been introduced. At 18:18 he learned Noah of the biblical character in a picture story book. All his common names referred to inanimate objects, real or pictured, or to pictured people and animals or to transient people and animals—that is, to ones whom he met casually. There can be no doubt about the salience of the semantic clues. Could it be that he also depended on linguistic clues? It is more difficult to be confident, but it seems unlikely. He did not become more accurate in his use of proper names; he seemed to start out with as much accuracy as his elders. It is certain that he had to learn, gradually, the force of the articles. Furthermore, since he did not for the most part use the articles himself, when speaking to him we did not either. When he first began to speak, more often than not we used to imitate him and say, "this is nose," "this is apple" etc. Of course we always dropped the article before mass nouns—milk, applejuice, etc.

The evidence is reasonably good that semantic clues preceded linguistic ones and guided the learning of linguistic ones, but it is not conclusive. I neglected to do the obvious experiment when he was young enough: introduce him to some indidivudal, say Tom, as *The Tom* or *A Tom*. If he had been depending on linguistic clues, he should have given evidence that he took Tom to be a name for the individual and been prepared to apply it to other similar individuals, as he did *boy*. If he had been depending on semantic clues, he should have either attempted to call the individual *The tom* or *A tom,* or ignored the articles and called him *Tom;* in any event treated the word as a proper name.

Conclusion

Let us take it that children as young as 17 months are able to distinguish between common and proper names. The evidence is clear from experimental and naturalistic observation. Already at that age they seem to grasp the semantic difference and to have noted the linguistic correlates, namely the presence or absence of the article. There is some evidence in the diary data, not in the experimental, that the semantic distinction comes first and, perhaps, forms the basis for learning the linguistic ones.

Notice the manner in which objects were introduced to the child and subsequently requested in the experiments, either as *Zav* or *a/the Zav* (I let *Zav* stand for all nonsense syllables). According to the theory of reference to be proposed in Chapter 11, the proper name *Zav* refers to the individual named; *Zav* in *give me the Zav* refers to both objects but the effect of *the* is to single out a particular one of the set called *Zavs; Zav* in *this is a Zav* does not refer. Since all testing was done with *Zav* or *the Zav, Zav* was always referring during testing. By adult standards the children, when asked for the *Zav,* should have given the one that had initially been classified as a Zav, but they did not. That may have been because they did not grasp the semantic force of the distinction between the articles, *a* and *the.* That is quite likely in view of what we shall see of children's learning of the articles in Chapter 9. This leads me to the conclusion that the manner in which an object was introduced had most impact, and either change from *a* to *the* was not noticed or not understood.

If we grant this, we have the children taking *Zav* as a proper name and *a/the Zav* as a sortal. The semantic distinction between proper name and sortal then seems to have drawn their attention to the presence or absence of an article, without leading them to distinguish between the articles.

The same line of interpretation suggests that even if they took *a Zav* as a nonreferring sortal whose semantic function was merely to classify objects, they had no trouble subsequently accepting it in referring position. When told *Give me the Zav,* they responded as though they had been instructed to hand over one of those objects that were referred to by the sortal, *Zav.*

The claim that the semantic distinction between proper names and sortals was prior to the linguistic distinction needs analysis. What it means is that by the time the child comes to learn language, he has already learned that objects in certain categories are important as individuals, those in other categories are merely exemplars of the category. Person is the preeminent category of the first sort, and when he is introduced to one, he will take the word applied to that person as a proper name. Words applied to objects in most other categories he will take as a sortal.

This may well mean that from the onset of speech a child is coordinating the notions individual and class. Only individuals of a certain class receive proper names. Remember that the children in the experiments did not automatically take all names for dolls as proper names; they noted the presence or absence of an article, thus revealing that they were aware that a doll might receive either type of name. The doll might be referred to as an individual or as a member of a class. Thus individuality is never just that, but the individuality of a member of a class. The two notions seem to be inextricably related from the start.

My interpretation, then, is that by the time he comes to learn vocabulary the child has learned not only to divide the world into classes, but to treat the individuality of the members of certain classes as important. The individuality of the members of most classes is usually not important. The cognitive distinctions guide him in making the relevant linguistic observations. Words applied to individuals as individuals are treated one way syntactically; those applied to individuals as class members are treated another. There will be a syntactic difference between the two in all languages, but how it is made will vary from one language to another.

To claim that meaning guides the child to a useful linguistic distinction is not to claim that it tells him the precise linguistic rules. These the child must discover for himself by closely observing how the semantic distinction is expressed. There are several relevant linguistic rules in English; the ones we have studied are the presence and absence of the articles *a* and *the*. Since ultimately the relevant linguistic rules must be stated in terms not only of articles, but of the plural, of quantifiers (*some, any, many,* etc.) and adjectives (*good, big,* etc.), the child's learning the rules depends on a great deal of syntactic learning that we will not go into.

What we have just seen is an account of how children learn the linguistic distinction between common and proper names, but if I am right we have not seen them learning the corresponding semantic distinction. It does not follow that they have not learned it. All that need be said is that by the time the child begins to speak, he seems in certain cases able to refer to the same material object either as an individual or as an exemplar of a class. If that distinction is learned, it is learned earlier. Anticipating the discussion of sense, that means that from the beginning of speech he can refer with and without accompanying sense. He can represent the same material object as different intentional objects: an individual in its own right and an individual of a class.

3.

I and *Thou*

I gave her one, they gave him two,
You gave us three or more;
They all returned from him to you
Though they were mine before.
    —*Alice in Wonderland*

In 1943 Dr. L. Kanner described a rare complex of symptoms in child psychiatry, and the children who manifest them he called autistic. The core of the complex is an emotional disorder that prevents a child from forming normal relations with people. Dr. Kanner called his article "Autistic disturbances of affective contact." Once I spent some time visiting the Child Guidance Centre at Dowan Hill in Glasgow, and I observed there a four-year-old boy, Ken, who met Kanner's description exactly. Ken was unusually bright; from the age of three he was able to take to pieces and reconstruct any small mechanical or electrical device in his home. He was uncannily quick with numbers. He was a handsome and healthy young fellow. What was odd about him was that he almost never looked at people. His eyes focused to left and right of them, never on them. And his speech was poor. In particular he used the personal pronouns the wrong way round. He called himself *You*, presumably because others addressed him as *you*. Similar misuse of pronouns has frequently been observed in such children.

  Children like Ken pose the problem of personal pronouns in an unusually forceful manner: how do other children learn to use them the right way round? They do it so young and make so few mistakes that one might not ask how they do it if one had not seen Ken. Having seen him, one asks oneself not how did he get them wrong so much as how do other children get them right? The crux is that if a parent uses a pronoun of the child, he says *you* and refers to himself as *I*. When the child speaks he must reverse them. He must exchange the parent's *you* for *I* and the parent's *I* for *you*.

These are the only variable names to be discussed in this book, and they will be discussed largely to illustrate a particular aspect of language. In every language there are terms whose choice depends critically upon the speaker and his position in space and time rather than on grammar. There are words like *here* and *there* which depend on the position of the speaker, as do *going* and *coming*. And there are terms like *now* and *then* and *henceforth* whose meaning varies with the time they are uttered. This type of variability with time, place, and speaker is called deixis by linguists. It contrasts sharply with the rest of language, whose interpretation is not so dependent. The creature who is a *dog* today is a *dog* tomorrow; and even if at times we refer to him with other words, such as *Freddie* and *animal,* the interpretation of those terms is fixed—or nearly so, because we must remember that over the centuries words change their meaning.

THE PERSONAL PRONOUNS IN ENGLISH

The pronouns that will concern us are the singular first and second person ones: *I, me, myself, my, mine, you, yourself, your,* and *yours.* Two of these are sometimes called possessive adjectives, *my* and *your;* but presumably they are abbreviations for *of me* and *of you.* Just as we regard the possessive elsewhere in English, e.g. *Harry's,* as basically a noun, we will regard *my* and *your* as basically pronouns; and indeed they are pronouns etimologically.

It is commonly believed that pronouns substitute for nouns, but that is not generally true. We can say *The man came to dinner,* but not *The he came to dinner.* We can say *He came to dinner;* but then we notice that *he* substitutes not for the noun, *man,* but for the whole noun phrase, *the man.* Only when a noun phrase consists of a single word, such as a proper name or a plural noun, does a pronoun substitute for a noun (see Gleason, 1965, p. 125). Unlike nouns, personal pronouns do not take determiners like *a, the,* or *some,* nor can they be modified by adjectives. Unlike nouns, *I, she, he,* and *they* have accusative cases: *me, her, him,* and *them.* In writing, personal pronouns normally refer back to noun phrases that have appeared previously. In conversation, where the referents for *I* and *you* are obvious, they usually do not refer back; they refer directly to speaker and listener.

There is much more to be said about the English personal pronouns, but that is enough for our purposes and for the discussion of baby talk in general. There has been a small number of careful studies of how children come to learn the personal pronouns from the point of view of both comprehension and production. The most recent of these is also the most thorough, that by Janet Strayer (1977); and she will be our main guide. She based herself mainly on spontaneous conversation between parents and babies, and like many other workers she examined the children's utterances. But in addition she made a serious attempt to find out what children understood of parents' remarks to them, remarks that contained personal pronouns. In addition she gave the children tests of comprehension. More formal tests of comprehension have also been given by deVilliers & deVilliers (1974). Children's spontaneous uses of personal pronouns were studied by McNeill (1963) and Huxley (1970), and blind children's uses were studied by Fraiberg & Adelson (1973). I have also kept a diary on my son Kieran's language learning and paid special attention to personal pronouns. These records, with the addition of some earlier ones reviewed in McCarthy (1954), will provide us with our data base.

We will begin by summarizing the findings and then go on to their explanation. We will attempt to determine whether first and second personal pronouns are learned as systematically related pairs. In other words, are *I* and *you* learned independently of each other or as a related pair? And since both *I* and *you* can refer to the child as well as to his mother, we will try to determine if they are first learned in one or other or both of their denotational uses. Besides being *I* and *you* as occasion demands, the child and his mother have proper names. We saw in Chapter two that even eighteen-month-olds are beginning to make some sense of the contrast between proper and common names. Here we will study how proper names relate to the personal pronouns. If the shifting sense of personal pronouns proves too much for a child, he has always the fixed proper names to fall back on. And what do his parents do to help him; how do they accommodate their speech? Are there any specially useful teaching links or circumstances that enable a searching child to solve the puzzle of shifting reference?

COMPREHENSION—STRAYER

Janet Strayer selected four first-born girls whose mean age at the beginning of the study was just under 22 months and at its close, 10 months later, just under 32 months. The girls were brought to a playroom in Simon Fraser University once every two weeks and there they were videotaped for half an hour. Parent-child pairs were taped individually and the parent (usually mother, but sometimes father) was asked to carry on with the child as though they were at home. Because the data were so abundant, Strayer confined the analysis to five well spaced tapes for each child, 20 tapes in all.

Averaged across the 20 taped sessions there were 66 occasions per session on which the parent asked the child to do something in such a manner that the child's response would show whether he understood. On 33 of these parents used neither a personal name nor a personal pronoun. On three parents used either their own name (*Mommy*) or the child's name. Interestingly, the parent used a second person pronoun over six times more frequently than a first person one. This means that when the parent used a personal pronoun, it usually referred to the child.

Utterances in which there was no overt personal reference were like commands: "come here," "put that down," "don't touch that," etc. Understanding on the child's part is difficult to assess, because failure to do as told could be due to other factors besides understanding. Two-year-olds can be willful. However, over the ten months of the study the mean number of compliant responses rose from 53 to 76 percent. In the early sessions children's appropriate responses to utterances that included first person pronouns were only about 10 percent on average; to utterances with second person pronouns, appropriate responses amounted to over 40 percent. To both types of utterance appropriate responses climbed to over 80 percent after 10 months. Initially the children responded correctly to the few utterances which included proper names over 80 percent of the time.

During the course of the study Strayer administered tests of comprehension of a simple nature: *point to my head* or *point to your leg*. Once again correct responses to *your*-type expressions were initially more numerous than those to *my*-type ones. Errors tended to be the child's pointing to his own head when asked to *point to my head*. These findings have the support of a study by deVilliers & deVilliers (1974) in which they tested children by telling them to look for an object on *my* side or on *your* side. The children were aged 2½ and responded correctly to *your* 90 percent of the time, to *my* 67 percent of the time.

PRODUCTION–STRAYER

When we look at children's use of first and second person pronouns, the pattern at first looks quite different. Over all sessions the proportion of all utterances in which children made reference to persons was 33 percent. Initially they referred to themselves by their personal names some 40 percent and by a personal pronoun about 60 percent of the time. Ten months later the corresponding figures were about 5 percent and 95 percent respectively. When referring to their parents, they initially used a proper name 95 percent and a pronoun some 5 percent of the time. After 10 months the corresponding figures were about 40 percent and 60 percent. Since the figures are a little confusing when so stated, they are presented again in Table 3.1.

Table 3.1   Percentage of Personal References in Which Children Used either a Proper Name or a Pronoun, by Age and Person Referred to (Strayer, 1977)

Age in Months	Refer to Self		Refer to Parent	
	I	*Name*	*You*	*Name*
22	60	40	5	95
32	95	5	60	40

The most striking contrast between the comprehension and production data is the reversal in predominance of personal pronouns. In comprehension *you* and *your* preceded *I* and *my;* in production *I* and *my* are far more frequent than *you* and *your*. Yet all this fits a thoroughly intelligible pattern. The personal pronouns that a child is most at home with, or at any rate deals with correctly most frequently, are those that refer to herself. She is accustomed to hearing herself addressed as *you* and to speaking about herself as *I*. Only later does she come to master the reciprocal pattern, of referring to her parent as *you* and accepting her use of *I* as referring to herself.

This way of interpreting the data is borne out by the errors that children made in the use of personal pronouns. A total of only 35 errors were recorded, and of these 19 consisted of the child referring to her parent as *I* and 16 of her referring to herself as *you*. At least, this is the number of clear errors: it is not possible to be certain in every case that a usage was an error. An example of a clear error is the child handing a book to its mother with the words "I read a story." Further proof that it was an error lies in the fact that the children seemed satisfied when their mother reformulated the statement in some such words as, "So you want *me* to read a story," and the mother went ahead and read one. Now the children's use of first person pronouns was far more frequent than their use of second person ones. In fact at the beginning of the study errors in the use of *you* were about seven times more numerous, proportionately, than errors in the use of *I*. That is why it is reasonable to take the error data as corroborating the correct usage. The child's use and understanding of pronouns that refer to herself is more accurate than that of pronouns that refer to another.

A second feature that emerges from Table 3.1 is that when they are beginning to talk, children use proper names very frequently, far more frequently than their parents do. As time goes by they replace proper names with pronouns, at least in the types of dialogues that Strayer recorded. This, too, makes a good deal of sense. Proper names are fixed, whereas pronouns shift meaning with the speaker.

All this has the support of an early paper by David McNeill (1963) in which he studied the use of personal pronouns by one of the children in Roger Brown's sample of three children. Eve, the girl he studied, responded appropriately to utterances with *you* in them more frequently than to ones with *I* in them across the age range of 20 to 27 months. Moreover, Eve tended to use proper names instead of pronouns early and to replace them gradually with pronouns. Eve's mother used pronouns much more frequently, but often combined both *Momma* and *I* as though indicating the equivalence to the child. And Eve used *I* of herself before she used *you* of her mother.

Huxley (1970) took weekly recordings of a boy and a girl from the age of two years and three months to the age of four years. She, too, found that they used proper names before pronouns; they used *I* before *you*. The boy was older before introducing *I* into his own speech and then often combined it with his own name as mothers sometimes do, "I, Douglas." The effect is a little like a last will and testament, though it undoubtedly reassured the boy and kept him from error. Indeed, Huxley never found her children erroneously reversing pronouns.

KIERAN'S DATA

Strayer's study was so thorough and so painstaking that it seems ungracious to register any disappointment; yet the children seem to have been too old at the beginning of the study. By then they were already responding appropriately to instructions that included *you* 40 percent of the time. Allow for occasional whims and inattention, and that may mean a fairly accurate grasp of the reference of *you* as used by a parent. Moreover, at the beginning of the study the children referred to themselves as *I* some 60 percent of the time; and there were only 35 errors in the children's use of personal pronouns across all sessions. All this implies that the children were well along in the learning of personal pronouns at 22 months, when Strayer began her work. McNeill's study of Eve began when she was 20 months old and Huxley's when the children were 27 months old. If we are to understand the process of learning, we must look to younger children.

My diary of Kieran begins with the beginning of his speech when he was 13 months. Though it lacks the experimental rigor of Strayer's study, it does help to fill in the earlier period. The relevant excerpts are given in full in Appendix 1; here I will just comment as best I can on how he progressed.

The first record of a personal pronoun suggests that already he had figured out the most difficult element of the pattern. At 15:19 (months:days) he saw a photograph of himself and he said *me*, pointing to himself. To grasp the significance of this I give a note I wrote when he was 10 months:

> Mirror Experiments: greatly interested in figures in the mirror (a shaving mirror on hinges). (a) Experiments with movements and seems to notice his control of baby's movements. (b) Reached out and touched mirror and baby's fingers several times. (c) Compares man in mirror to me (I was holding him—) he can't see himself, but seemed to recognize me in mirror. (d) Swung mirror on its hinges—controlling entire mirror space. (e) Looks behind mirror and seems surprised.

All this took place in the space of about 10 days and I could not help concluding that he had figured out that the mirror somehow presented his real environment to him in a new way, and that he himself was part of what he saw in it. He thus learned to identify his appearance.

Similar experiments and experiences with mirrors continued at frequent intervals, so that by the age of 15 months he was quite familiar with his own appearance. There can be little doubt that he recognized himself in the photograph by the age of 15 months. What is surprising is that he referred to himself as *me*. That he did so is borne out not only by the subsequent record of his use of personal pronouns, but by his pointing to himself when he first used *me*. For long after this period he pointed to the objects he named, as though to ensure the listener's comprehension of his intent to refer. On this interpretation of his *me* it follows that he had already made the jump from his parent's use of *me* to its potential for referring to himself. We will come back to how he managed it.

An important exercise in establishing his use of the personal pronouns was a game in which he and one of his parents took turns. The first entry about the game is at 16:9. No doubt he had noticed that we frequently removed things from him with the words *No, that's mine*. He then, in a spirit of fun, began to grasp whatever we happened to have in our hands, a pencil or book for example, and tug it towards himself, saying *mine*. Our part was to tug back saying *mine*. At 16:26 a variant of the game began: I pointed to myself and said *me;* he pointed to himself and said *me*. The two versions were frequently played, one after the other. About a week later, at 17:2, the exercise bore fruit:

> In bed this morning he began his *me/me* game. When he said *me* [pointing to himself], I said *yes, you*. Then followed one exchange, *me/yes, you*. Then he pointed to himself and said *Kieran*. Joyce, [my wife] had told me that he had begun to say his own name but that was the first time I heard it.

At the time when this was recorded he had long grown used to responding to instructions with *you* and *your* in them, and he had long since learned that *Kieran* referred to him. He seemed to use the game as a means of drawing all his learning together: *me* used by him referred to himself; *you* used by me referred to himself; *Kieran* used by him (and presumably anyone) referred to himself. That this is the right interpretation is shown by his reaction a week later:

> 17:9. This morning we went through the *me/me* routine. I quickly changed to *you*; but when I changed the *you* to *Kieran* he was overcome with delight and shouted out loud.

Later entries show that he gradually learned to understand *I*, as used by us and to use it of himself. There were numerous routines that gradually contributed to his learning to say *you* and so refer to other persons. Among them was a game in which he and one of us said in turn *I see you*—beginning at 17:21. Another was *thank you*—beginning at 18:8, and *see you* (good-bye)—beginning at 18:25.

Early in this 19th month he began to show systematic confusion. At 19:4 when shown a photograph of himself and asked *Is that you?* he responded *you*. At that time he used to say *no* as a negative answer and as an affirmative repeat the last word of the question. Hence the answer, *you*. The rule for affirmative answers seems to have dislodged the rule that *you* in his mouth referred to another person and *me* to himself. However, the disorder was only partial for at 19:17 we find him responding to a series of questions, *you did?* with *I did*. On the same day he showed that the *see you* routine was bearing fruit by saying: *See you, Martha; See you, George; see you Anne*. Here the reference of the *you* was specified.

LEARNING

At the very least Kieran's record shows that we must begin our study when children are only about 15 months if we hope to catch the early stages. But I think the interest of the record is more than that. The chief importance of the personal pronouns is that in learning them the child gives the lie to all standard psychological theories of learning. In the first chapter we discussed various theories that depend basically on an association between an observed object and an uttered sound. Take an object, the child himself, and a sound, *you,* and take learning as the establishment of an association between the two. That would lead to errors more than half the time. Everytime someone other than the child is addressed as *you,* he would take it as referring to himself. The child is *you* only when he is addressed; when he speaks he must not refer to himself as *you*. Though the records show occasional lapses in which a child did just that, they are rare. In any case the child must correct them.

Imitation, another favorite construct of learning theory, is also of little account. Undoubtedly, imitation of some sort plays some part in language learning. Children do not create their language *ex nihilo*. But it is an imitation guided by a highly intelligent appreciation of the intentions of speaker and listener, and of their changing conversational roles. Mindless imitation would lead to error on all occasions when the child uses the first and second personal pronouns.

Strayer remarks that through all the sessions she recorded, and they were far more numerous than those she analyzed for her report, she never observed a parent attempting to teach correct usage of the pronouns. I do not remember either my wife or myself correcting Kieran. Children change from proper names to pronouns that refer to themselves and later to pronouns that refer to their parents, but they do so on their own. As mothers, hard pressed by psychologists, might say, they just pick it up.

The evidence that they learn *I* and *you,* referring to themselves, as a systematically related pair is convincing. There are many records of a child addressed as *you* responding with *I.* However, it is not simply the case that *I* is some sort of superficial associate of *you,* in much the sense that black is of white or *top* is of bottom. In Table 3.2 are set out the frequencies with which Strayer found children replying with a personal pronoun when addressed with one. Children are not under the control of anyone or anything quite to the extent that some behaviourists imagine. Sometimes they simply ignore a remark, or say something quite different, as anyone knows who has ever watched the strategems of a child who

Table 3.2 Percentage of Parent *I* and *You* Utterances Responded to by Children with *I* and *You* Utterances (Strayer, 1977)

Parent	Child's Response	
	I	*You*
I	3	2
You	8	1

is being sent to bed. And children are often stubborn. Strayer gives examples that ring all too familiar: Parent, "you do it"; Child, "You do it."

Another conjecture is that frequency of adult usage partially explains at least the pattern of development in personal pronouns. This is almost certainly wrong. In general, Roger Brown (1973) found little correlation between the frequency with which adults used particular morphemes when speaking to children and the order in which the children began to use those morphemes. But nowhere is the discrepancy so great as in the personal pronouns. Strayer found that parents used *you* almost seven times more often than *I* when speaking to children, yet children used *I* very much more frequently than *you*. So, frequency of use by parents is not related to frequency of use by children in any simple fashion. Yet it may be related in some way. If we look up any of the word counts for English, Thorndike & Lorge (1944) or Kučera-Francis (1967) or Carroll, Davies, & Richman (1971), we find that *I* is used almost twice as frequently as *you* outside the realm of child-parent talk. It follows that in speaking to young children, parents adapt their use of pronouns considerably. Instead of talking so much about themselves, they make the child the center of attention. It is commonly known that parenthood serves to make men and women less selfish, but it is not generally appreciated how all pervasive the effect is and in particular how it manifests itself in speech.

The parents' selflessness and focusing on the child does, probably, make the child's task simpler. It enables him to concentrate on sorting out the use of *I* and *you* while holding the referent (himself) constant. Once that is done, he is in a position to let go the constancy of referent and apply the personal pronouns to himself. In the meantime he refers to the other persons by their proper names, whose referents are fixed. Only when he has pinned down *I* and *you* in relation to himself does he gradually replace *Mommy* with *you*. Perhaps unwittingly parent and child have worked out an excellent strategy for dealing with the shifting pronouns.

But when all is said and done, parents' accommodations are only a crutch and do not explain how children grasp the correct rule. How then do they? We simply do not know, anymore than we know how we induce the correct answer in a thousand other situations. But let us be clear about what the child does. He begins by interpreting *you* when used by others as referring to himself. Now he does not take *you* as another proper name for himself. At 19:15 Kieran said *I love you* and a little later *I love Freddie*. We were convinced that *you*, in the first referred not to Kieran but to his mother; and *Freddie* in the second definitely referred to Freddie. There are several other examples in the early record that rule out *you* as a proper name. It follows that Kieran had already discovered that *you* could refer to several people. Yet it was not a common noun either; he never used it of anyone apart from the person he was speaking to or himself (incorrectly).

By a parallel argument it is clear that Kieran did not take *I* as either a proper name or as a common one. So it must be that very early he saw that both pronouns were intimately related to the immediate participants in a conversation.

But that merely shows that he had the generalization almost right; tottery, perhaps, but almost right. How did he avoid the generalization, also well supported by the evidence, that *I* referred to everyone except himself? Or the even better supported generalization, that *I* referred to any participant other than himself? It seems clear that he never made such a generalization, and so we are forced to the conclusion that that is not the sort that occurs to children. Not that a child is incapable of forming the class, participants other than myself; that is more or less what he needs as referent for *you* as used by himself. What does not seem to occur to him is that there should be a useful class consisting of persons from which he himself is always excluded. Others can refer to him as *you*, so that does not count. Others never refer to him as *I,* so the incorrect generalization would have it that he was always excluded from the class that could use *I.* I believe this conjecture about his hypotheses is right, but of course I do not know why the incorrect generalization is excluded. Perhaps it has to do with the child's appreciation that he is a person just as much as any others who take part in conversations, and so has as much right as any of them to be an *I* sometimes.

There is very little evidence on the matter, but I suspect the child pays more attention than is imagined to conversations in which he is not himself engaged. For example, he might notice that when father and mother talk to one another, each says *I* of themselves and *you* of the other as they speak. That would give him the correct rule, relating the pronouns to conversational role, provided he was prepared to include himself. And perhaps it never occurs to him to exclude himself.

One can also think of situations that must be particularly illuminating for the child. Suppose mother says: "Mommy will do it; I will do it," and by her actions indicates that both sentences mean the same, she has given the child a clue that she can refer to herself as *Mommy* and as *I.* That would be a start. On other occasions the child says "Mommy" and mother replies "Here I am." This strengthens the interpretation that *Mommy* and *I* are equivalent. Yet the bond between *I* and *Mommy* does not become close because the child bears similar exchanges from other persons. In each the word *I* refers to a different person and only that person. It is never used as a common noun, like *person,* to refer to a whole class.

Then there are numerous exchanges of the general sort: (Child) "Mommy, up"; (Mother), "No, *you* get up yourself." On many such occasions it will be clear to the child that Mommy is not going to do as asked, but the child must act himself. Then it must be apparent to him that the change from *Mommy* to *you* is accompanied by a change in referent, *you* referring to the child. Indeed *you* is the pronoun he hears most frequently: "pick up your toys"; "time *you* were in bed"; "are *you* thirsty?"; "did you hurt *your* knee?"

We are so accustomed to hearing that children's thought is egocentric and that they cannot consider situations from the point of view of another person, that we are distracted from the most obvious examples of evidence to the contrary, speech. One common test of egocentricity consists in asking a child how many brothers his brother has; he often forgets to count himself and gives an answer that is one short. Other tests require the child to visualize a scene from some point of view other than that which he occupies. He frequently fails such tests. Undoubtedly the tests mark some difficulty of a cognitive nature. But we must not exaggerate. The child who fails such tests at the age of five has almost certainly learned the pronouns the right way around by the age of two. And that involves seeing that the meanings of *I* and *you* depend on who is being addressed. Moreover, getting them right involves being able to see their meaning when used by another and making the necessary reversal when he uses them himself. If he was as egocentric as he is frequently portrayed, he could not make that reversal. In Chapter 9 we shall encounter a charge of egocentricity in connection with the use of the articles *a* and *the*, but we will see that it is not well grounded. From the evidence of language I am forced to conclude that children do not lack the ability to consider matters from the point of view of another. If they fail on tests of egocentricity, the likelihood is that some other factor, such as memory load or unfamiliarity with the test concepts, is tripping them up.

To sum up. Children as young as the youngest who were tested for knowledge and command of the personal pronouns have never shown any problem with the notion of self-concept as distinct from the concept of another person. At first they appear to rely on personal names to establish who is being referred to. By the age of 22 months their understanding of such personal names appears to have been nearly perfect. They learn the first and second personal pronouns first as they relate to themselves. That is, they understand that *you* when used by another and *I* when used by themselves both refer to themselves. A little after the age of 2½ most of them had learned to use *you* of another person.

The personal pronouns, because of their shifting reference, pose a special problem for children. That they come to master them is revealing and excludes solutions based on mere associations, on mere imitation or on frequency of usage. We considered some incorrect generalizations that could be supported by the evidence and concluded that such generalizations do not occur to the child. In particular we concluded that he will never form a hypothesis that includes everyone else, and always excludes himself; perhaps because he believes himself a human being and so not to be excluded. However, the process whereby a child induces the correct rule for the personal pronouns is really not well understood.

One of the aspects of the problem that we did not dwell on was a recurrent theme in the first part of the book. I assumed, throughout, that the child had means of knowing whom a speaker referred to when he used *I* or *you*. That is a large assumption but no larger than the assumption that he knows what is being referred to by any name. Presumably the abilities that reveal to him what *dog* and *animal* refer to on a particular occasion reveal what the pronouns refer to. The difference is that the personal pronouns shift reference in a way that *dog* does not, and the child must make pronominal reference depend on conversational role. In fact that is the reason for considering pronouns separately.

We began by referring to autistic children and their failure to get the personal pronouns right. Unfortunately, we cannot say with confidence what their difficulty is, but the foregoing leads to one or two conjectures. Autistic children, as described by Kanner, are highly intelligent, so their failure is unlikely to have its source either in a failure of inductive inference or inability to take a point of view different from that of the observer. The most likely source is a failure in personal relations. For some reason autistic children try to avoid human contact. It follows that they will not attempt to analyze whom the personal pronouns refer to. And having failed in that, they have no basis for making the pronominal shift. Conversely, normal children are able to make the reversal because of their intense interest in personal relations.

4.
Things Have More than One Name

In old maids' albums, too,
Sticks seaweed—yes, and names it.
—W.S. Gilbert, The Rival Curates

If I had met Evelyn Waugh I dare say I would have called him "Mr. Waugh" but I also dare say that his wife called him "Evelyn." When I meet new people I have to solve the problem of what to call them. I usually begin with a formal title if the person is older than myself, *Mr. Higginbottom,* and sometimes on better acquaintance change to first name, *Tom.* At any rate, we are quite accustomed to people having several names.

All these sorts of names designate a person as an individual. Others assign them to a class, e.g., *person, man, pope.* And there are hierarchical relations among some classes. All popes, with the dubious exception of Joan, have been men; but not all men have been popes. All men are persons, but not all persons are men. These hierarchically related classes will be the center of attention in this chapter and the next. They must cause a problem for the infant who surely wonders why a thing needs so many words attached to it. Why is the family pet not content with *Freddie;* why does he have to be *a dog* and *an animal* besides? How do all these relate to one another?

Here is prime material for the study of cognitive psychology. We will begin by examining the extent to which children are acquainted with hierarchically related terms. Since they learn them from their elders and betters, we will look at what those elders and betters call objects both when they are talking to adults and when they are talking to children. We will go on to a preliminary inquiry into what various levels of terms mean to children, paying particular attention to overextensions and underextensions, e.g. calling cows *dogs* and refusing to call chihuahuas *dogs*. And finally we will discuss certain criteria proposed by Inhelder & Piaget (1964) for deciding whether children have arranged related categories in true hierarchical order.

Children's Knowledge of the Terms

The most recent study that I have seen on this topic is in Anglin (1977, pp. 52 ff.). He chose the following hierarchies for particular attention:

I	II	III
animal	plant	food
dog	flower	fruit
collie	rose	apple

He collected a large number of pictures with which to exemplify each term and had them rated for typicality by adults. This was a precaution suggested by certain studies done by Eleanor Rosch (1973, 1975). She began with the observation that certain creatures are more typical of a category than others. A robin, say, is a more typical bird than a penguin. Rosch showed that this typicality dimension had an important effect on availability of names and ease in recognizing and naming objects. Anglin chose the three pictures that received the highest ratings for typicality as examples of a particular term. He showed these pictures to two groups: 20 children ranging in age from two to five years; 10 adults.

Each person was asked to name the object in each picture, and then to give a general name for the three objects in a group of three. So he might correctly have said that each collie was a *collie* and that all three were *collies;* similarly, he might have named a *pointer,* a *german shepherd* and a *husky* and called all three *dogs;* and he might have named a *dog,* a *cat* and an *elephant* and called all three *animals.*

Some of the two-year-old children responded strangely, allowing that each of the apple pictures showed an apple, but unable to say what all three together were. This is not surprising, since Roger Brown (1973) found that children do not consistently use the plural form until they are 2½ years or older. But for the most part Anglin's subjects answered appropriately.

The main differences between adults and children were these. The adults called the collies by that name and the children called them *dogs*. The adults called roses by that name; the children called them *flowers*. The adults called the group of three plants, *plants;* the children called them *flowers*. The adults called the group of three fruit, *fruits;* the children either could not give them a common name or called them *food*.

The usual order of acquisition was *dog* first, followed by *animal* and then *collie; flower* first followed by *plant* and then *rose; apple* first followed by *food* and then *fruit*. As Brown (1958) and Stross (1969) had found, there was no clear tendency for the children to begin with the specific and proceed to the more general, or to follow the reverse order. However, there was marked agreement between the relative frequency of the nine terms in child language as a whole and the proportion of children who gave them in Anglin's test. In fact, the rank-order correlation between frequency as found in Rinsland (1945) and the percentage of children who gave them in Anglin's test was 1.0 (i.e. perfectly correlated).

Anglin (1977, pp. 35–52) had found similar results in an earlier, less well-controlled study. Most children in that experiment knew *car* before *Volkswagen* and *Volkswagen* before *transportation; money* before *dime* before *coin; fish* before *animal* before *shark; animal* before *monkey* before *primate; boys* before *children* before *people*. Much of this fits nicely with the findings of Eleanor Rosch. In a series of ingenious experiments she has shown that in a number of hierarchical categories there is one which she calls *basic*. It is the first level as one descends a hierarchy at which most people can conveniently form a visual image. For example, people generally have difficulty visualizing a fruit, but none visualizing an apple. Rosch, Mervis, Gray, Johnson, & Boyes-Braem (1976) have also shown that the basic label is the one that normally occurs first to a person when he sees an object, and indeed that it is the first one learned by children.

Mother's Speech to Babies

There is one puzzle in the foregoing related to certain differences between adult and child speech. Adults named a flower by the most specific name they knew, *rose* or *daisy*. At first glance this suggests that children have not picked up the name for an object their parents use, but choose a more generic name, like *flower*. It would be odd if young children adopted more generic names than they hear.

The puzzle is really only apparent. In fact, most adults failed to give a specific name to two of the flowers and named them, just as the children did, *flowers*. They also failed to give specific names to two of the dogs, and like the children named them just *dogs*. Even more telling, the adults gave specific names to the three fruits: *apple, banana,* and *strawberries*. Children gave the same specific names, but failed to give *fruit* as a generic name for all three. From this we can conclude that children adopt closely the usage of their parents. Parents do not know the specific names of many varieties of dogs and flowers, and so children hear them called *dog* and *flower* very frequently. On the other hand, parents do know the specific names of many varieties of fruit, and they use them. The children hear the generic, *fruit,* much less frequently and so are not likely to use it.

Anglin also explored the possibility that mothers do not always call an object by the same name when they are talking to children and to adults. He selected pictures of 25 objects: pineapple, sandal, pigeon, collie, carnation, cantaloupe, typewriter, hammer, grasshopper, pomegranate, mint (candy), dime, ant, cat, mint (sic), knife, ring, table, gun, snake, elephant, refrigerator, automobile, ruler, and record. He asked 20 mothers to name the pictures once for their two-year olds and once for the experimenter. In addition he asked 18 children between the ages of three and five to name them. He found that in six cases most mothers changed from a specific name when speaking to the experimenter to a more generic one for a child: *sandal (shoe), pigeon (bird), collie (dog), carnation (flower), mint (candy),* and *dime (money)*. For the rest they used the same names; and those names corresponded well with what the children said when they were able to name the objects. Most children used the generic names, *shoe, bird, dog,* and *flower,* though most said neither *mint* nor *candy,* nor *dime* nor *money*. So overall there was close correspondence in usage between mothers and children. And mothers did in some instances change to a more generic name when speaking to children, usually to the name that the children themselves used.

Overextension and Underextension

So much about the words that children know; it is time to begin a closer examination of what the words mean to them. Clark (1973) has made a study of the numerous diaries that linguists have kept of their children's early speech, and she has classified a number of "overextensions," i.e. words used by children of a wider range of objects than adult usage normally allows. For example, many children seem to use *dog* of both cats and dogs. They give the impression that they take *dog* to mean domestic quadruped. Of course we cannot be sure that they have actually classified dogs and cats separately as distinct species under the generic name, *dog.* If they have not, and if they mix up the objects cats and dogs, their term, *dog,* is merely specific waiting till the proper distinctions are made for its extension to be settled. However there are times when it is highly likely that an overextension is a higher-order word. Luria & Yudovich (1959) cite a child who called carrots, turnips, plums, and watermelons all *carrot.* For that child *carrot* surely functioned like *flower* in most people's vocabularies. Adults know there are many varieties of flower, but through ignorance of names they often have to make do with *flower.* And probably the child was in the same case in the matter of vegetables, knowing that there are many kinds but having to make do with the single term, *carrot.*

Clark has argued that perceptual similarity is the normal basis for children's overextensions, and she suggests that the main deciding factors are shape, movement, size, sound, texture, taste, and function (Clark, 1975). Labov & Labov's (1976) study of the features that one child employed in determining whether an object was a cat or not lends support to Clark's suggestion. However, one must not discount the possibility of a sense of metaphor as opposed to the type of confusion that the word overextension suggests. Clark (1973b) tells of a child who called a doorknob *apple,* presumably because the doorknob was round like an apple. It would be asinine to say Shakespeare overextended the term *breath* when he wrote of "summer's honied breath" meaning the summer air. And after all Shakespeare was a baby once. Clark wisely recognizes the likelihood that *apple* on that occasion was a metaphor. On the whole subject of metaphors in child speech see Winner (1978).

Anglin (1977, p. 104) makes an interesting observation about linguistic diaries. He noted that they tend to leave out under-extensions (failures to use a term where it would have been appropriate), because they are not so easily detected. If a child calls both a cat and a dog by the name *dog,* down goes that fact in the diary. But supposing he meets a chihuahua and does not know what it is, the child says nothing and nothing is entered in the diary. That amounts to a bias in favor of overextensions. Nevertheless, Anglin did locate some underextensions in the diaries. He cites one of a boy who called a large dog *hosh* (horse) even when he called most dogs *goggie.*

Anglin (1977) reports several studies of under- and over-extensions in connection with hierarchically related terms. In one he showed children pictures of the three categories that we have already seen:

I	II	III
animal	food	plant
dog	fruit	flower
collie	apple	tulip

There were 120 pictures and they were shown to three groups: children between 2½ and 4; children between 4½ and 6; and adults. As each picture was shown, a subject was asked, "is this an animal?" (or collie, or dog). Some of the pictures exemplified the object named in the question and some did not. Anglin found that underextensions outnumbered overextensions by about the same amount at each age level. It seems that people tend to caution rather than temerity in their use of words. That corresponds with the common observations that children tend either to get a grammatical construction right or not to use it. In view of the possibilities for error that grammar affords a child, he makes few errors.

In further studies, Anglin (chap. 5) adduced evidence that familiarity with an object or its picture was not an important factor in leading to underextension. Far more powerful was whether the object looked like a typical (in Rosch's sense) member of the class. In yet other studies (chap. 6) he found that the same factor was the most powerful one leading to overextension, far more powerful than the function that an object served or an association of contiguity. In general Anglin found that the factors that lead to underextensions in prompted speech are those that Clark (1973, 1975) found leading to overextensions in spontaneous speech.

The Meaning of Animal

Anglin's main concern was the hierarchical relation between terms like *dog* and *animal.* However, he and Clark, as we have just seen, examined the rules for applying such terms to objects in the environment. Neither one looked at meanings as such. There is a large literature on the subject associated with the name of Jean Piaget, and we must glance at it now, relying on the excellent analysis given us by Susan Carey (1978).

Piaget (1929) betrays his philosophical leanings in his approach to the word *animal;* like Socrates he demanded a definition. That is, he looked for the child's beliefs about necessary and sufficient conditions for something to be an animal. But he also asked whether various objects—e.g., the sun, a clock, a table, and a cat—were alive, and he asked for justifications for answers. If a child said a clock was alive but a table wasn't, he was asked to explain why. The central assumption in this work is that meaning consists in a set of conditions for applying a term. The literature is not at all clear, but as I see it, the difference between Piaget on the one hand and Clark and Anglin on the other is this: Piaget is looking for conceptual conditions of application whereas Anglin and Clark are looking for sensory ones. For example Piaget pays most attention to a condition like "moves autonomously," where autonomy is a conceptual interpretation. Anglin paid attention more to sensory similarity among objects.

Piaget's early work must be seen as exploratory. Its most authoritative successor is Laurendeau & Pinard (1962), which establishes norms for placing children in various developmental stages distinguished by criteria for attributing life. There are several major problems with this type of work. The request "tell me what an animal is," however phrased, makes sense only to someone who knows the word *animal.* Then one wonders how children construe such questions. A glance through the "correct" answers for the vocabulary items of the Stanford-Binet test shows that two interpretations are standard. When asked what an X is, nearly all children say (1) how you could tell it from something else; or (2) what you could do with it. Both interpretations are quite natural, but each lays aside the central matter that Piaget is after: what is the internal representation of the concept "animal" itself? It follows that one has to be more subtle if one wants to find out whether children have the concept "animal." Indeed, when attention is focused on "animal" rather than how you know them or what they can be used for, even an intelligent adult may fail to give a reasonable account. For the moment I will use *concept* and *meaning* interchangeably.

My own view is that no psychological work has addressed the core question of what "animal" (and the like) means. Most of the work has confined itself to the set of sensory attributes whereby we recognize that something is an animal. Now I may be able to distinguish lobsters from all other creatures, and demonstrate adequate sensory tests for lobsterhood; yet I may believe that lobsters are just peculiarly repulsive clothes brushes. In other words I may be sound on discrimination and quite unsound on meaning. The rest of the work on concept formation or meaning acquisition explores the set of phenomena that people attach to the category. For example they ask children whether worms breathe and have babies. That is more to the point, but it is only an initial step. The meaning of the word *animal*, I will argue in Chapter 12, is the meaning or sense we make of a certain set of creatures we call *animals*. Presumably the sense we make of them is that they are things capable of walking, breathing, having babies, etc. We attribute to them a nature which, however dimly, explains how they can walk, breathe, etc. Presumably we want the meaning of *animal* to be a representation of that nature. There is no easy road to the form of the representation. To ask whether worms breathe, walk, etc., is to ask if they are animals. Even if a child says a worm is an animal but denies that worms have babies, are we to say that for the child the word is ambiguous, or that he does not take having babies as an essential property of animals?

But I am rushing ahead to issues better left for Chapter 12.

All and Some

Whatever the content, we can inquire whether children's concepts are related hierarchically. That is, are such pairs as "dog" and "animal" related in children's minds as they are in adults'? Is every dog an animal but not every animal a dog? The findings so far reported constitute a prima facie case that children's concepts are so related. When asked, most three-year-olds and older children agreed that a particular creature was both a *dog* and an *animal*. On the other hand they would not allow that certain creatures, such as an elephant, was a *dog*, though they agreed it was an *animal*. That is, they said all dogs are *dogs* but only some animals are *dogs*, though all animals are *animals*. This indicates that implicit in the use of names by three-year-olds is the logic of quantification. In the next chapter we will see that this is the result of an interesting development.

There is, however, a well known attack on the position I take, which cannot be ignored. Inhelder & Piaget (1964) claim that children do not normally form "true concepts" and so cannot cope with classes or the relations among classes until the age of about seven. Strange as it may seem, they discount the evidence of language.

> The main finding of these investigations may be stated thus: the fact that the language of adults crystallizes an operational schema does not mean that the operation is assimilated along with the linguistic forms. Before children can understand the implicit operation and apply it, they must carry out a structurization, or even a number of successive restructurizations. These depend on logical mechanisms. (p. 4.)

Now it is reasonable to be suspicious of language. A child might simply have been taught that certain creatures could be called *dog* and *animal* and other creatures *cat* and *animal.* He might then treat them somewhat as we treat certain combinations of proper names. Certain girls are called *Betty Jane,* and certain others are called *Mary Jane.* We have to learn which are which. When we know, we can correctly identify the Bettys, the Marys, and the Janes. Yet *Jane* does not behave cognitively like *animal.*

Nevertheless, it is folly to disregard spontaneous language altogether, as Inhelder & Piaget do. As a matter of fact it is a simple matter to show that a three-year-old does not always use terms like *dog* and *animal* in rote fashion. Show him, as Anglin did, pictures of dogs he has not seen previously, and he will agree to call each one *dog.* Show him, as Anglin did (p. 141), pictures of an aardvark, an anteater, and a wombat and he will agree to call each of them *animal.* (By the way, he agreed, usually, only when it was right to do so.) He is not responding as he would if his learning had been of the *Betty Jane, Mary Jane* variety.

Inhelder & Piaget err in the other direction also. Language does not "crystallize" any logic, if this means that it conveys a logic ready made, albeit in an unsatisfactory form. Language and logic are autonomous systems, radically autonomous, even for a child. The linguistic structure that yields *all dogs are animals* yields also *all dogs are dogs, all animals are dogs,* and, slightly modified, *all dogs are not dogs.* Some of these are pointless and some are false, even necessarily so, but all are fully grammatical sentences. Language may be used to express logical relations; it cannot "crystallize" them.

Inhelder & Piaget turn their back on the child's spontaneous speech and place all their trust in specially designed tests. Their first is to place a variety of objects before a child and ask him "Put together the things which are alike," or "Put together the things that go together" (p. 18). Most two-, three-, and four-year-olds arranged the objects in what Inhelder & Piaget call "graphic collections." In other words the children did not put together objects of the same shape or color, but made various designs with them. Five- and six-year-olds often made small "non-graphic collections" but did not employ a hierarchical design. For example, one boy grouped the men together, made a separate group of chairs, another group of jugs, and a fourth group of animals (p. 57). He did not show any evidence that men and animals could go together as animals or chairs and jugs as household furnishings.

There has been some question about the replicability of the results (see Denny, 1972), yet Nelson (1973a) obtained similar results when she used Inhelder & Piaget's technique, and I am inclined to think that replicability is not an important problem. What is a most important problem is the sense that the children make of the instructions. They are as vague as one could imagine. What does "together" mean? Inhelder & Piaget noted that children often placed objects together in pairs; for example, two men, or two chairs. That is certainly putting objects together. The instructions did not say to place together *all* objects of a particular class. And what does the expression "things that go together" mean? Surely a man and a chair go together just as well as two men.

The point is not just critical for the sake of being critical, and it is vital for my case to get the matter straight. Nelson (1973a) varied the method slightly. She placed before the child eight objects that in her view made just two groups. She observed what the child did, and if he did not conform to her standards of grouping she grouped the objects for him. She repeated this pattern with various sets of objects, and she found reliable evidence of ability to copy the grouping in children between the ages of 12 and 24 months, that is, younger than the youngest that Inhelder & Piaget tested. Nelson's work confirmed an earlier finding by Ricciuti (1965).

Even more telling, Glucksberg, Hay, & Danks (1976) made the instruction explicit. They tested children between the ages two years and eight months and three years and three months. They asked them, among other things, "Give me one that's the same color as this bead." All children always responded correctly. Particularly when dealing with children who may not have learned the unstated expectations for certain adult routines, one has to spell out what one means.

In any case Inhelder & Piaget (1964) seek to establish a negative: that children under six are unable to classify objects in virtue of their similarities. Negatives are notorious. They can be overthrown by a single counterexample. And the counterexamples are legion, as we have seen in Anglin's work and as experience of three- and four-year-olds daily testifies. Against that, no amount of negative test results can cause a moment's hesitation.

Even if Inhelder & Piaget were to concede the weakness of their first line of tests, they would fall back on a second and more famous line. They claim, not unreasonably, that if a child really has a concept that enables him to classify objects, then he ought to be able to apply it to all the appropriate objects. In other words, classifications of objects partition them, and that affords an entrance to the quantifiers *all* and *some*. So *all birds have two legs; some animals have two legs.* How do we find out whether a child conforms to the logic of such quantifiers? Inhelder & Piaget's answer is a most extraordinary series of tests which I will exemplify by just one.

PRIMULAS AND FLOWERS

In one test the children aged 5–7 were shown a number of pictures that included eight primulas and some other flowers. They were asked several questions, which included: "Are there more primulas or flowers?" (I assume that *primevère* is more familiar to French-speaking children than its equivalent, *primula,* is to English-speaking ones.) Many children under 7 answered incorrectly, according to the testers, that there were more primulas.

There is little difficulty in replicating the result; it has been done thousands of times. But what does it mean? Inhelder & Piaget conclude that the children could not manage the class relations: all the primulas are some of the flowers. They claimed that having classified the primulas as such, the children could not simultaneously classify them as flowers. That is, a failure in class logic led them to interpret the question as, Are there more primulas or flowers other than primulas?

Much ink has been spilt on this and similar studies, but now, owing to the work of Ford (1976), we are in a position to settle the matter. He constructed a series of tests in which both the content questioned and the question form varied. First the questions, in three forms:

1. Give me *X*s or *Y*s. (e.g. "Give me cats or brown things"—where some cats might be brown).

2. Give me *X*s or *Y*s, or both. (e.g. "Give me blue things or dresses, or things that are both"—where some dresses might be blue).

3. Give me Xs or Ys, but not both. (e.g. "Give me clothes or dresses, but not both").

The second and third forms resolve an ambiguity in the *or* of the first. If you ask me what I would like for my birthday and I say, "Something to wear or something inexpensive," I might be happy with something that was both wearable and inexpensive. On the other hand, if I ask whether Nancy had a boy or a girl, I would be astounded to hear that her baby was both (a hermaphrodite). In some instances *or* is intended inclusively (wearable and inexpensive) and in others exclusively (boy or girl).

Ford's test items took account of such ambiguity. In some the Xs were cats and the Ys dogs. In others the Xs were dogs and the Ys animals (like the primulas, which are flowers). Of course, he employed more pairs than that, but I will content myself with illustrating. He tested 20 five-year-olds, 20 seven-year-olds, 20 eight-year-olds, and 20 adults.

The essentials of his findings are: (1) All age groups tended equally to interpret *or* exclusively (boy or girl) no matter whether the objects mentioned formed discrete categories like dogs and cats, or whether they formed overlapping ones like dogs and animals. The only important age differences occurred when the objects formed overlapping categories (dogs, animals) *and* the question took the form: Give me X or Y or both.

Now let us see what that means for Inhelder & Piaget's primulas and flowers. Ford's findings indicate that there is a strong assumption, equal at all age levels (except infant, presumably) that *primulas or flowers* means primulas or flowers other than primulas. Outside of logic class, in ordinary language, that is what the expression means to everyone. To overcome that assumption one must be explicit; one must say something like, primulas or flowers or both. Ford found that on hearing such an expression his older subjects were able to lay aside the normal assumption, but his youngest ones were not.

There is also a study by Markman and Seibert (1976) that supports this interpretation. They thought of a new way to ask the question, using such words as *bunch, family, class,* and *pile.* These are all names for collections, and contrast with the key expressions used by Inhelder & Piaget. They compared the effect of the two by asking children two types of question:

1. Who would have more to eat, someone who ate the green grapes or someone who ate the bunch?

2. Who would have more to eat, someone who ate the green grapes or someone who ate the grapes?

The children had been shown a bunch of grapes some of which were green and some purple. The pair of questions just given illustrates the lot. They found that the children they tested, kindergarten and first grade, gave significantly more correct answers to the questions with the collection words. The differences were significant, but not enormous: the mean number of correct answers to questions of type 2 was 1.57; to questions of type 1 it was 2.14 (MAX = 4). My reading of the finding is that the collection term helped the children to overcome their tendency to interpret *or* exclusively; a collection term like *bunch* urges a holistic interpretation more strongly than a plural like *grapes* (see also Markman, 1979).

This all throws new light on Inhelder & Piaget's results. Their younger children assumed that the tester meant primulas or flowers other than primulas. No more, no less. They interpreted the question as adults generally do. That did not mean that they were lacking in the logic of disjunction. Curiously, one result that puzzled Inhelder & Piaget has escaped most people's attention. It tells us the answer to the children's logic. Inhelder & Piaget included two other questions with the ones reported above. They asked: (a) "If you take all the primulas, will there be any flowers left?" (b) "If you take all the flowers, will any primulas be left?" (p. 101). They report (p. 104) that most of the children who had given a "wrong" answer to the questions with *or* in them gave the right answer to these. Notice that neither contains the fatal *or*. When the children were not misled by an *or* in the question, they answered rightly. They handled the quantifiers correctly. They responded in a way that recognized that all the primulas are some of the flowers.

Summary

One of the curious things about certain groups of names, like *chihuahua, dog, animal,* is that they are hierarchically related, at least for an adult. That means, among other things, that the entire class "chihuahua" is encompassed in the class "dog," and the entire class "dog" in the class "animal." Names go with the classes and so there are parallel relations among the names. The language learner is confronted with this early. He knows that he is a boy and a person. He hears talk of his trucks and his toys, some of the toys being trucks. Similarly he hears of clothes which subdivide into pants, shirts, sweaters, etc.; and food which subdivides into bread, meat, potatoes, etc.

This chapter begins the exploration of the child's knowledge of such hierarchical relations. We began with a study of the specific and generic terms that children know, basing ourselves mainly on Anglin's (1977) work. We found that such sets of terms increase in number from the age of about 2½. There is no clear tendency for the child to go from the specific to the generic or from the generic to the specific. It depends on the particular set of terms.

Anglin's findings support those of Eleanor Rosch (1973, 1975, and Rosch et al., 1976) in the relevant ways. Rosch argued that in hierarchies of classes one level is basic—that is (by one criterion) the first level as one descends the hierarchy at which one can readily form a visual image suited to the name. She claims that the name for the basic level is the first that the child learns, and Anglin's work bears her out.

Rosch also claims that the basic level name is the one that usually occurs to a person when he sees some object. This may explain Anglin's finding that there is a close correspondence between what mothers normally call an object and the one name that children usually have for it. In other words, adults may have many names for an object, but they usually use one, and that one, not surprisingly, is what children learn first. There were a few discrepancies between what a mother called an object and what a child called it. Anglin was able to show that in those cases mothers when speaking to a child usually used the child's word.

We began our study of what hierarchically related names mean to a child by looking at underextensions and overextensions, i.e., departures from adult standards in the application of terms. Both in diaries, which record spontaneous productions, and in Anglin's study of comprehension we found examples of both. Overextensions were more common than underextensions in diaries. That may well be due to an unconscious bias that notes the overextensions but fails to note when a term is not employed. In Anglin's study of production, underextensions were considerably more numerous than overextensions, though both types of error seemed rare. We concluded that children are cautious in formation of hypotheses. The most frequent source of underextensions and overextensions was perceptual form. If an object did not have the typical form associated with a class name, underextensions were common; if it did have a form close to that typically associated with a name, overextensions became common.

We went on to criticize the work done by Piaget and his collaborators on the meaning of the child's superordinate terms. The conclusion, largely anticipatory of later chapters, was that, valuable though it may be in other respects, it throws no light on meaning.

We ended with a critical analysis of Inhelder & Piaget's (1964) attempts to show, experimentally, that most children lack "true concepts" before the age of seven, and as a result they cannot perform the basic operations in the quantified logic of classes. We saw that their two main experiments were vitiated by ambiguous or misleading instructions. We also saw that when the ambiguities and the confusions were removed, other experimenters were able to show that children could perform the operations they failed for Inhelder & Piaget. But in any case, the spontaneous utterances of children from the age of three show a command of those operations. Indeed it is difficult to see how Inhelder & Piaget could have come to their conclusions if they had been attentive to language.

I have not attempted to account for how the child acquires hierarchically related sets of terms or applies to them the logic of quantification. That must wait until we have seen more clearly what it is a child learns in connection with such sets of terms.

5.
What is a Gorgon?
(Subordinate/Superordinate Names)

"Mamma," said Amanda, "I want to know what
Our relatives mean when they say
That Aunt Jane is a Gorgon who ought to be shot
Or at any rate taken away."
—Hilaire Belloc

Part I

In our effort to discover what sense the child makes of two
sortals for the same creature, e.g., *dog* and *animal,* we would do
well to tune in to nursery talk. Where there is a two-year old there
is chaos, and he is often told to put it to rights. One of the most
frequent instructions is, *pick up your toys, you heard Mommy say
put away your toys.* Does the child realize that each stuffed animal and each truck is a toy? Anglin (1977, chap. 5) asked two interesting questions aimed at finding out. He showed 20 children,
who ranged in age between 2 years and 10 months and 6½ years,
three pictures, one of a cow, one of a horse, and one of a cat. Of
each picture he asked, *Is this an animal?* And later, in a long series
of test items, he asked of each, What is this? With very few exceptions the children agreed that each was an animal and also identified it as a cow, a horsie, and a cat. The answer this gives to our
question is that by the age of about three most children realize
that the individual members of at least some categories can be described by both subordinates (like *cow, horsie,* and *cat*) and superordinates (like *animal*). In the last chapter we also saw that Anglin
(chap. 2) found that children of the same age range mostly describe

a group of three animals (dog, elephant, cat) as *animals*. So from the age of three, most children seem to have made the same sense as adults of the relation between subordinates and superordinates. Of course an adult may know much more about cows or horses than a three-year-old, but the hierarchical framework seems to be the same.

Let us go back to the nursery and ask if children can make sense of hierarchical relations among words as soon as they learn them. Do children younger than those tested by Anglin know that an individual truck is a toy; or does *toys* mean to them the chaos of objects that they are so often told to tidy up? Does *animals* mean just the group of creatures that they look at with their mothers in a particular animal book? Does *birds* mean a group whose individual members are robin, sparrow, and crow? Does *food* mean that mashed mixture that is made up of meat and potatoes and spinach? English itself, in certain of its terms, would seem to suggest the answer *yes*. Mother puts on the child's *clothes*, but a pair of pants is not a *cloth*. *Clothes* can be used of the group, but not of the individual. On the other hand the word *thing* seems to apply to anything you can bump into or pick up; and each is a *thing*.

It is quite unlikely that children can sort all this out as soon as they become familiar with pairs of words like *dog* and *animal*. Many objects have pairs of names that are not so related: *Thomas* and *Tom; Richard* and *Dick*. A bilingual child may learn that an individual dog is both *dog* and *chien*. Even a unilingual is liable to hear his baby brother called *Cecil* and *monkey;* yet it does not follow in any serious sense that Cecil is a member of the race *Simia* (or monkey). Nature would, then, be unwise to build into a child too immediate an impulse to seek hierarchical relations among pairs of terms applied to an individual. As with everything else in language, the child is obliged to use his intelligence to figure out how terms are related, discover or identify a hierarchical relationship, and determine which sets of terms are hierarchically related and which are not.

The rest of this chapter will be devoted to some studies that Nancy Wargny (1976) and I carried out of how two-year-olds interpret superordinate names. We did several tests which lead to the conclusion that at about the age of 24 months many children take a term like *animal* or *toy* as applying only to a group of objects, not to an individual object. Moreover the group is not just a plurality. Ten dogs are *dogs,* not *animals;* but a group consisting of some dogs, cats, sheep, horses, and cows is *animals. Animals,* then, at one stage signifies a plurality of type rather than a plurality of token. However, the matter is complicated. We found some evidence that the children had the idea "animal" though not as the meaning of the word *animal*. We also found that in a forced choice, they took the word *animal* to mean an individual animal. This led to a partial understanding of how they progress.

TEST 1: *IS-THIS-AN-ANIMAL?*

This whole line of investigation was prompted by curiosity to know what sense children make of hierarchically related terms applied to an individual. We soon became convinced that such pairs of terms do constitute a problem for a child. One day Nancy Wargny pointed to a two-year-old's toy box and asked him, "What's in there?" He replied without hesitation, "Toys." She then took out an airplane and asked "is this a toy?" With equal assurance he responded, "No, that's an airplane." He responded so when questioned about other individual toys. An even more striking example is the following exchange between Wargny and a 28-month-old boy to whom she showed her live goldfish:

Wargny:	What's this?
Child:	A fish.
Wargny:	I got him yesterday. He's so new that I don't have a name for him yet. What do you think I should call him?
Child:	Fishy.
Wargny:	Fishy. That's a fine name. I'll call him Fishy. Is Fishy a fish?
Child:	No, not Fishy a fish.

Though *Fishy* and *fish* in that conversation were a proper name and a common one, respectively, the boy's responses illustrate the general point.

All this suggested a very simple test, showing objects to children and asking, appropriately, *Is this an animal? Is this a toy?* The terms *animal* and *toy* seemed highly suitable. Nelson (1972) in a study of the first 50 words of 18 children between one and two years of age found that most in that range knew three specific animal names, like *dog, cat, horse.* In fact all 18 children knew some animal names, though not the term *animal.* Animals and food apart, no other category was represented in all children's vocabulary, but clothes, toys, vehicles, and household items came next in frequency.

The objects we used were plastic animals brought by the tester (Mrs. Erica Baker) and occasionally a stuffed animal or two from the child's own collection. The toys were small plastic boats, cars, blocks, and balls brought by the tester as well as some of the child's own. These were shown one at a time to a child and he was asked, appropriately, *Is this a toy?* or *Is this an animal?* Each child was also shown one object that was not a toy, e.g., a diaper or a shoe, and asked, *Is this a toy?* He was also asked of such objects, *Is this an animal?* This was a check on response bias.

The children tested were 12 boys and 16 girls from middle-class homes in Montreal. All were native speakers of English and all were tested in their own homes. The boys' mean age was 28 months and the range was 24 to 35 months; the girls' mean age was 29 months and the range was 24 to 33 months. Each child was tested about eight times for *animal* and eight for *toy*. The objects were shown as far as possible in random order and so the order of questions was varied randomly.

We counted the following types of response as correct: "Yes," "Yeah, animal," "Yeah, doggie," "Toy." We counted the following wrong: "No, it's a dog," "No," "No, truck," "Doggie." We were obliged to form a third category of response, "irrelevant," in which we placed all responses that we could not categorize as right or wrong.

The results are summarized in Table 5.1. There we see that about half the total responses were right and half were wrong. From Table 5.1 are excluded the responses to objects that were neither a toy nor an animal. The data taken en masse do not suggest a response bias in favor of *yes* or *no*.

Table 5.1   Numbers of Responses in the Three Categories.

	Right	*Wrong*	*Irrelevant*	*Total*
Animal	119 (51.3%)	110 (47.4%)	3	232
Toy	106 (48.4%)	110 (50.2%)	3	219

What of the individual children? Their responses are set out as concisely as possible in Appendix 2. Only three children gave fully consistent responses: two answered all questions correctly and one answered all incorrectly. A more useful summary of the data is given in Table 5.2 in which a cut-off point of 75 percent is taken. That is, the table shows the numbers of children who answered 75 percent of the questions correctly and the numbers who answered 75 percent incorrectly. In a third category are placed the vacillators, i.e., the remaining children. The numbers in parentheses under *right* and *wrong* are the mean number of

Table 5.2   Response Patterns to the Questions of Test 1.

A. *Is this a toy?*	(Mean number of trials per child = 7.8
	$N = 28$)

Number who correctly accepted the superordinate on at least 75%
of trials   9
    Number of those who also, incorrectly, accepted *toy* for at least
    one non-toy   4
Number who incorrectly rejected the superordinate name on at
least 75% of trials   9
Number who vacillated between *yes* and *no*   10

B. *Is this an animal?*	(Mean number of trials per child = 8.3
	$N = 28$)

Number who correctly accepted the superordinate on at least 75%
of trials   8
    Number of those who also, incorrectly, accepted *animal* for at
    least one non-animal   4
Number who incorrectly rejected the superordinate on at least 75%
of trials   7
Number who vacillated between *yes* and *no*   13

responses per child in each of those categories. For example, the eight children who 75 percent of the time or more answered correctly that certain objects were animals did so in fact on 91 percent of trials—see the figure in parentheses in the top lefthand corner. We see thus that our cut-off point gives us fairly homogeneous groups: children who answered correctly nearly all the time; children who answered incorrectly nearly all the time; and a group who wavered almost randomly between *yes* and *no*. About one third of the children are in each of the three groups.

Table 5.3   Numbers of Children Who Answered 75 Percent of Questions
Right or Wrong. (In parentheses under *right* and *wrong* are
the mean number of responses per child in those categories—
under *vacillators* in parentheses is the number who correctly
answered Yes (Y).)

	75% Right	75% Wrong	Vacillators	Total
Animal	8 (91%)	7 (90%)	13 (50%Y)	28
Toy	9 (92%)	9 (90%)	10 (43%Y)	28

Matters are not quite so simple though. Of the eight children who in Table 5.3 consistently accepted the superordinate category (*toy,* or *animal*) four allowed, wrongly, that a diaper or a shoe was a toy and the same four also said it was an animal. Those four may just have been of an agreeable disposition, answering *yes* to all questions. On the other hand none of the children who consistently rejected the superordinate category said a diaper or shoe was a toy or animal. Could it be that they were just crossgrained and responded *no* to all questions?

There are several indications that those who consistently refused the superordinate category were not just crossgrained. Many of them were quite emphatic in their denial. One boy later mimicked the tester's style, picked up a plastic horse, and asked, "What's that?" The following argument took place:

Tester:	It's an animal.
Child:	No.
Tester:	Yes it is.
Child:	No. (laughs)
Tester:	Yes.
Child:	No.
Tester:	This is an animal too.
Child:	No.
Tester:	Yes.
Child:	Horsie.
Tester:	It's also an animal.
Child:	No.
Tester:	It's an animal and a horse.
Child:	No.
Tester:	Just like you're Brian and you're a little boy.
Child:	No.
Tester:	Yeah.
Child:	No.
Tester:	You don't believe me.
Child:	No.

Just for the record that boy had previously taken the animal in six out of six trials in which he was offered two objects, say a spoon and a dog, and asked to take the animal.

Besides the emphasis with which they rejected the superordinate category, children were rarely content to say just *no*. They supplied what they thought was the appropriate word, as though to correct the tester. Eighty-one percent of rejections were of that sort—e.g., "No, piggie." Notice that they were supplying information that was not in the tester's question. They had not been asked, *Is a piggie an animal?* Just, *Is this an animal?*

It seems, then, that some children really meant to deny that a dog was an animal or that a ball was a toy. And it seems likely that at least a few really did accept both terms of a single object. Perhaps it would be wise to treat the others as vacillators, children who just had little idea what to make of these paired terms and responded either randomly or as agreeably as they felt was polite. So we have a small number, perhaps 5, who knew how to handle the pair; about 9 who had a clear idea, but by adult standards a wrong one; and 14 who were just puzzled or lost.

TEST 2: *WHAT-ARE-THESE?*

We guessed, when children consistently denied that a dog was an animal or a ball was a toy, that they had an idea that *animal* and *toy* were normally plural in their semantic force.[1] The reason for our guess was that mothers seldom use *toy* when they have a single object in mind.

In thinking about the matter, we noticed that plurals are sometimes ambiguous. *Chemicals* might sometimes mean several portions of the same kind of chemical, though more likely it would mean several types of chemical. *Dogs* on the other hand usually means several members of the species, dog. Let us use *plural of types* for one (e.g. *chemicals* in its normal interpretation) and *plural of tokens* for the other (e.g. *dogs* in its normal interpretation).

To be on the safe side we devised two tests. In one we showed a child a transparent plastic bag containing 10 plastic dogs. In the other we showed him a transparent plastic bag containing 10 assorted animals, two sheep, two cows, two horses, etc. Of each bag each child was asked, What are these? If he did not say *animal,* he was asked, Could you call them animals?

The questions were put to 20 children whose average age was 29½ months with a range of from 25 to 32 months. None of them had taken part in Test 1. There were 10 boys and 10 girls, all native speakers of English in Montreal. They were all tested in their homes by Reesa Benderoff.

The results are summarized in Table 5.4. I have divided the responses by what the child said and what he accepted. About half the children called the dogs *dogs* but denied that they were animals. About half called the assorted animals *animals* but nearly all accepted that they were animals. Of course the 11 who spontaneously called them *animals* were not asked the second question. There was no need to.

Are there any problems in interpreting these data? We can at least be sure that responses to question 1 were not random. It was

Table 5.4   Numbers of Children Who Gave Various Types of Answers
to the Questions of Test 2. N = 20.

	said	*accepted*
Question 1	20 said *dogs*	11 accepted *animals*
Question 2	11 said *animals*	19 accepted *animals*

not a *yes/no* question; children had to supply a name for the
objects. Question 2 was a *yes/no* one. However it was not put to
the 11 children who called the assorted animals *animals,* and yet
they are included in the 19 in the bottom lefthand corner of
table 5.4. Their responses at least were not random. What of the
others? We know that the responses are stable. We had an oppor-
tunity to test all the boys with the bag of dogs one month later
and they all responded in the same manner as previously. So
random responding seems most unlikely.

What of response bias? If children did not know the answer,
did they tend to say *yes*? If we look at the 8 children who did not
spontaneously call the assorted bag *animals* but answered *yes* to
the question if they were animals, we find that 5 said *yes* to the
corresponding question about dogs, and 3 said *no.* This does not
support the response bias hypothesis, but neither does it rule it
out. In fact, we do not have very good evidence against response
bias when children answered *yes.* When they answered *no* we had
the same evidence against such bias as in the first test. The *no*
was usually emphatic and accompanied by, "doggie," or "bow-
wow," as though to correct the tester.

Eleven agreed that the dogs were animals. They were not the
same 11. Only six of those who agreed that dogs were animals
spontaneously called the assorted bag *animals.* There is not, then,
as close a correlation as the figures might lead one to imagine
between correct responding to those two questions.

The girls answered better than the boys. Only three of the
children who spontaneously used *animals* were boys; eight were
girls. Only four of those who accepted *animal* of the dogs were
boys; eight were girls. It is not uncommon to find girls more
advanced than boys in language.

What does this tell us? If we lay aside the details, it tells us
that about half of our children avoid the word *animal* except as
referring to assorted animals. They do not allow its use of several
animals of a single type, e.g. several dogs. On the other hand, about
half the children accepted *animals* of a single species, and they also

accepted or spontaneously used the word of the assorted animals. Their usage matches an important part of adult usage of hierarchically related terms: *animals* comprehends a single species as well as a variety of species.

I have suggested that the children who refused *animal* of a single species saw the semantic force of the word as normally plural, and thought it inappropriate to use of an individual—compare *clothes*. Another possible explanation is that such children always employ the lowest term in a hierarchy. That would explain why a child would one moment call a creature *a fish* and, having named him *Fishy*, insist on the proper name. Such a strategy would guarantee the maximum of information in most circumstances. At table a request for bread is more likely to produce the desired result (if it's bread you want) than one for food. Could it be that these children were employing the strategy of maximizing information?

That does not fit the data as well as the "plural" explanation. It does not explain the vehemence of the denial that a horse is an animal. Some children strongly suggested that they thought it wrong, not just inadequate, to call a horse an *animal*. They responded as I might if asked whether a single cow is a herd. However there are other data that rule out the suggested strategy.

When my son, Kieran, was 2 years and 1 month he was clearly at the stage when hierarchical terms were a problem of the sort described. The following is an extract from my diary of his speech:

25:10	This evening I asked: "What's Puppy (his proper name for a stuffed animal)?" He repeated the question.
Self:	"Is he a dog?"
Kieran:	"Yes," firmly.
Self:	"Is he an animal?"
Kieran:	"No," firmly.
Self:	"Is Freddie a dog?" (Freddie is the family dog.)
Kieran:	"Yes," firmly.
Self:	"Is Freddie an animal?"
Kieran:	"No," firmly.

I showed him pictures of two animals he did not recognize, a giraffe with head bent and a polar bear. "What's he?" I asked pointing to one. Kieran didn't know and gave the wrong answer, and I said "no." "Is he an animal?" I asked. Kieran firmly responded, "no," to the questions about both. I placed four stuffed animals in his bed—Puppy, a koala bear, a dog, and a squirrel. I said: "Give me an 'animal'." He paused and gave me the koala. He immediately picked up Puppy and hesitatingly hugged him. Then he asked of each if he was an animal.

Several features of this are worthy of note. Kieran had long called Freddie a *dog,* so he had no reluctance to use a term for Freddie that conveyed less information, *dog.* What he refused to do was call him an animal. Now there is a longstanding dispute about whether proper names have sense and stand as the lowest terms in a hierarchical classification that might run *Freddie, dog, animal.* For the sake of argument let us suppose that proper names are very different from common names, and take the lowest term in Kieran's hierarchy to be *dog.* That would explain his agreeing that Freddie was a dog and refusing to allow that he was an animal. In that case Kieran ought to have agreed that an animal for which he did not have a specific term (giraffe, polar bear) could be called *an animal.* He did not agree to this. Therefore his responses cannot be explained by a strategy to employ the lowest term. On the other hand he did not inevitably take *animal* as a plural or collective noun. When asked for *an animal,* he gave just one. My interpretation of his mind is that he was sure of *animal* only as a plural (of type), but allowed his interpretation of it to be guided by the presence of the article *an,* for him a sure marker of singularity.

I am confident of Kieran's pattern of responses, but I also questioned two other children who were at the same stage in their use of *animal.* The two were at a baby-sitting center in Montreal. One was a boy aged 35 months; the other was a girl aged 26 months. Both children could name several varieties of animals. Both refused to allow that any single animal was an animal. Some of the *animals* about which I questioned them they were able to name an *elephant* or a *monkey.* Even when they did not know a name, and I picked some rather uncommon varieties, they would not allow that any was an animal. On the other hand each child allowed that three toy animals—a dog, a squirrel, and a koala bear—were animals. Their responses bear out my interpretation of Kieran's.

For these reasons I rule out the explanation that certain children refused to allow that a dog was an animal simply because of a strategy to employ the lowest term in a hierarchy.

TEST 3: *SENTENCE-IMITATION*

The crucial development that we are looking for is the recognition that an individual of a subordinate category is also an individual of a superordinate category. The English structure *an X is a Y* can be used to express that relationship. Of course it can be used for other functions. *A wet day is a pain* does not really classify wet days in a superordinate category, pain. *A puppy is a young dog* does not classify puppies in a superordinate category, young dogs, but expresses an identity. Nevertheless, the form *an X is a Y* is the normal way to express a hierarchical relation between terms.

We were interested to know if two-year-olds had a command of this structure. One way to find out is to ask children to imitate sentences of that form. The test has been used extensively in the study of child language. For the test to be maximally useful it must tax the child's memory span. The idea is that if a sentence is taxing, knowledge of syntax will help. For purposes of comparison we also asked each child to imitate a phrase of the same length as our main sentences, a phrase which does not contain the key structure. For that purpose we chose phrases of the form *an X and a Y*.

We tested 38 children who had not taken part in any of the tests so far mentioned. They were 24 boys and 14 girls, all native speakers of English. The mean age was 30 months, the range from 24 to 38 months. Each child was tested in his own home by Mrs. Erica Baker.

The results are synopsized in Table 5.5. The key sentences were difficult, and about one third of the children failed to imitate them. The length of the key sentence does not seem to have been the explanation for failure, because fewer failed to imitate the control expressions, which were of equal length. If two-year-olds find a structure strange, they usually try to change it to conform to their own syntax. We found no such attempts. The reasons for failing to imitate the key sentence seem to have had nothing to do with syntax. Several children refused to imitate because they thought the key sentences were false. Some when asked to say sentences like *A pig is an animal* simply said "Pig not animal." One child refused to say *A giraffe is an animal* and retorted "No, it's a giraffe." This is the pattern we are familiar with.

Table 5.5   Numbers of Children Who Imitated Criterion and Control Expressions in Test 3.

	Criterion *an X is a Y*	Control *an X and a Y*
Imitated	25	29
Failed	13	9
Total	38	38

We have found, then, no evidence that two-year-olds find the syntactic structure *an X is a Y* strange. Could it be, for example, that they always interpret it as the *is* of identity (a puppy is a young dog) and never as the *is* of class inclusion. For example, Kieran Macnamara answered "Yes" to "Is Freddie a dog?" and "No" to "Is Freddie an animal?" It is the same *is* in both questions and it is the *is* of class inclusion. A giraffe is not an animal, we can now interpret them to say, because *animal* does not mean an individual of any sort.

TO SUM UP

What prevents certain two-year-olds from saying that a dog is an animal does not seem to have anything to do with syntax. It has to do with the meaning of such words and how they are related. We found a good deal of evidence that some do not know how adults relate certain objects hierarchically. Some of them guess that the superordinate term is a plural of a special kind. Being a plural, it cannot properly be used of any individual. Such plurals are of a special kind in that they refer to multiplicity—not of individuals of a single species, like most plurals, but to multiplicity of species. *Animals* means a set of creatures that vary in species. *Toys* means a collection of objects that vary in type. In Test 1 we saw that perhaps one third of the two-year-olds were of that frame of mind. In Test 2 we found that about half the two-year-olds refused to accept *animals* as applied to a group of dogs, but almost all accepted the term when applied to a bag of assorted animals.

In Test 2, however, we found that about half the two-year-olds responded in a manner that agreed with adult usage and adult understanding of the relation between subordinate and super-ordinate terms. In Test 1 we found that only one third of them so responded when the terms *animal* and *toy* were applied to an individual. In that test we found that about one third of the two-year-olds did not reveal any clear solution to the problem of hierarchically related terms. It seems that more children are willing to accept a term like *animal* as a plurality of type than as applicable to an individual.

No doubt these findings are modest and might have been anticipated by any parent who is attentive to how one talks as a child. However, they do show the child as actively seeking explanations for puzzles, and hitting on explanations that differ not at all from the type an adult would be satisfied with. How he moves from interim solutions to adult hierarchical classification is the business of the next section.

Part II

When we find that a child does not use some word that we think
appropriate to describe an object, the difficulties might be:

(a)   He does not know the word.

(b)   He does not have the corresponding idea.

(c)   He fails to construe what precisely is being asked of him.

(d)   Some combination of (a)–(c).

Let us explore these possibilities. We can rule out (a) as applying
to the 2½-year-olds who would not agree that a dog was an animal
or a truck was a toy. Almost every one of the 2½-year-olds who
took part in the test agreed that assorted animals were animals.
They knew the word *animals,* but they did not allow it the scope
that adults do.

Could it be that 2½-year-olds do not have the idea (used rather
loosely) adults have of toys and animals? In one trivial sense the
answer is certainly *yes.* Adults in general know more about animals
and toys than 2½-year-olds do; so adults have richer ideas of
animals and toys. For our purposes it is more to the point to
inquire if 2½-year-olds have formed an idea that, like an adult's,
classifies certain types of creatures as animals and certain others
as toys, and if those ideas are applicable to individual objects. We
have part of the answer. Nineteen out of twenty 2½-year-olds
agreed that a bag of assorted animals were animals. Many 2½-year-
olds refused to allow that an individual cow or horse was an animal,
or that an individual truck or doll was a toy. Less than half a dozen
out of 28 tested gave a clear indication that an individual object
could be called *animal* or *toy.*

Why? We have already considered the force of the adult's
clothes, which is a plural-only word. It resembles our interpretation of the child's *animal* in that it does not apply to an individual; it differs from the child's *animal* in that *clothes* is not
necessarily a plural of type. Two shirts are clothes. Nevertheless
clothes helps to make the point. Doubtless my concept of clothes
is quite as applicable to an individual shirt as my concept of animal
is to an individual dog. Indeed I have a word, *garments,* to prove
it. *Garments* refers to an assembly of which each member is a
garment. The restriction on calling a shirt or jacket a *cloth* appears
to be mainly a lexical matter not a conceptual one. In other
words there appears to be no conceptual reason to make *clothes*
a plural only. Could it be, for the 2½-year-olds that most interest
us, that the restriction on calling a dog an animal was also linguistic,

rather than conceptual? I will try to deal with that recondite matter before going on to the third of the possible difficulties suggested as explanations for the children's responses.

To clarify the issue Nancy Wargny and I carried out two experiments. One was of object sorting and the other was a forced-choice test. In the latter a child was shown a pair of objects, say a hairbrush and a toy dog, and he was asked to *take the animal.* That, we imagined, would urge the child to apply a generic name to an individual far more than asking him, *Is it an animal?* The object-sorting task was designed to serve two functions. The skill it elicited was more nonverbal, or independent of language, than that elicited by any other of our tests. Secondly, it required the child to handle objects and, in order to perform correctly, to apply a principle of classification (a concept) to individual objects. Calling a bag of assorted animals *animals* does not involve calling the individuals in the bag *animals.* Choosing the animals from an array of objects does involve embracing them individually under a principle of classification. We will begin with the object-sorting.

OBJECT SORTING

The objects for the test can be grouped as *animals* and, for want of a better word, *machines.* The animals were small plastic figures of a horse, a cow, a pig, and a dog. The machines were small plastic toys: a boat, a truck, a tractor, and an earthmover. Care was taken, as far as possible, not to permit the groups to be distinguished by irrelevant criteria. So all the objects were plastic, and all were roughly of the same size. Colors varied in each group, and no simple color rule could be used to distinguish between groups. There were several relevant discriminators. The animals all had legs and the machines did not. The machines, like real ones, were of a smooth texture; the animals, like real ones, were rough in texture.

The eight objects were spilt out in a random array on the floor before a child. The tester, Reesa Benderoff, then told the child to watch what she did, and she placed half the objects back in the box. She then asked the child to do just as she had done, and she noted what he did. There were two conditions. In one she placed the four animals in the box. In the other she placed the cow, the pig, the boat and the tractor, picked in random order, in the box. That was a control condition to ascertain if the children were able to memorize the four objects that the tester selected. If they showed evidence of being able to memorize in that fashion, when there was no single previously established category to cover all four objects, there would be no need to invoke a category, animal, to explain success in sorting out the four animals. Notice that in the control condition a conjoint category defined as two animals and two machines would not help the child very much. He would have had to memorize which two animals and which two machines. On the other hand if children fail the control test and succeed in the experimental condition, we can be confident that memorization does not explain the success. To rule out memorization is to strengthen the case that the children have a classificatory category—to which adults attach the name *animal*—that they can employ to pick out all and only the individuals that fall under the category.

The children who took part in this experiment were 24 boys between the ages 24 and 30 months, with an average age of 28 months. All came from middle-class Montreal homes and were tested individually in their homes. Each was tested in his home under only one condition, and he was given only one trial.

Results. We counted responses as either right or wrong. A right response was one in which the child placed in the box the four objects that the tester had done and no others. All other responses were classed as wrong. In Table 5.6 are given the number of children who responded correctly in each condition.

Table 5.6   Number of Children Who Sorted Objects Correctly.

	Experimental *4 Animals*	*Control* *2 Animals, 2 Vehicles*
No. Correct	9	0
N	12	12

Table 5.7   Numbers of Objects Correctly Sorted.

	Experimental *4 Animals*	*Control* *2 Animals, 2 Vehicles*
No. Correct	40	25
Total Sortings	48	48

The first thing to notice is that these children were unable to sort correctly on the basis of memorizing the individuals. No child in the control group succeeded in placing the correct two animals and the correct two machines in the box. So the task was too much for their short-term memory for individuals.

Nine of the twelve in the experimental group put all the animals in the box. Actually I suspect that that underrates their performance. One of the other three put all the machines in the box. Only one other child did that, a boy in the control group. I suspect that at least the boy in the experimental group was following some such rule as, place all the nonanimals in the box. He might have done that in order to give them their turn, or because he misunderstood the game: the tester puts in the animals and you put in the machines. Such rules would suggest the concept "animal", by exclusion.

In any case we now have good evidence (9 out of 12, or on a more liberal interpretation 10 out of 12) that 2½-year-olds can sort animals. To do so they had to select individual objects according to some classificatory principle. They almost certainly could not have merely memorized the individuals. The classificatory principle enabled them to pick the appropriate individuals. In other words, it was a principle that embraced a certain range of varieties, not just any varieties.

We will discuss the broader implications of this finding after we have seen the next experiment. The object-sorting test was nonverbal; the next one is largely verbal. It is designed to reveal whether 2½-year-olds can make any sense of a generic name applied to an individual. If they can, we have thereby an indication of how they progress to adultlike use of generic terms.

TAKE THE ANIMAL: TAKE THE TOY

In this test a child was shown two objects only one of which was either an animal or a toy. The animals were plastic figures brought by the tester, although occasionally one of the child's own stuffed animals was used. The toys were also brought by the tester, although again occasionally one of the child's own toys was used. None of the objects I call *toys* was an animal. On each trial an animal or a toy was paired with some object that was clearly neither. For example, the other object might be the tester's shoe, a cup from the kitchen, and such like.

Each child was tested five or six times with animals and the same number of times with toys. So as to hold the child's attention the pairs of objects were varied randomly from trial to trial. In pilot testing we discovered two useful hints that guided us throughout. The tester should hold the two objects far enough apart so that the child could not reach both of them at once. Unless "forced" to choose, many children will ignore instructions and simply take everything that is held before them. The second hint was that one had more success with children if the instruction was to *take* an object rather than to *give* it or *show* it. It is wise to use the child's possessiveness rather than fight it. In addition, the tester was careful not to look at either of the objects she was holding while waiting for the child. That was to avoid prompting. Those were the only precautions we took. There was no possibility of using a double blind, because there was no possibility of concealing the correct response from the tester. Mechanical devices for presenting the objects might have eliminated unwanted bias, but they would probably have eliminated a good deal of responding too.

Altogether 66 children were tested individually in their own homes. Each was a native speaker of English from a middle-class home in Montreal. There were 38 boys and 28 girls. The average age was 29 months and the range from 24 to 36 months. The testing was done by Mrs. Erica Baker.

Results. In these tests we showed children objects in pairs, and we were confident that they knew specific names for at least the key object in each pair. We named that key object with a generic name to see if they could understand it as applied to an individual object. Table 5.8 shows that in most trials they responded correctly and took the object referred to with a superordinate name. If instead of the general finding we look at the individual performances, the results are equally impressive. Since on each trial a child has to choose between two objects, the probability of choosing right by chance was .5. No more than three children gave a clear impression of responding at random; the others seemed to be able to comply with the instructions, and gave the impression of momentary lapses of attention or of being momentarily distracted by the "wrong" object.

Table 5.8. Responses in Forced Choice Tests.

	N	No. trials	No. correct responses	% correct responses
Take the toy	66	382	337	89
Take the animal	66	423	375	89

These results indicate fairly clearly that 2½-year-olds are able to make some sense of a generic term, like *toy* or *animal,* as applied to an individual object. From the rest of what we have seen of them, we know that many of them are not happy about applying a generic term to an individual and in fact refuse to do so. Yet when offered a choice and told to take an individual referred to with a generic name, they do so. Presumably many of them felt that the generic name was being used somewhat strangely. But the strange usage had adult authority and could not be dismissed out of hand. Those who would not themselves approve of that usage were then forced to see which of the pair of objects best fitted the instruction. They chose correctly about 90 percent of the time.

That result shows that even children who see the words *animals* and *toys* as meaning only plurality of type are able to place an appropriate restriction on the range of types. In other words, they do not take the terms to mean plurality of any types, but plurality of types over a certain range. This supports the finding of the object-sorting task, where again children were able to choose all and only the animals showing that they had a category that specified an appropriate range of objects, namely animals.

The result also suggests that the step of employing a generic term to refer to an individual cannot be too far off or too difficult. After all, they were able to function correctly when generic terms were so applied. In chapter four we saw that Anglin (1977) had good evidence that they themselves would be able to say that a dog was an *animal* from about the age of three.

CONTEXT

At the beginning of the section, I suggested three possible explanations for why a large number of 2½-year-olds might refuse to allow that an individual dog was an *animal* or an individual doll a *toy*. I have discussed two of the three: they might not know the word; they might not have the appropriate higher-order concepts. I was able to rule the first out from what we had seen of children in the previous section. I produced some experimental evidence (object sorting) that they do have the appropriate higher-order concept. That points to the conclusion that what they lack is a linguistic rule that allows the terms *animal* and *toy* to be applied to individuals. We have just seen that they can be "bullied" into relaxing whatever linguistic restriction they have imposed and can in a forced-choice task take the animal and take the toy. Before discussing the matter further, I would like to take up the third possible explanation.

The idea was suggested by a paper of David Olson's (1970) in which he pointed out that what an object is most appropriately called depends on context, nonverbal as well as verbal. We have seen ourselves that if an object is the only one of its kind in the environment it will usually be called *the X—the dog*, for example. Otherwise it will first be called *an X—a dog*. Olson showed that what people will call a circular white block depends on what other blocks are in its neighborhood. If there is a black circular block in the neighborhood, the key block will generally be called *the white one*. If there is a white square close by, the key block will generally be called *the round one*. If there are several blocks close by, including a black circular one and a white square one, the key block will most probably be called *the white round one*.

We asked ourselves if a similar principle might not have been guiding our 2½-year-olds. After all, they chose the animal or toy as told to when the other object in the neighborhood was a nontoy and a nonanimal. They agreed to call an assorted bag of animals *animals*. Could we explain along those lines the numerous refusals to call an individual object a *toy* or an *animal*? Olson (1970) said: "a word specifies a perceived referent relative to a set of alternatives." Could it be that lacking an appropriate set of alternatives, they simply refused to call either an individual or several objects of a single type (dogs) by a generic name? Whenever we supplied "an appropriate set of alternatives," they handled the generic name correctly.

That did not seem a likely explanation. Notice that Olson chose to illustrate his point with articles like a white circular block that do not have a linguistically simple name in English. We do have simple names for dogs and cats and the like. Nevertheless Nancy Wargny (1976) put the matter to the test.

She tested eight children in a Montreal day-care center. They were aged three and four, and were seen individually. Wargny showed each child four boxes the contents of which were as follows:

(a)   several plastic animals

(b)   several small toys

(c)   one plastic animal and several toys that were not animals

(d)   one toy car and several objects chosen because they did not look like toys: plate, cup, knife, fork, spoon, and an adult's tennis shoe.

She opened the boxes one at a time, in random order, and asked the child to look at the things inside. She then pointed to a toy or an animal and asked, *Can you tell me what that is?*

All the children, no matter what else the box contained replied with the relatively more specific words, e.g., *car* or *tiger*. None used the generic name, *toy* or *animal,* even when it should have been preferred by Olson's criterion.

On the basis of this evidence we decided that Olson's hypothesis did not explain certain children's refusal to apply a generic name to an individual object. We had always felt confident that our 2 to 2½-year-olds understood quite well what we asked of them and had not been misled by establishing cognitive contexts different from ours in posing the tests. Wargny's findings strengthened our beliefs.

Conclusions

I do not wish to obscure the fact that several 2½-year-olds gave evidence of having formed hierarchically related concepts and of using the related words in the manner of adults. And I do not wish to suggest that all those who failed to reveal that response pattern use the terms *animals* and *toys* as adults use *clothes* (a plural only). Only about one third of the children seemed to treat the terms in this way.

Let us be quite clear about the questions we have asked in this and the preceding chapter. We have not really looked at the content of the children's concept, but at the formal relations between terms that for adults form hierarchies, *dog* and *animal* or *truck* and *toy,* for example. We have attempted to do that by tests of whether 2½-year-olds would apply terms from different levels to the same object; and when certain of them failed, we tested whether they would apply a superordinate term to a single species or only to a variety of species. To extract the conceptual relations from language we carried out a nonverbal test.

The conclusions we come to can now be summarized. Children have some idea of "animal" that embraces several subordinate categories (cats, dogs, horses). That follows from the *What-are-these?* test; it showed that children are prepared to call a variety of species by the term *animals.* Their notion, "animal," embraces individual members of the subcategories. That follows from the results of the object-sorting test, because there they had to pick out the animals one by one. It also follows from the results of the forced-choice test; when asked to *Take an animal,* they took an individual dog or cow. There was abundant evidence that many 2½-year-olds are reluctant to apply a superordinate term to an individual object. The main source for that conclusion is the *Is-this-an-animal?* test, in which many refused adamantly to allow that an individual dog was an animal. This sums to the following:

children have formed adult-like relations among certain hierarchically related ideas, yet something stops them from applying a
superordinate term either to a subordinate species or to an individual object. They treat superordinate terms like collectives.
Two problems immediately follow: (1) What is the form of the
constraint that results in children treating a superordinate term as
a collective and how do they relax it? (2) How do children manage
to relate concepts hierarchically? The second of these I will put
aside until a later chapter. In the remainder of this chapter I will
attempt to answer the first.

One likely explanation is that children consider terms like
animal as collective nouns. It would not be surprising if they
should because that is how they hear them used. Recall Anglin's
(1977) finding that in speaking to a child, adults call a rose
a *flower*, but not a *plant*. To call an individual flower a *plant*
sounds odd in many contexts, and so too does calling an individual
dog *an animal*. Small wonder if young children thought such usage
modeled a linguistic restriction.

How do children who have come to the collective-noun interpretation shed it? The evidence of our *Take-the-animal* test is that
shedding it will not be a very large step. Nearly all those whom we
tested were able to interpret a generic term when it was applied to
an individual. Though they may not have so used the term themselves, they were able to divine what it meant when so used.

It must be the case that a great many children become acquainted
first with the terms *toy* and *animal* as used of assortments of
objects. Later they will notice that they are used in describing
individual objects too. The child who asks, "What is a yoyo,
Mommy?" will hear something like, "It's *a toy* with a string
attached that you can make go up and down." Or "It's a sort
of toy." The child who asks "What is a yak?" will be told "It's
an animal, a bit like a cow, and it lives in Tibet." In the explanation of many words that describe individuals there will occur the
expressions *a toy* and *an animal*. On other occasions the child
will hear such remarks as "The poor animal is suffering from a
rash" used of the family dog. Again *animal* is being used of an
individual. But such explanations and such observations will not
normally be made to children until they are well advanced in
syntax.

If I am right in concluding that 2½-year-olds who fail to apply a
generic term to an individual are confused on a linguistic point,
not a conceptual one, the cure must be relatively simple. They

already have concepts appropriately related—say, the individual pet, which is a dog, which is an animal. All that needs to be done on encountering the necessary linguistic evidence is allow the words *dog* and *animal* to match those conceptual structures. The only change is the relaxation of a linguistic restriction.

Once again we see how conservative young children are in forming linguistic hypotheses. And once again we see the advance of conceptual development on linguistics. The child learns language so as to be able to express the things he has to say; and as he is learning, he has more to say than he can express.

PART II
MATTERS MAINLY LINGUISTIC

6.
Sound Sense

No belly and no bowels,
Only consonants and vowels.
  —John Crowe Ransom, "Survey of Literature"

Why do foreigners speak so quickly and indistinctly? It can hardly be that aside from English speakers the world is full of gabblers and mumblers. The explanation must be a perceptual one; over years we have learned the sounds of English and the words, and we can recognize them rapidly and easily. But even though we know a little French, we find we cannot keep pace with those who speak and perceive French as their native language. Foreigners, therefore, only seem to mumble, and any other explanation must sound parochial. Now there is a real sense in which we must sound to our infants as foreigners sound to us. Doubtless the parallel is not exact, since we have learned perceptual biases in learning English whereas the infant is, auditorily, a *tabula rasa*. Nonetheless, the infant has not as yet grown accustomed to and mastered the sound patterns of English, and until he does, much of what we say to him must sound like gibberish. Since names are part of this gibberish, learning them involves among other things sorting out those sound patterns that are names. In this chapter we shall be concerned with how he does it, and we shall begin with the question how sharp are the infant's ears? Is he able to detect all those contrasts in sound that are important in English, or do some of them have to be thrust upon him, in the way that the Scots and Irish thrust on the English the distinction between *loch* (lake) and *lock*. Part of the Englishman's trouble is that he doesn't seem to hear the difference. The study of such phonological problems is of central importance to cognitive psychology. Failure to come to grips with them has led the two main branches of contemporary philosophy—phenomenology and the logical analysis of language that stems from Frege—into seriously simplistic proposals about concept formation. The standard position is that the problem of how to categorize objects is solved for the child by the names he hears applied to them. That presupposes that the problem of categorizing those phonological entities that we call names is psychologically simpler than that of categorizing nonlinguistic objects. To examine this presupposition will require a detailed analysis of phonological learning.

The first question we will ask is this: In learning the set of sound contrasts of English is the infant learning mainly to ignore certain auditory distinctions of which he is capable and settling for those that are essential in the system? Or is it the other way about; does he have to increase his acuity so that he can detect them all? Put this way, it is evident that the question is about the capacity for distinguishing among speech sounds that nature endows a child with. Is the capacity too sharp or too blunt initially?

Before answering, we may wonder that the question arises at all; why do we suppose that the capacity is not exactly right for English? The answer is that children of English-speaking parents are just as capable of learning Chinese or Tagalog as English. The sounds of English match those of other languages only in part. It follows that the set of speech sounds that the child learns depends on which language he learns. Nature, then, could not equip a child equally well to learn any natural language and at the same time set him up with a linguistic capacity to distinguish all and only the sounds of his mother tongue.

Experiments on Auditory Acuity in Infants

The past fifteen years or so have seen a remarkable increase in ingenious techniques for studying the abilities of very young infants in their first months. Some of the ingenuity has been applied to the infant's acuity in distinguishing speech sounds. The first studies were carried out by Peter Eimas and his colleagues (see Eimas, Siqueland, Juszych, & Vigorito, 1971), and others have followed. Several were carried out at McGill by Sandra Trehub, and since I had the good fortune to witness some of these, I will describe them.

The main item of apparatus was a special nipple which was attached to a pressure transducer. This enabled the automatic recording of the number of times it was sucked in a given space of time. The nipple was placed in an infant's mouth and a pair of headphones over his ears. The infant's sucking controlled a tape recorder and determined whether or not he heard anything in the headphones. He heard a single speech sound until he grew tired of it and stopped sucking. Then came the interesting part of the experiment. At that point the tape recorder was started again. Some infants heard the same sound as before, but some heard a different sound. Interest attached mainly to whether the new stimulus provoked more sucking than the old one.

In one experiment Trehub & Rabinovitch (1972) contrasted the syllables *bah* and *pah,* and *dah* and *tah.* There were 30 experimental infants and 30 control ones aged between one and four months. Sucking patterns subsequent to the change of sound showed that the experimentals responded differently to the new sound. Infants who heard the same sound sucked little, those who heard a new one sucked vigorously. They must have noticed the change. Of course much more technical skill in phonetics is required to run this experiment successfully than this brief description suggests. Nevertheless the method does enable us to explore differences in sound to which infants are sensitive, and the experiment just described shows that they are sensitive to whether an initial consonant is voiced or not.

Even more interesting, this sensitivity was probably not learned in the brief period during which the infants had been hearing English. Streeter (1976) repeated the experiment with Kikuyu infants and obtained very similar results. The Kikuyu are a Bantu tribe whose language does not make the same voiced-voiceless contrast as English. Moreover, Trehub (1976) found that infants in English-speaking homes were sensitive to the contrast between [ža] and [ra] that is made in Czech, but not in English. Infants were highly sensitive to the contrast, though adult English speakers find it difficult to detect. The result is interesting, but there are difficulties with its interpretation. Perhaps adults could detect the distinction if there was some way of getting them to believe it wasn't speech, so that they did not attempt to bring their speech perception rules to bear.

So far the results suggest that the infant comes to speech with more acuity than he needs. However, there is a study by Eilers & Minifie (1975) in which infants did not react to the difference between [sa] and [za], a contrast that their native language would require them to attend to later. So the overall result is that infants appear to have more acuity than they need in some acoustic regions and perhaps less than they need in others. It would follow that they must be able to increase their acuity in some regions. There are only two ways in which this could happen. One is that their auditory systems become more sensitive with time. This happens because we know that the sound-frequency range to which infants are sensitive increases with age, perhaps owing to developments in the bone formations of the ear. The only other way is that they attend to finer differences. We know that this happens in the visual domain. Not everyone can read a thermometer at first, for example. Presumably infants must learn to attend to differences in certain sounds that their ear registered but that escaped their attention. (For a much more complete review of the literature on infant speech perception, see Jusczyk, 1980.)

What about those acoustic regions where the infant appears to have more acuity than he needs? One might be tempted to say that in learning his mother tongue he has to blunt the acuity. But this may be a mistake. After all, as we grow older we do not lose our ability to detect slight differences in accent, and we can even recognize our friends by the sounds of their voices. There is something puzzling about this, but at the same time we must recognize that the difference between, say, an Irish /r/ in the word *girl* and that of a Scotsman, though detectible, forms no part of the phonological system that we call English, or even of an Irishman's English, because that distinction is not built into the system.

The point is subtle, but it comes up again and again in psychology. For example, Corballis & Beale (1976) have written about the ability of various animals, including humans, to discriminate between simple figures and their mirror images, e.g., the letters *b* and *d*. They draw a sharp distinction between the ability to notice that the two are different when they are presented together and the ability to tell which is which when they are shown one at a time. Ability to *tell* which is which is difficult to pin down. For example, one could train an animal to seek food on the right when he encountered an arrow in this orientation →, and to seek it on the left when he encountered one like this ←. But he might merely learn to move to the side where the arrowhead is, without really knowing which is which. By varying his behavior consistently, he shows that he is responding to differences in the arrows, but he may have nothing equivalent to such labels as our "right pointing" and "left pointing." True discrimination, then, as distinct from merely noticing differences, involves knowing which is which. It seems to involve some sort of cognitive labels that attach absolutely to the different stimuli, though the perceiver need not be conscious of the label.

To speak English with an Irish accent does not involve knowing the difference between an Irish /r/ and a Scottish one. It merely demands the ability to pronounce /r/ in the Irish fashion and to discriminate between it and all the other sounds that form the phonological system of an Irishman's English. Of course matters may be complicated in several directions. An Irishman may learn to mimic a Scottish accent and may know very well which pronunciation of *girl* is which. In that case he is clearly able to discriminate between the two.

An infant is not much concerned with accents, but he must learn the set of sound contrasts that are made in his mother tongue. It is not enough to learn to distinguish between them; he must learn to discriminate and know which word is which. For example, he must learn to tell which his mother is saying, *bad,* or *pad.* When he talks, though at first he is allowed much latitude, he must eventually produce the appropriate sounds.

By the example I gave of accents, we must not be misled into supposing that within a particular accent the child's task presents no theoretical complications. His trouble, in a way, is the opposite —of discriminating between an Irishman's /r/ and a Scotsman's. He must learn to discount, phonologically, variation in speech sound that is accidental. He must, for example, discount difference in pitch, so that he does not assume a word is different just because his father pronounced it an octave lower than his mother. He must not assume that he is dealing with two different words because once a sound pattern was pronounced slowly or loudly and once quickly or softly. This is not to say that he cannot notice whether his mother spoke to him sharply or softly, and that he does not know what the difference means; neither is it to suggest that he cannot discriminate between his father's and mother's voices. The point is that he must not build such discriminations into the phonology of English, i.e., that system of speech sounds intrinsically involved in deciding which words are which in English. In other languages, like Chinese and Vietnamese, certain differences in pitch are built into the phonological system; not in English. The child's task in learning the phonemes of English is much more complicated than that of discriminating figures and their mirror images. The child must discriminate among discriminations; he must keep the discrimination of his father's and mother's voices separate from the discrimination of the phonemes.

What I have to say is made awkward by the fact that the word *discriminate* tends to suggest an awareness of differences, and I am uneasy about the notion that infants become aware of phonemes. In fact I very much doubt that they do, since phonemes are theoretical constructs in linguistics. For example, the English phoneme /p/ has several allophones or different phonological realizations. At the beginning of a stressed syllable, it is heavily aspirated, as in *pit* or *appear*. In a consonant cluster it is almost entirely unaspirated, as in the word *spit*. The phoneme /p/ is a construct to explain the similarity between $[p^h]$ and $[p]$, the aspirated and unaspirated forms respectively, and to explain too the fact that English phonology does not employ the differences between the two to discriminate among words. Doubtless some readers will not remember having adverted to the difference between the two, and thus illustrate the perceptual collapsing of the two sounds into a single phoneme. However, what children must become aware of is which words are which, and presumably it is only at the level of words, or perhaps syllables, that awareness enters. The mechanisms of articulation do recognize the distinction, but they are largely unconscious in their operation.

The illustration just given serves a second purpose in drawing attention to a type of variation that, if he noticed it, an infant must discount in mastering the phonemic system of English. It is distinctly possible that the infant at first notices the difference, because in Hindi /p/ and $/p^h/$ are phonemically distinct. The ability to detect the difference would help a baby learning Hindi, but if the same baby were learning English, he would have to learn to ignore it.

The Role of Meaning

Hitherto I have represented the child as pitting his auditory system against the phonology of English more or less in a vacuum. This is misleading because—certain maternal urgings to pronounce words aside—he encounters the words only in attempts to communicate. His mother's speech is usually trying to tell him something, or to do or stop doing something. Usually the environment, distinct from her words, provides a clue to what she means, and so can guide him to the phonemic system.

Take a Spanish speaker who is trying to learn English. He provides a lot of fun, and some embarrassment, in being unable to tell which word an English speaker is saying: *slip* or *sleep, dip* or *deep, pip* or *peep*. Unlike English, Spanish does not contrast /i/ as in *ship* and /I/ as in *sheep*. In view of what we know about the infant's auditory acuity, it seems that the Spanish speaker has learned to discount variations in the pronunciation of the Spanish /I/, and he has learned it so well that he now has difficulty in detecting a contrast that seems so clear to us. It is not just that he is unwilling to make a phonemic contrast between /i/ and /I/; he does not notice the difference that we make. I would like to claim that one good reason he does not is that it is never associated in Spanish with a difference in meaning, and luckily Roger Brown (1958a, pp. 213–216) reports an experiment that gives some support.

Brown performed an experiment on the salience of vowel length for two groups of adult subjects, one in whose native language, English, vowel length is not phonemic and one, Navaho, in whose it is. There were fifteen subjects in each group, and the task was to classify colored chips as described by nonsense syllables. There were eight chips which varied by gradual degrees from red to blue. There were four nonsense words: [ma], [ma:], [mo], and [mo:]. It was believed that English speakers would readily notice the change from [a] to [o], but not the change in vowel length (increase in vowel length is denoted by a colon placed after a vowel). As expected, the English speakers made two classes of the chips corresponding to what they heard. The Navahos generally made four classes, corresponding to the four nonsense words.

When the English speakers had completed their task, Brown rejected their classification as erroneous. They then set to work again and all, eventually, made four classes corresponding to the four words. That is, they began to discriminate between words on the basis of vowel length. It is tempting to conclude that infants can hear many discriminations but tend to ignore those that do not make some difference to sense. The early discrimination would explain the accuracy of production; the collapsing of distinctions in perception would be a function of meaning. This seems highly probable, though we remind ourselves of what we have already noted, that difference in meaning does not always imply phonemic difference. *Stop* pronounced softly may mean something quite different from *stop* shouted, yet loudness is not phonemic in English; the word is the same.

I will conclude the case for meaning as a guide to phonology with some examples from Irish. I list some nouns under the headings nominative, genitive, and dative, and indicate changes in the initial sound that, granted certain syntactic conditioning, regularly occur in those cases:

Nominative	Genitive	Dative		English
[pobal]	[fobail]	[bobal]	=	people
[bád]	[váid]	[mád]	=	boat
[tarv]	[hairv]	[darv]	=	bull
[daul]	[gʰauil]	[naul]	=	blindman

The phonetic representation is rough but it will suffice for my purpose, which is to show that the infant who sets about learning Irish encounters a great deal of phonological variation in the sound of initial consonants. How does he cope with it? I suggest that he will be helped by the fact that he often knows what is being spoken about, whether because of some action of the speaker or of something in the environment. In other words, he is able to guess that the speaker is talking about the same thing and using the same word, though its sound changes quite a bit. For example, his father may say to him, "Look at the boat [bád]", and go on to speak of "the size of the boat [váid]" and of "the sail on the boat [mád]". Surely the meaning will be a clue that there are phonological rules at work on what is basically the same word. The form of the rule for the dative, for example, is roughly: change an unvoiced consonant to the corresponding voiced one: [p] → [b]; [t] → [d], and replace a voiced consonant by the homorganic nasal: [b] → [m]; [d] → [n].

The Irish examples are particularly interesting in that on the one hand [p] and [b] are phonologically (actually morphophonemically) related in the foregoing examples, and on the other hand they can also be phonemically distinct. For example, [paul] = *hole* and [baul] = *limb* are different words. The same holds for each of the other pairs in the set of examples as well as for many other pairs. It follows that the child must learn, on the basis of nonphonological cues—such as syntax and context—whether [baul] is the nominative of the word which means *limb* or the dative of that which means *hole*. He must learn to treat a single sound contrast now as a syntactically conditioned variation, now as a phonemic contrast. To a lesser extent the same is true of English. *Leaves* may be the present tense, third person, singular of the verb *leave,* or the plural of *leaf.* So we must not regard Irish as extraordinary in the demands it makes on infants.

The role of meaning must not be exaggerated, however, because if a child were guided by it alone he would soon be in serious trouble. *Small* and *little* mean very nearly the same thing, but a child who for that reason attempted to derive one from the other phonologically would be a phonological anarchist. Presumably, the child is endowed with a phonological similarity metric that tells him that *small* and *little* are too different to be related phonologically, but *leaf* and *leaves* are not. So both sound and meaning play a part in guiding the child to the phonology of his language.

One may wonder why I have so far ignored the many studies of phonological development in infants. The reason is that all the studies of child phonology that I have come across deal with the sounds that children produce, not with the sounds they can cope with when they are listening. These are quite different matters. If one is taking violin lessons, one can hear perfectly the sounds that the master plays but fail miserably to reproduce them. The perception and production of violin music are, alas, related by a tortuous chain of events. And so with speech sounds. We will not delay over their production, important though that may be in its own right. However, I feel compelled to draw attention, fleetingly, to one development in child phonology:

Kiparsky and Menn (1977) studied theories of how children learn to pronounce the speech sounds of their native language. The theories they studied had in common the belief that development is deterministic; that development follows a predetermined path. Kiparsky and Menn showed that the data refute all such theories. All children in a speech community do not follow the same path. An individual child will progress and backtrack in a curious manner. They cite, for example, Werner Leopold's daughter, Hildegarde, who when still very young learned the word *pretty* and pronounced it correctly, initial consonant cluster and all. Though she continued to pronounce that word correctly, for a long while she pronounced no other consonant clusters. All words with such clusters she simplified in pronunciation. It was as though she could manage such clusters, but only with great difficulty, and so she adopted a strategy of simplifying.

Kiparsky & Menn (1977), and in a more detailed form Menn (1977) and Ferguson (1977), propose a highly "cognitive" theory of the development of skill in phonology. The data lead them to conclude that phonology presents children with a set of articulatory puzzles, and children achieve temporary solutions of great ingenuity and originality. All this is in close harmony with the stance I am taking throughout this book; but to pursue their argument further would lead us too far from our theme.

Segmenting the Sound Stream

One of the problems that confronts the infant word learner in any language is that words are not normally given him distinctly in the flow of parental talk. What I mean is that the words are dovetailed together without clear indications of when one begins and ends. Nothing in speech corresponds to the spaces between words in print. There are short pauses, but they are occasioned by the stop consonants like /d/ and /b/. In pronouncing them we stop the airstream for a brief period that shows readily enough in a sonographic printout of speech. But such pauses are as likely to appear in the middle or end of words as at the beginning, so they are not much use as guides to segmentation. Indeed a speaker who is not being artificially pedantic normally modifies the end of each word and the beginning of the following one, so that the transition from one to the other can be effected without a pause and as effortlessly as is compatible with the requirement of being interpretable by his listener. Pauses are not a likely means of segmentation into words.

In some languages that stress the initial consonant of a word, stress can be a clue to the beginnings and, by implication, the ends of words. But English, to take just one language, provides the baby with no such regularity. Stresses can occur almost anywhere: e.g., *possible, impossibility, political, politics*. So English babies must have some other clue to words.

One possible clue has been explored by Hayes & Clark (1970). They followed up a suggestion of Harris (1955) that there are more constraints on phoneme combinations within a word than across words. The idea, which they call clustering, is simply this. The phonemes that occur within a word must always be pronounced together. There is not an equal obligation to place words side by side. It should follow that the number of different phonemes that can follow a particular phoneme within a word should be smaller than the number that can follow the final phoneme of a word. Hayes & Clark constructed a language of unutterable sounds, without syntax or meaning, but with just the constraints that they call clustering. They asked adults to segment continuous strings into wordlike segments. And they found that adults could, within the space of about three quarters of an hour, do so. It seems likely, then, that human beings come equipped with a system for using clustering effects for segmenting speech strings.

In an unpublished experiment Professor A. L. Bregman of McGill Psychology Department studied a different type of clue. He wondered whether frequently repeated patterns of sound, without clustering characteristics, are not readily detectible. He composed a sequence of eight pure tones as the pattern to study. To make sure they did not form a tune and thus exhibit clustering character-istics, the intervals between the tones were not those of any known musical scale. To make the pattern continuous and in that sense similar to speech, the tones were all connected. He embedded the pattern hundreds of times in a long series of randomly chosen pure tones. The intervals between occurrences of the pattern were ran-dom; each repetition of the pattern fitted into the stream without obvious trace.

The entire tape, about an hour in length, was played to listeners who were told that there was an eight-note pattern repeated at frequent intervals. Their task was to press a button every time they identified the pattern. There were some very slight indications of learning after long periods of listening, but it is virtually true that no subject identified the pattern.

However, if Bregman made one slight change, nearly everyone identified the pattern right off and continued to do so. If he played the pattern a few times in isolation, people had little difficulty in detecting it in the continuous string. In fact the effect is so powerful that Bregman has frequently used his tape for demonstra-tion purposes in lecturing and whole audiences react as he expects them to.

Suppose a mother wants her child to say *cat*, it is very likely she will go through some such routine as the following:

Look at the cat, pet.

Look at the cat.

This is a cat.

A cat.

Say, *cat.*

Cat.

Cat.

All the time the mother is narrowing down the context until the word is isolated. Most of us know from experience that mothers go on like this, but recently there has been intensive study of how mothers modify their speech when talking to young children, and it has been observed, not surprisingly, that they do single out words in the manner illustrated—see Snow (1976). In my opinion this combines well with Bregman's work to show that infants must be greatly aided by such isolation. It remains a problem, however, that the same words sound different when isolated and when embedded in speech. There was no such contrast between Bregman's isolated and embedded patterns. Still his work suggests a partial solution of how the child solves the problem. He must have a remarkably tenacious memory for patterns of speech sounds, and a remarkable skill in detecting them even though modified to fit into speech contexts.

For an excellent account of how adults manage to recognize familiar words in fluent speech, see Cole and Jakimik (1978). The interest of such work in the present context is that it shows the end product of the learning process—competence—that the child must eventually acquire.

Categorizing Objects

There is a well known hypothesis in philosophy and linguistics that is commonly referred to as the Sapir-Whorf hypothesis. It suggests a view of child language learning that is largely incompatible with what I have said above about the role of meaning. The hypothesis rests on assumptions about the perception of speech sounds which, so far as I know, have gone unnoticed. I will discuss the hypothesis only insofar as it is related to phonology, and in order to give my remarks focus I will concentrate mainly on the writings of the phenomenologist, Merleau-Ponty. The general empirical and theoretical grounds for rejecting the hypothesis are well set out by Professor Joshua Fishman (1960).

Merleau-Ponty wrote extensively and interestingly on language, but he did not write much about language learning in infants. What he has to say on the matter is to be found in *The Structure of Behavior,* chapter 3, the section headed "The Human Order." There he states that the child is dependent on language for guidance in forming those conceptual categories in which he describes objects and events. He believes that words guide the child to form a conceptual category under which cats fall, another under which dogs fall, another for knives, and so on. The theory fits quite well persons who have already learned a language. We can then tell them how we think plants and animals can be classified and give them names for the classes. But Merleau-Ponty claims that the same holds of the child who is just learning his mother tongue:

> But even then it is out of the question to suppose in children the perception of objects defined by an ensemble of "visual", "tactile" and "sonorous" properties. This could be to forget the role which language plays in the constitution of the perceived world.   (1963, p. 167)

There is something naive about this position. It could only have been proposed by a person who had never seriously considered what problems phonology presents a child with. That is the main reason I devoted so much space to phonology. Most philosophers assume that the child's difficulty is to pin down the objects which words refer to; they seem to think that the words themselves are much simpler perceptual units. However, all that we have seen suggests that words present just as much of a perceptual problem as objects. Merleau-Ponty gives no reasons for believing his position right. To him it seemed self-evident. While I cannot produce an apodictic argument to show he is wrong, I believe I have undermined his position. Furthermore, an infant does not normally give evidence of understanding words before 12 months, or of saying them with meaning until later. During his first year he seems to have been observing the world about him, noticing what things look like and what they are for. It seems highly likely that the knowledge he has thus acquired guides his early language learning. That was the point of my earlier remarks about Irish phonology. Moreover, there is some evidence, albeit not quite satisfactory, that deaf babies can learn to make signs younger than hearing babies can use words (Schlesinger & Meadow, 1972).

To show that the point of view here associated with Merleau-Ponty is by no means confined to phenomenologists, I will add a quotation from Michael Dummett's (1973) book on Frege and on the tradition of linguistic philosophy to which he has given rise. The quotation should be read as picking out not a view made explicitly by Frege, but one implicit in his thinking and subsequently made explicit:

> The picture of reality as an amorphous lump, not yet articulated into discrete objects, thus proves to be a correct one, so long as we make the right use of it. It serves to emphasize that, in learning the use both of countable general terms and of proper names, we have to learn the criterion of identity associated with them, where this means primarily learning the sense of statements of identification of the form: "That is

$a-$" thus of sentences involving demonstratives. Such a picture corrects the naive conception, found for example, in Mill, that the meaning of a general term consists just in its connotation . . . and that of a proper name just in its denotation . . . : for this conception presupposes that the world presents itself to us already dissected into discrete objects, which we know how to recognize when we encounter them again, in advance of our acquiring any grasp of language at all. It is precisely this misconception . . . against which Wittgenstein wages war in the early part of *Philosophical Investigations*.   (pp. 577-78)

Dummett himself subscribes to the position advocated in the passage, and I hope it will itself now be seen as naïve, without thus throwing oneself into the hands of Mill. I will not delay longer with Frege and Wittgenstein, but return to Merleau-Ponty.

There is another issue involved in Merleau-Ponty's discussion. It is altogether too vague to speak, as he does, of words "constituting" the child's conceptual categories. Concepts are not constituted for the child; he forms them himself. Words could never be more than hints to what is really an enormously complex process, one which we scarcely understand even vaguely.

There is an even more implausible thesis that Merleau-Ponty puts forward citing the early Piaget (1926) in his support. The theory has the support, too, of Vygotsky (1962) and, surprisingly, of Neisser (1976). It is that at an early stage the child actually imagines that an object's name is one of the object's attributes as much as is its color. One can understand why Vygotsky thought so; he was an associationist, and for him objects were bundles of associations, of its visual attributes, its feel, its taste, and so on. It is natural on this account to place the name with other associations. However, it is not so easy to understand why theorists who do not confine themselves to associations should believe the thesis.

The evidence in its support is that if young children are asked, in a game, whether one might change an object's name for a while, they usually say no. They do not want to call cows *horses* and horses *cows* even for a while. Older children usually agree to switch names. Vygotsky concluded, and the others agree, that the child imagines the name to be as inalienable as an object's shape.

It is impossible to see what useful theoretical conclusions such facts lead to. In the child's experience many objects change their shape; Daddy is sometimes sitting, sometimes standing, and sometimes engaged in that form of continual shape-changing we call walking. Books are sometimes closed, sometimes open; butter can be spread; water spilt. Color changes too, as when milk is poured in tea, or when crayons are applied to paper. Porridge is sometimes too hot to eat and one must wait till it cools. On what grounds would anyone suppose that in the child's world attributes are necessarily immutable? And names? Listen to the names a child himself is called: *Henry, Harry, good boy, pet, little monster, rascal* and a hundred others. Does that mean that the child has as many extra attributes as he has names? And what, in the face of such evidence, can be made of the idea that for children names are immutable? Far simpler to say that young children refuse to allow names to be changed in the manner Vygotsky suggested because they know that it is only too easy to confuse them; older children have more confidence. Just imagine how you would feel if you were learning German and the teacher said, "Today as an exercise, we will call a cow *'ein Pferd'* and a horse *'eine Kuh.'*"

Summary

The phonological aspect of learning names for objects is one that has usually been neglected by philosophers and psychologists. As a result they assume that learning the sound pattern is straightforward, and that assumption is implicit in several positions, such as the Sapir-Whorf hypothesis, and in Merleau-Ponty's view that words establish for the child the conceptual categories into which he places objects. For this reason I devoted considerable space to sketching the variation in speech sounds from which a child must quarry those linguistic building blocks, phonemes. The variation is of several kinds, and some are accidental in relation to phonology, such as the difference between men and women's voices, differences in loudness, differences in speed of articulation. Other variation is phonologically conditioned but still does not establish phonemic contrast; such is the phonic difference between the /p/ in *spit* and that in *pit*. The remaining contrasts are phonemic: those that enter into deciding which words are which. I showed that a single contrast may sometimes be phonemic and sometimes not. For example, that between /f/ and /v/ in *leaf* and *leaves* is phonemic if *leaves* is a verb; if it is a noun, the two sounds are morphophonemically distinct. I argued that in such cases, and in many others too, meaning is an aid to the child. Meaning can help him to see whether he should introduce a phonological rule of the sort [f] → [v] in certain contexts, or whether he had to do with different, and phonologically unrelated, words. This, so far as it goes, is the opposite of the Sapir-Whorf hypothesis, of Merleau-Ponty's position, and of the Frege-Wittgenstein-Dummett one. Instead of words being the guide

7.
Nouns as Names

O Beer! O Hodgson, Guinness, Alsopp, Bass,
Names that should be on every infant's tongue.
—Charles Stuart Caverley

Benjamin Lee Whorf (1956, p. 215) claimed that Nootka, an Amerindian language of Vancouver Island, does not distinguish between nouns and verbs. He claimed further that this portrayed "a monistic view of nature"—one in which there was no distinction between "temporary events," like actions and "long-lasting and stable events," like objects. Whorf then took the apparent absence of a noun/verb distinction as evidence that Nootka Indians did not, as we do, distinguish in reality between objects and actions. From this it would follow that they did not have words that referred to objects. I would like to claim, on the contrary, that in all languages one can refer to objects and be understood as referring to them. If I can handle Whorf's counterclaim for Nootka, I hope that an indulgent reader will allow my very general principle to stand.

To begin with, Whorf's claim does not seem well grounded at the linguistic level—see Hockett (1958, p. 224). The basic division in Nootka is between stems that are inflected and those that are not. However, many stems when without inflection have "noun-like syntactical uses": when certain inflections are added, the same stems "are used syntactically in verblike ways" (Hockett, 1958,

p. 225). Elsewhere Hockett (1963) remarks that Nootka shows "something very much like the noun/verb contrast." These are the linguistic facts; there is really little to comment on at the semantic level. In Nootka it is possible to refer to the class of objects, men, /qu'?as/. By adding the suffix /-ma/ the word acquires verblike functions. I am not expert enough in Nootka to know if the semantic result of adding the suffix is much the same as the contrast in English between using *man* as a noun and as a verb. In any event, many English words can surface in different form classes. We can police the house or house the police. This does not in any way impair our ability to speak of either houses or policemen. I do not see how a similar linguistic flexibility on the part of the Nootka Indians could impair theirs.

In this and the next chapter we shall engage in, I fear, a lengthy discussion of how a child comes to place his words in grammatical categories. The matter is of great importance, not only as an aspect of name learning but as the beginning of syntax in which names play so large a part. The problems are unusually subtle and have not, to my knowledge, been previously discussed in sufficient detail. That must be my excuse for allowing them so much space. In the present chapter I will confine myself mainly to laying out the problems and the data; in the next I will attempt to reach a solution and to extend it to three subdivisions of noun; those based on gender; those based on classifiers; and the division of nouns into count and mass. The distinction between common and proper nouns has had a whole chapter to itself, Chapter 2.

Names and Nouns

Whorf's mistake was to equate the linguistic and the cognitive. It is true that in English we often use nouns when we refer to objects: *house, man, dog, cat.* We also use nouns for other purposes. We speak about *a walk, a talk,* which are events; we speak about *the red on a wall,* which is an attribute; we speak about *the outside* and *the inside,* relational terms, and so on. English does not set up a one-to-one correspondence between nouns and objects.

The traditional definition of noun—"the name of a person, place, or thing"—leaked so badly that it had to be thrown out. The main trouble was *thing;* it embraced every word that is a noun and is not the name of a person or place. That made the definition unusable in linguistics; but we shall see more of it in the sequel.

Modern linguistics has two ways of defining noun, both captured in Hockett's (1958, p. 221) definition of a part of speech: "a form-class of stems which show similar behaviour in inflexion, in syntax, or in both." Applied to noun, the idea is that any stem is a noun that either (a) takes noun inflections or (b) performs noun functions in a sentence. As noun inflections one thinks mainly of the plural and possessive, both written *s*. But if one were to cling to them as the sole means for deciding if a word was a noun, one would make many mistakes. One would fail to count *man (men), child, (children), sheep (sheep)* as nouns. Moreover, one would find words that took an *s* and were not nouns: *walk*(s), *run*(s), etc. Besides, *Dad's* in *Dad's gone* is neither a plural nor a possessive, in fact it isn't even an inflection. The trouble is compounded by such facts as that both *walk* and *walks* can be either nouns or verbs. One can *walk* or take a *walk;* one *walks* sometimes and sometimes one takes *walks.* This complicates the interpretation not only of final *s* but of other endings too, such as *-ing.* Both *walk* and *walking* can be verbs, but in *Walking hurts my feet, walking* is a noun. Such formations are common enough in some transcripts I have seen of adult speech to very young children: *Do you want me to spank you? Do you want a good SPANKING?* Ultimately children must know that the same word may be used in different grammatical categories; even that the same morphemes, *-ing,* or similar sounding morphemes, *s,* may be used in different grammatical categories. However, at the initial stages sounds attached to words will not solve the problem of fitting words into grammatical categories. They could do so only if the child had independent access to a set of morphemes categorized precisely as noun morphemes, verb morphemes, etc. I take it he does not have this.

Hockett's second criterion fares no better. It distinguishes nouns by their grammatical functions in sentences. How would the child know the functions that are peculiar to nouns rather than other parts of speech? It would seem that he might be able to if he knew which were the nouns. But this is circular. It is hardly necessary to give examples, or to show that a combination of grammatical function and inflection class will not solve the child's problem.

Could it be that the notion "noun" along with that of other grammatical categories is innate? The short answer is no. The notion "noun" in English is different from that in most other languages. That is, the morphological endings that can be combined with nouns in English are different not only in phonological shape but in semantic function from those of many other languages. Japanese, for example, has no plural morpheme corresponding to /-s/ in English. And the phrase-structure rules in which nouns play a part vary from language to language. It follows that nature would not equip a child with an innate notion "noun" that was at once adequate for all natural languages.

That does not preclude innate constraints of a purely linguistic sort on what can be a noun in any language. I imagine there are such, and Bresnan (in press) is one who has some interesting suggestions. Before admitting them to innate status, however, one would naturally want to be satisfied that they could not be learned. So far, I know of no evidence to that effect. [1]

Even if we allow some innate linguistic constraints on grammatical categories, the child still has to learn the categories themselves for his own language. How does he break into the linguistic circle? The answer is complicated and will take the rest of this chapter and the next. In outline the solution is close to the old definition of noun; the child initially distinguishes among words with respect to semantic function. Semantics leads him to morphologicial divisions and to divisions in phrase structure. Semantics leads him to distinguish noun morphemes and noun functions in sentences. The distinctions form the basis for the notion of the grammatical category, noun.

Interestingly this may provide a solution to the vexed question whether there are nouns in Chinese, say, as well as in English. The answer would depend on whether children learning the two languages make use of the same semantic rules to make initial classifications of words—classes, that is, that eventually become grammatical classes as defined linguistically. That may seem perverse and awkward, but unfortunately there is little evidence that in allowing languages to develop as they did, men were attentive to the needs of linguists and psycholinguists.

A beginning to the study of how children learn to apply grammatical categories was made by Roger Brown (1957), a beginning indeed that might have been suggested by the medieval doctrine of the modes of meaning (see O'Mahony, 1965, and Trentman, 1973). Brown examined the vocabularies of children aged about four or five (by then they used sentences) and found that their nouns referred more often than adults' to concrete objects, like sticks and stones (as distinct from truth or justice). Their verbs more often than those of adults meant actions.

Brown was interested in the possibility that grammatical category might be the child's clue to meaning. It also seemed possible on the evidence that meaning might be the clue to grammatical category. I pursued the latter possibility by studying the vocabularies of younger children and also the vocabulary that is used in speaking to them. The main line of my case will be first that children arrange their words in semantic, not syntactic, categories. The principal categories will be words for objects, words for attributes of objects, and words for actions. Evidence for the existence of the categories, apart from their semantic basis, will at first be flexibility in using a word within a semantic category but not across category boundaries—for example, *shoe* of boots, shoes, and sandals, but not of any action. As the child grows older, evidence not only for the existence of the categories but for their relevance to language will be twofold: the use of inflections respects the category distinctions; the combination of words respects the category distinctions. The argument will be that the child initially constructs categories on a semantic basis and later rejects that basis in favor of a purely linguistic one.

Children's Vocabularies

The literature contains lists of the first 50 words or so of several children: Nelson (1972, 1973a and b), Brown, Fraser, & Bellugi (1964), Braine (1963), Gruber (1967), Menn (1976), Miller & Ervin-Tripp (1964). They divide the words into two main categories, one associated with actions, the other naming objects. Though suggestive, the lists raise as many questions as they answer. Entries in them are almost invariably based on the first usage of a word by the child under observation. We would like to know if the child used a word sometimes of an object and sometimes of an action. Are there any characteristics of the object names to suggest that they are leading the child in the direction of the class of nouns? To answer that type of question I studied the vocabularies of two children and I also studied the remarks addressed to one of them by adults. One of these children is my son, Kieran, on whom I have kept records. The other is Sarah, one of the three children Roger Brown describes in his book *A First Language*. Roger Brown very kindly made the transcripts available to me when I was a Visiting Professor in Harvard in the spring of 1978. In addition, I consulted Melissa Bowerman, whose linguistic records on her own two children are the most complete in existence.

KIERAN MACNAMARA

I have chosen for study Kieran's language up to when he was 21 months, the time of writing. The corpus given in Appendix 3 is by no means all he said; it is all that my wife and I noted in our journal. The list of words is very nearly complete, but the set of word combinations is not. We simply found it impossible to keep up. However, the combinations we recorded are probably highly representative of his speech.

I made three divisions of the material: (1) before the 20th month; (2) the 20th month; (3) the 21st month. I neglected to tape-record all he said over a fixed period of time, so I cannot accurately assess mean length of utterance (MLU) as Roger Brown (1973) did. Nevertheless it is clear that the three divisions correspond roughly to MLU's of 1, 2, and 3 respectively. I will refer to these as stages 1, 2, and 3, respectively. Kieran is a highly verbal child.

I have categorized the words on semantic grounds, distinguishing them by what they referred to or described or by the effect the child wanted to produce. That was generally easy, though it is not easy to say *how* one does it. Quine (1960) has shown us that we cannot "operationalize" the interpretation of what anyone means by anything he says (see below, Chapter 11). For all that, we seem to succeed in understanding one another nearly all the time. The psycholinguist studying the child is in a position like that of the art critic who must judge the authenticity of a painting or the musicologist who judges whether a certain flute sonata was written by J. S. Bach. Somehow through long experience of their art they come to recognize which are genuine. Likewise, parents, much more than visiting experimentalists, come to know what their children intend when they speak. While mistakes are possible, parents are the best sources we have in the area. I hope, then, the reader will be disposed to accept my own judgements and those of my wife in respect to Kieran. Some decisions were doubtful and these I have indicated with a question mark. The category names speak for themselves. I will comment only on those entries in a category that might cause surprise or on those I think doubtful.

CATEGORIES OF WORDS

Under *Exclamations* I have listed expressions that were used impishly as attention gainers or in verbal games. Each was used as an unanalyzed cliché. For example, *I see you!* was used in a peekaboo-type game before there were any other complete sentences. There are no more grounds for analyzing it than for analyzing *Oh gosh!*

"Action demands" increased in length over the three stages, but I have treated them as unanalyzed for the same reason that I did exclamations. *Thank you* as an action demand at stage 1 was a request to take some object that Kieran offered as he said it. This use is distinguished from the use of *thank you!* as a mark of politeness, when Kieran offered nothing. *See,* from about the age of 13 months, was frequently placed before a name—e.g., *see Freddie.* It could not always have meant "look at" because the object named was not always visible. It seems to have been a call for attention to an object, and so the action demanded was a very abstract one.

Among "action descriptions" pass over *bel$_2$*, which was taught for experimental purposes. *Mine* was used in a game of tugging in turn at some article, each participant saying *mine* as he tugged. I have glossed it "I take," but since a few days before the game began Kieran first used *me* to refer to himself (see Chapter 2), there is a slight possibility that *mine* might have been a personal possessive. *Shave,* in stage 1, applied to the set of activities that included my going to the bathroom to wash my face and teeth and to shave. *Sleep* and *sleeping,* seem to have been an activity for Kieran. When requested to sleep he would put his head on something, close his eyes, and remain still. It is impossible to be sure, of course, but we had the impression that sleeping was as much an activity for Kieran as, say, standing still on one's hands is for an adult. *Rain* and *raining* were used of rain only while falling. It is somewhat arbitrary whether to place them under action words or under object words. *Fun* and *funny* (at stage 2) I have glossed as "laughing" because they were used only of people while laughing. Similarly, *good time,* at stage 3 was used only of people laughing, and at that point Kieran never spoke of time in any of its more common meanings. *Like,* at stage 2, was used only in connection with eating. At stage 3 it developed new meanings of which one was "want" and the other, with *no,* was "stop." I listed *going to* at stage 3, but it may have had no meaning apart from the verb it preceded. *Happened,* at stage 3, may not have had any meaning either; it may have just been a phrase picked up from us; *what happened to X?* Kieran used it only in that context.

There are a great many proper names. Kieran never once used any of them, mistakenly, as a common name. *Breakfast* was food rather than eating; at 18:27 (months:days) when he began to use the word, I asked him what it was and he slowly said "egg" and "grapefruit." *Combing,* I will come back to. I placed question marks after *food* and *home* because I do not know what they referred to. *Pee pee* meant both urine and penis. *Sky* he always used appropriately when pointing to pictures or in connection with airplanes, but it is unclear whether he conceived of the sky as an object or not. Two words in the list, *music* and *noise,* were always used appropriately, but they did not refer to objects and they certainly did not refer to actions.

The rest of the common names, there is little doubt, refer to or apply to objects. Occasionally when I was in doubt I was able to check the matter out. For example, at one time when asked to show his teeth he used to open and close his mouth. Wondering whether *teeth* described the action or the objects, I pointed to my, stationary, teeth and asked what are those, and he said "teeth." I also touched his teeth with my finger and asked him what are those, and he said "teeth." That, for me, placed the matter beyond doubt.

Animal, at stage 2, may cause some surprise in view of the discussion in earlier chapters. He first used the term at 20:30. At 21:21 my wife said "animal" to him and paused and he said "see horsie; see hippo." He seems to have figured out what it meant. *Another one,* pronounced /onoman/, became his name for a frozen yogurt stick, used for nothing else. *Ones* usually meant nappies in the expression *dry ones, wet one. Some* meant "a piece of" or "a portion of" and was a pronoun in that it could refer to many different objects. Yet it was not a simple action-demand word, because Kieran occasionally said something like *more some. Work* he sometimes said, but I did not know what it meant to him.

Words listed as modifiers were used of objects but not to name them. My reasons for claiming that are (1) that even at stage 1 he usually knew a sortal for the object of which the modifier was used, and sometimes used the modifier in combination with the sortal; (2) they were used of sets of objects that he showed no evidence of otherwise associating in a class; (3) he seemed often to use them to describe variable states of objects rather than objects themselves. The first reason is not strong because he often had several sortals for a single object. However, when modifier and object word were combined, there can be little doubt about the matter, e.g., *big bus; big belly.* It is quite unlikely that *big* was a name for a class that included bus and belly. *Clean,* as a single word, was used mainly of hands and feet when there was a question of cleanliness, as in connection with washing. *Wet* and *dry* he said of nappies only when they were as he said. At stage 1 most modifiers connoted attributes of objects, but even then *all, all-gone, gone, other* and *two,* can scarcely have done so. At later stages several modifiers expressed relations among objects—*my, new, our, different, his* and *last,* for example.

At stages 2 and 3 I introduced the category "locative" to designate interesting relational terms, though they might have been put with the modifiers. The class "miscellaneous", also introduced in those stages, consists simply of those words that did not fit naturally into any existing categories, and yet were not numerous enough to subdivide.

INTEGRITY OF KIERAN'S CATEGORIES

We will now go on to ask a series of questions about these categories aimed at whether they had psychological reality for Kieran. (1) Did Kieran have a rule of the sort, one word for one object? The answer, in general, is clearly, no, though for a time such a rule seemed to apply to his use of proper names. For a time each individual was given only one name and it was peculiar to that individual. Later, from the age of 17 months, that was relaxed in two ways. As he found other people called by the same proper name, he used the name, at first reluctantly, of them too. And he also learned alternative names for certain individuals like *Joyce* for Mammy and *John* for Dad. Thus there was considerable flexibility within the category, proper name. No proper name was used of an attribute or action, but there was some interchange with common names. For example, Freddie, the dog, was sometimes referred to as *he* or *him;* and several people whose names he used were described as *friend.* Curiously, Kieran never used *Dad* for anyone except myself. The one exception was *moon,* first learned at stage 2. He called a variety of shapes *moon.* This may mean that *moon* was not a proper name at all; or more probably it was an abbreviation for *like the moon.*

(2) For the rest Kieran did not seem to expect a one-to-one correspondence between names and objects. *Button* he learned early and he spent a lot of time pointing to one button after another on my shirt and calling each *button.* We may then ask, did he have a rule of the type, one sort of object, one name? Though there is a fairly general one-to-one correspondence between common names and classes of objects, it is by no means perfect. When he was 16:10 (months:days) I recorded that he was

calling shoes *boots;* a month later he called them *shoes.* One name did not replace the other; both were used in the same conversation of the very same objects. Other such cases are *plane* and *airplane, chick* and *chicken, cock* and *rooster.*

There seemed ample evidence in spontaneous speech that Kieran readily learned two sortals for the same kind of object, but none that he learned to use a single sortal of two kinds of object. Many of his pronunciations collapsed two different adult words to a single phonological shape; for example, at one stage *hand* and *hen* were both pronounced /hən/. That was probably due to articulatory difficulties, and the words probably sounded quite different to him. I wanted to know if he would accept a single sound, as I pronounced it, for two different sorts of object. I chose objects for which he had as yet no names, "blankets" and "shaving cream." When he was 17:2 I taught him *ban* for shaving cream in the morning and the same word for blanket in the evening. He immediately learned the word of both sorts of object, and though his pronunciation fluctuated somewhat he settled on one for both objects. His performance convinced me that he had no resistance to learning a single sortal for two kinds of objects as well as several sortals for the same class of objects. That implies flexibility within the category, common name.

(3) Did he have a rule that an attribute word could not be used as an object word or an object word as an attribute word? I have no experimental evidence on it, but the data suggest the answer, yes. There is almost no confusion whatsoever between those two categories. There are a few pairs of object words, e.g., *apple, apple juice; ear, earring;* and *belly, belly button,* where for an adult the first element of the complex word may function semantically as a modifier of the second, but I see no reason to believe that for Kieran they did. Only one word, *dirty,* seemed to jump semantic boundaries. He began using it of his hands when they were dirty but soon extended it to the floor and to tables. Then he would pick up bits of fluff from the floor and say "dirty," while still using the word of his hands. Nevertheless I am inclined to believe that there was a powerful tendency to keep the two categories of word distinct.

(4) Did he have a rule not to use an object word of an action or an action word of an object? I am using action word to cover demands for action and descriptions of action. The answer is in general, yes, but it is complicated.

One of his earliest words, *nana,* he invented himself, and at first it meant "give me that object" and "do what I want" (pick me up, for example). When he was 14:7 I noted that my wife had begun to interpret *nana* to mean milk. A month later it suddenly struck me that Kieran now used *nana* only in requests for objects including milk, never in requests for actions such as to be picked up or put down. In demands for action he used one of the words listed in that category or he just cried. This struck me as an interesting division of linguistic labor between actions and objects.

There are 42 words in the combined categories Action Demands and Action Descriptions at stage 1. Forty of them, I am confident, related to activity and not to an object; they were never used of an object. These include *sleep* and *sleeping,* which I have already commented on. Two possible exceptions are *rain* and *raining,* which, as I noted, could have meant drops of water rather than the process of falling. However, there was no evidence that they changed meaning, signifying now drops and now falling.

Melissa Bowerman sent me notes on her daughter Eva's vocabulary when Eva was about 1½ years. There were two fairly clear examples of words that she used for actions and objects, *sit* and *wipe.* Sit seemed to mean sometimes the action of sitting and sometimes stools or chairs. *Wipe* seemed to mean the act and also paper and cloths used for wiping. For example, at 17:4 Eva, who mostly meant by the word an action, said *wipe* while looking at a dead wasp on a kleenex that her mother was holding. No wiping occurred just before or after the utterance. So it seems probable that though children have a strong tendency to keep action and object words distinct, the rule is not inviolable.

To try and settle the matter I conducted a little test on Kieran. When he was 17:12 I taught him the nonsense syllable *bel* for my briefcase and continued to teach it for a day or two until he had learned it. When he was 17:15 I taught him *bel* as meaning a special sort of jumping when he and I held hands and jumped. I would say, "Would you like to bel? Let's bel." He liked the activity and said "bel" without difficulty. Three days later there is the following entry:

17:18 He seems to have learned *bel* both of my briefcase and of jumping. This morning I asked him, holding out my hands in the ritualized manner, if he would like to bel, and he did. He said "bel" though he had to be prompted. This afternoon I asked him "what's that?" pointing to my briefcase and he replied "bel"-/bəm/: Later, without any gesture I asked him if he would like to bel, and he immediately began to jump.

Curiously, when I asked him about the briefcase and he said "bel," he paused and began to jump. The following day I noted that, when questioned, without prompting, he called the briefcase and the action *bam.*

At that point I decided to keep on testing him but not to prompt him any more. At 17:23 he began to make a clear distinction, calling the briefcase *ban* and the action *bam.* For five days he maintained the distinction and then dropped it as suddenly as he had instituted it. My conclusion was that he had no absolute prohibition on using the same word for an object and action, but he had a tendency not to do so. This conclusion was supported by a further observation.

When he was 17:27 I taught him *comb* of both the object and the action. He knew the object well and when I showed it to him he said "hair." The following day I noted that *comb* for him referred to the object, nevertheless I continued to teach him the word for both action and object, saying each morning "I'm combing my hair." I have several notes of his saying "comb" when I showed him the object. For 17:30 I have the entry that he said "combing" when he saw me combing my hair. By now he had begun to use the progressive ending quite commonly. Two days later I showed him the comb and asked what it was. To my amazement he said "combing," and he stuck to it for a long time. This was the only exception to his using *-ing* with an action word. I believe that when the newly acquired morphological rule was set in competition with older rules, not to interchange action and object words, and to attach a salient word to a salient and invariant object, the older rules won out, thus revealing their strength. Not until Stage 3 did he sort it out and speak of the action as *comb* and *combing.* When he did this, of course, he had to violate the rule of keeping object and action words distinct.

One highly interesting case is the learning of *shave* and *razor.* *Shave* initially was a word for a whole sequence of events; I never attempted to specify its meaning. Gradually I taught Kieran many of the objects and acts involved—*soap, toothbrush, toothpaste, washing.* When he was 20:19 I noticed that he seemed to call the razor *shave;* I tested him and found that that was indeed the case. I then tried to teach him *razor.* It was only at 21:1, a week and a half later, that he succeeded in recalling the word when asked— though I had taught it to him almost daily—and only later still that he learned *shaving* for the action. There are several points of interest, the most striking being that he came to the conclusion him-

self that *shave* must be the word for the only other salient object
in the sequence of events. Second, he had difficulty in laying aside
his conclusion, probably in part because he had come to it himself
but mostly because the correction meant jumping the semantic
boundary between object and action. He normally learned new
words the instant he was told them and showed a tenacious memory for them.

Over the three stages Kieran used 136 action words, and of
these only one seems to have been used occasionally as object
word as well. Bear in mind that in Roger Brown's analysis of the
vocabulary of 4- and 5-year-olds, some 33 percent of verbs referred
to something other than an action. To sum up, then, we find considerable flexibility within the major category that interests us
most, names for things. Kieran learned the same proper name of
different people and different proper names of the same people.
He used sortals of people whose proper name he knew. He scarcely
ever used a sortal of an attribute or action, or an attribute or action
word of an object. This is prima facie evidence that the category,
word for an object, played a part in his language.

(5) Are these grounds for the belief that Kieran saw the words
in the object-word list as similar to one another in a sense that an
object word and an action word, say, are not similar? In other
words, is there any evidence that he took the words in the object-
word list as forming a category of words rather than a category of
objects? There is, of course, the evidence we have already seen that
he easily accepted several object words for a single object or class
of objects and only with difficulty accepted a single word for an
object and action. This tells us about his attitude to words as distinct from his attitude to objects. It is some evidence that the
words themselves form a category. But, I must confess, it is not
overwhelming evidence.

Additional evidence, as we shall see when we study Sarah's
speech and the speech of adults to her, is the fact that Kieran
heard the same word applied to an object and to an action: e.g.,
bath used of a tub of water and of the action of being washed in
it. He did not adopt such linguistic liberties in his own speech,
which again reveals that his restriction, though based on nonlinguistic materials, was related to a linguistic attitude.

I am not anxious to argue, however, that the lists formed distinct linguistic categories in Kieran's mind rather than distinct
semantic categories. My general argument is equally well served
in either case.

THE COMING OF INFLECTIONS IN KIERAN'S VOCABULARY

Even if we agree that Kieran divides his words into categories that are semantically based, we must ask how this will aid his forming of grammatical categories which must be defined linguistically. So we must see how Kieran's semantic word categories serve him in specifically linguistic tasks. Recall that Hockett pointed to inflections and to syntactic roles as clues to grammatical categories. We will look at both and ask, does Kieran respect the integrity of his word categories in his use of inflections and in his word combinations? We will begin with inflections. I will call the inflections by their names in the grammar of adult English. That does not mean that I believe an inflection is functioning in Kieran's English, as it does in an adult's; I use the name for convenience.

1. *The possessive.* When Kieran was 17:21 he and I were sitting in bed one morning and he suddenly touched my wife's nightdress and said "Mammy." I took it as an attempt to say that the garment was peculiarly associated with his mother; he clearly did not think it was her. The following day I showed him the nightdress and again he said "Mammy." For some time he continued to point to objects and, appropriately, mention someone's name. When he was 18:18 he brought me his mother's wallet and said "Mammy's," the final -*s* being new. From then for a short while he used the final -*s* spasmodically in similar situations. And then my diary has this entry:

> 18:21 He is now using the possessive quite frequently and appropriately of a variety of inanimate objects most of which he knows another word for, like shoe, pin, bottle, shirt.

This -*s* was attached only to proper names and the proper name so modified was only said of inanimate objects. For most of the inanimate objects he already had a word, and he continued to use the proper name, appropriately, without the -*s*. This is evidence that the semantic class, proper name, was serving a truly linguistic function, namely, the class of words to which the possessive morpheme is attached.

At Stage 2 (see Appendix C) he continued to use both forms: *Daddy's sandal* and *Daddy cake*. He also began to use *my* and *our* with an object word. So in initial position he could place either a proper name or a possessive adjective. In second position, too, the scope enlarges to include, besides inanimate object, part of animate object and proper name. We have

Freddie's ball
Freddie's nose
Wanako's Mammy
Peggy Anne's Daddy
Our Car
Our Mammy
My Mammy

The new rule looks something like this, the braces signifying a choice among the elements within:

$$\left\{ \begin{array}{l} \text{Proper name} \pm s \\ \text{Poss. adj.} \end{array} \right\} \quad + \quad \left\{ \begin{array}{l} \text{Inanimate obj. word} \\ \text{Word for animate part} \\ \text{Proper word} \end{array} \right\}$$

And that is how it remains throughout State 3.

2. *Plural.* The plural *s* came in about the same time as the possessive, but its use, throughout the three stages, was far more sporadic than that of the possessive. At 18:20 he pointed to one foot and said "feet," and to the other and said "feets." At 18:27 he spoke of "horsie" and went on to say "horses." This was very different from the possessive. *Feets* and *horses* classify the objects pointed to; *Mammy* and *Mammy's* did not classify the nightdress or wallet.

I have not made a special list of the words that were used in both singular and plural form. However, the plural was used only with common, count nouns, never with proper names or mass nouns. This can be explained partly if we assume that he tended not to use a plural *s* with words unless he heard us do so. But that cannot be the full explanation because he never heard us say *feets.* It follows that besides our example he was guided by something else. I submit that that was a semantic category, given him by his perceptual-conceptual system, of objects with characteristic forms. We will come back to the count-mass distinction later.

3. *Progressive.* About the time he began to use the possessive he also began to use the progressive. He had been using words to describe or demand action from the time he began to speak, but now he began to add *-ing* to those words or to learn new words with the *-ing* attached. Appendix 3, where Action Descriptions are listed for Stage 1, contains 32 entries; 15 are in the progressive form, and 7 of these are side by side with the corresponding nonprogressive form—e.g., *cry, crying; fly, flying.* There can be little

doubt that Kieran saw -*ing* as a bound morpheme that could be added to Action Descriptions. He began to use -*ing* forms when he was 18:13, just five days before he began to use the possessive. It seems that at that point he caught on to the idea of bound morphemes, because he began to use not only the possessive and progressive at the same time, but the final -*s* of the singular, third person, present tense, and the -*s* of the plural all at the same time— the last two only very spasmodically. It is interesting in passing to note that Brown (1973, p. 274), who studied the order in which children master morphology, found that the present progressive, the plural, and the possessive are among the first mastered. He did not study the -*s* of the present tense.

Further evidence that Kieran saw -*ing* as a bound morpheme is that when he said "sleeping," his first progressive, he had just said "sleep." The next day he said "playing," "barking," and the following day "sneezing," all appropriately to describe ongoing activities. From that time the progressive became common. One other piece of evidence is the fact that he had long grown accustomed to the imperative forms of certain verbs and would respond appropriately: *cough, cry, dance, eat, kiss, sing, sleep, sneeze, wink,* and *yawn.* For some of these he produced both forms and for others no; but he clearly knew them both.

At Stage 2 there are 38 action descriptions, and of these 11 are progressives. What is interesting at this stage is a division of labor: progressives are used only as action descriptions; the corresponding nonprogressives are often action demands or imperatives. For example, *kiss* is an imperative; *kissing,* an action description. This continued through Stage 3. However, the nonprogressive was also used as an action description.

Most important is that -*ing* was added only to action words, never to object names or modifiers. The two apparent exceptions both occur at Stage 1, *morning* and *combing.* But *morning* has no accompanying form *morn,* and so it is not a real exception. *Combing,* we have seen, is a special case. It replaced *comb* completely and referred, in Stages 1 and 2, only to the object. It thus resembles *morning* in being an invariant, for Kieran. We saw that he took a long time to learn *comb* as an object word and *combing* as an action description, thus showing the inflexibility of the category, object word.

Stan Kuczaj (1978) has written an important paper on the learning of the progressive that does not agree with the foregoing. He notes that in the early stages of language children do not misuse the progressive as they do the plural morpheme. Indeed Kieran said *feets,* but nothing comparable with a progressive ending. Kuczaj is of the opinion that the early learning of the progressive is listlike: the child learns /-ing/ forms by rote and does not learn a rule that enables him to produce forms he has not heard. For a later stage Kuczaj has examples, such as *sticking* (striking with a stick) and *shirting* (putting a shirt on), that demonstrate a productive rule.

Against this, Kuczaj himself points out that there are no irregular progressives corresponding to such irregular plurals as *feet.* This weakens Kuczaj's case. His case is further weakened, if my earlier analysis is correct, by the near impossibility of Kieran's using such forms as *sticking* and *shirting,* because they violate the prohibition on using an object word to describe an action. This leaves only the stative verbs to account for (*own, have,* etc.), which do not readily take the progressive ending. But Kieran, as the list reveals, had no statives in his vocabulary at the time when he began to produce progressive forms. These facts undermine Kuczaj's argument, but they do not, of course, disprove his conclusion. It is in fact impossible, on the evidence, to disprove it. Nevertheless there is something significant in the fact that Kieran all of a sudden began to use four different bound morphemes, one of which was /-ing/. It does seem that he suddenly grasped a general fact about English. His application of the endings was conservative, though he produced novel forms of the plural. The absence of novel progressive forms is no evidence that he had not spotted the morphological rule, although his appropriate use of such pairs as *fly/flying* and *run/running* suggests that he had. All that is needed is that he saw that *run* and *running* were different forms of basically the same word.

KIERAN'S WORD COMBINATIONS

No area in child language has been as intensely studied as two- and three-word combinations in children's speech. The main bones of contention (see Bowerman, 1978b) have been: does the child establish a fixed order for combining words; do all children follow the same pattern of development; do their words show evidence of belonging in grammatical categories (noun, verb, etc.); and are the combinations governed by a phrase-structure grammar that specifies *NP*s and *VP*s and grammatical relations between them? Martin Braine (1976) made a very thorough analysis of the data and of the arguments. He examined the corpora of utterances from 16 children and concluded that there is not sufficient evidence to give an affirmative answer to any of the four questions. What seems clear is that the cognitive categories of children's experience (objects, attributes, actions, and the like) and the relations among such categories play an important part in guiding early word combinations. I agree with all this, and since my task is somewhat different from that of other workers in the area, I can sidestep the controversies. My main task is to determine if the semantic categories of words that we have already seen in Kieran's speech play a part in his two- and three-word combinations. I believe they do, but even if I am right, that does not prove that those categories are grammatical ones, or that Kieran had learned anything equivalent to English phrase structure. As far as I know, other workers in child language have not concerned themselves with the same issue in their data. Moreover, being interested in word combinations they usually began their studies at a time when the children were older than Kieran, and so there was no possibility of comparison with usage at a younger age (see, e.g., Schlesinger, 1974). Maratsos (1979) places us on our guard against simplistic semantic categories even in very young children's speech.

MARKERS FOR NAMES

Even when he knew only a dozen names or so, Kieran usually prefaced them by a rather mumbled /əs, əz/, which we interpreted, perhaps fondly, as *this is*. The diary entry is:

> 15:10 When he spontaneously speaks he very often, in naming objects, says /əs, əz/X. It sounds awfully like *this is* X. Whatever the significance, it is pretty regular.

Kieran continued so for over a month, and the interesting thing is that whatever the preface was, it was used only with words for objects and proper names. A later entry runs:

> 15:29 For about four days I notice that he no longer prefaces his attempt to name things while pointing to them with /as az/, but with /si/, *see*.

See became very common before names of persons and objects but before no other category of word. Though once, at 16:2, he said "see crying." Still it is evident that Kieran distinguished names from other words linguistically, and that for some purposes he collapsed the categories proper name and object word.

Between *see* and an object word Kieran often placed a mumbled vowel that I represented as /a/. At 14:26 I distinctly heard him say "see a bus," and at 14:29 "see a car." From then on, *a* was used spasmodically before count words for objects but before no other category of word. For example at stage 3 he frequently used the form *like a X,* but he never put *a* before a proper name or a word for a mass object. Thus we get *like a crab* but:

> Like Freddie
>
> Like you
>
> Like a boat on water

The before an object word occurs a few times at Stage 1: *the grass, the puppy, the other shoe.* In Stages 2 and 3 it occurs quite frequently but not consistently. It is used only with object words both mass and count. For example, at 21:16 he said in rapid succession:

> I find the comb
>
> I find the juice

His use of *a* and *the,* then, distinguishes object words from all other word types. *A* distinguishes words for mass and count objects, and *the* collapses the two, appropriately.

Modifier words were common in single word utterances from an early age, and in combinations from about 15:0. With a few exceptions at Stages 2 and 3 they occur only before an object word or proper name so the rules look like this:

$$\text{modifier} \quad + \quad \begin{Bmatrix} \text{proper name} \\ \text{object word} \end{Bmatrix}$$

The exceptions such as *Mammy great,* seem to be modeled on the adult sentence *Mammy is great.* Evidence for this is that at Stage 3 we find a few such sentences fully expressed: *I'm tired, they're wet.* From our point of view, the important fact is that with only one exception modifiers were used only with words for objects and proper names. This is evidence that those semantic categories are functioning in Kieran's early linguistic combinatorial rules. The exception, *biting bad,* at 21:12 was merely said repeating his mother who said "Biting is bad." Interestingly, the use of modifiers shows that Kieran is able, appropriately, to generalize across object words and proper names.

The nearest Kieran came to complete English sentences at Stage 1 was in utterances like:

18:17 He fly
18:21 Kiss him (Freddie)
18:24 Eat the grass (of a cow)
18:27 Freddie barking
18:27 I kick it

Bloom, Lightbown, & Hood (1975) distinguish between children who use pronouns and proper names in word combinations. Kieran used both quite freely. He always used a personal pronoun or a proper name in subject position. In object position he used a pronoun, not necessarily personal, or an object word. The general form of his sentence can best be captured by some such semantic chain as:

$$\text{Proper name of agent} \; + \; \text{Action word} \; + \; \left\{ \begin{array}{l} \text{object word} \\ \text{personal pronoun} \end{array} \right\}$$

The braces signify a choice between the elements within. This is not untypical of what Braine (1976, pp. 56–57) found in children's speech. Our interest is that it shows the semantic word categories, especially that of name, playing a part in Kieran's earliest sentences.

Someone might ask, how do you know Kieran distinguished between action words and modifiers in linguistic combinations (as well as semantically), seeing that he frequently placed both types of word before object words and proper names? The data provide a clear answer. We find numerous sentences of the type *kick the ball, find a shoe* but none of the type *big a bus, dead a bee*. We do find *a nice hat* and *a dead bee*. Further, action words frequently come before the pronouns *it, them,* and *you;* modifiers never do. There are other clues, too, apart from the fact, pointed out earlier, that *-ing* is added only to action words, never to modifiers.

In the interest of showing the role of the semantic classes in leading to grammatical categories and to the structure of the English sentence, I suggest a few of Kieran's sentence rules at Stage 3:

1. Proper name + action description $\pm$ *ing*

2. Proper name + action description $\pm \left\{ \begin{array}{l} a \\ the \end{array} \right\}$ + object word (count)

3. Proper name + action description $\pm$ *the* + object word (mass)

4. Proper name + action description + $\left\{ \begin{array}{l} it \\ them \\ you \end{array} \right\}$

5. Action demand + *the* + object word (count)

6. Action demand + $\left\{ \begin{matrix} \text{proper name} \\ it \end{matrix} \right\}$

These are not the only types, nor is order followed as strictly as they suggest, but they cover the most common sentence types. They clearly indicate roles for the semantic categories.

Throughout this section I have been playing hard and fast with such terms as *object word* and *action word*. Michael Maratsos (1979) in a highly instructive paper warns against such glibness. He points out that while a review of the literature reveals some generalizations at the level I suggest, it also reveals certain combinations that are restricted to particular lexical items. He takes this as suggesting that the child may be working with something much less general than the broad semantic categories I have been using. Melissa Bowerman (1976) also points out that her daughter Eva began to use *want* in combination with a great many words ("want juice," "want bottle," "want see"), though she did not so combine any of her 25 other action words or action demands. In addition, Maratsos warns us against lumping together in a single semantic category what may really be quite complex. He points out that the subject of a sentence may be a physical object and agent and also the subject of an attribute (as in *nice dog running*). The very same noun in another sentence, while still subject, may have none of these semantic properties (e.g. *dog resting*). Both these observations must be considered.

The second does not affect my analysis of Kieran's speech because I did not attempt any refinement of the semantic categories. Nor did I attempt to relate them to a case grammar by subdividing them into such categories as agent, dative, and the like. On the other hand each object word seems to have functioned as just that, a word for a physical object, in Kieran's speech during the stages we have been studying. One of the main arguments throughout is that at that level of analysis the semantic categories are invariant.

Maratsos' first point, about the restriction of combinatorial rules to one or two lexical items, is indeed true of many children's speech. It is not true of Kieran's. In Appendix 3 the complete lists of his recorded word combinations for his 20th and, separately, his 21st month are given. He simply did not behave as Melissa Bowerman's Eva did. It follows that there is some justification in using broad semantic categories to characterize Kieran's word combinations. Eva seems to have taken *want* as a prototype for certain combinations. Kieran didn't do that sort of thing. We must leave the matter at that, though we can allow the final word to Maratsos, who warns us about the variability of developmental patterns.

Some of my combination rules may suggest that I favor the idea that children delete words to produce what used to be called telegraphese. For example, Rule 10 for Kieran's 20th month combination reads: "Object word ± *for* + proper name." This is to characterize such utterances as "Kisses for Mummy" and "Medicine Freddie." Braine (1976) has argued against the idea that children delete words. I do not wish to take sides on the issue. My usage is meant to suggest nothing more than that Kieran sometimes did and sometimes did not say *for* where his intentions seemed to demand it.

At this point one might inquire how we know that at least at Stage 3 Kieran's word categories are not fully grammatical and no longer semantic. The answer is that we can't be sure they aren't. The scholars who have worried about this have not been able to suggest any criteria for deciding when a category goes from being semantic to being grammatical. It would be misguided to demand that there should be evidence for all the phrase-structure rules discussed, say, in Jackendoff (1977) before allowing they were grammatical. My view is that the child will shift from a semantic generalization to a grammatical one only when he is forced to, and I see no evidence, even merely suggestive, that Kieran has reached that stage for any of his categories. Moreover, as we turn to Sarah's utterances we find that the strict separation of object and action words is preserved to a much later age than Kieran's 21 months.

Sarah's Vocabulary

Sarah was one of the three children whom Roger Brown and his coworkers recorded for half an hour once a week for a period of a year—for full details see Brown (1973). The recordings began when she was 22 and ended when she was 34 months old. She thus gives us data for a period of a year after the data we have seen for Kieran end.

1. *Nouns and verbs.* I paid particular attention to the use of nouns and verbs in the first 10 sessions. I use the words nouns and verbs, basing myself mainly on the adult's (usually mother's) usage, which was always easy to determine. Sarah, too, often provided a syntactic environment that suggested one category rather

than the other. Besides, in the conversation as one participant picked up from the other, the general context nearly always suggested one rather than the other. I do not claim that Sarah had by then mastered the grammatical categories, noun and verb.

In Table 7.1 are the numbers of nouns used by Sarah and the adult divided by whether they applied to a physical object or not. In Table 7.2 are the numbers of verbs divided by whether they were used of an activity or not. As we expect, most of the adults' nouns applied to physical objects, but some 17 percent do not, and most of their verbs applied to activities, but some 28 percent do not. When we look at Sarah's use of the same words, or rather subsets of them, we find that about 3 percent of the nouns did not apply to physical objects and about 10 percent of the verbs do not apply to activities. It seems that at least to the age of 24½ months Sarah is maintaining the semantic integrity of the two categories that Kieran did. Adults who spoke to her did not. The record is full of remarks like *Do you want a good spanking?* where the verb *to spank* has been nominalized, and though a noun it still means an action. Adults used the following nouns in the first five sessions, none of them for concrete objects: *air, bites* (actions), *housework, ideas, loving, matter* (the), *minute, name, practice* (out of), *rest, ride, song, sense, Tuesday, way, year.* Of these the only one that Sarah used was *air.* In the first five sessions adults used the following verbs, none for activities even broadly interpreted: *bless, can, dare, got* (own or have), *has, have, know, let, like, lives, looks like, loves, make believe, minds* (notices), *remember, see, should, stuck, stay, supposed to, take* (it easy), *think, want, wanna.* Of these, Sarah used only *got* and *like.* At this age it just seems that Sarah did not in general learn words that did not apply to physical objects or physical activities. The next question is: does she use object words for activities and activity words for objects?

2. Integrity of Sarah's word classes. In ordinary English we *comb* (verb) our hair with a *comb* (noun); *soap* (verb) our faces with *soap* (noun); *slide* (verb) on a *slide;* etc. Did adults avoid such grammatical flexibility in speaking to Sarah? No, they did not, though I cannot be sure if they did it less than they do when talking to one another. I have an impression that they were just as flexible in speaking to Sarah, because I found no tendency for flexibility to increase with Sarah's age and linguistic progress. The following words were used as nouns and verbs in speech to Sarah, some many times:

Table 7.1 Nouns Used by Adult and Child in the First Ten Sessions with Sarah

	First 5 sessions			Second 5 sessions (new nouns)		
	Physical object	Other	Doubtful[a]	Physical object	Other	Doubtful[a]
Adult	133	16		111	28	
Child	111	2 (story) (air)	1 (light)	78	3	1 (heaven)

[a]"Doubtful" means that the child's utterance left in doubt whether the word was being used as a noun.

Table 7.2 Use of Verbs by Adult and Child in the First Ten Sessions with Sarah

	First 5 sessions			Second 5 sessions (new verbs)		
	Activity or Event	Other	Doubtful[a]	Activity or Event	Other	Doubtful[a]
Adult	63	24		52	10	
Child	15	2 (got) (like)	3 (see) (stay) (wanna)	24	2 (can) (want)	2 (rain) (hurt)

[a]"Doubtful" means that the child's utterance left in doubt whether the word was being used as a verb.

Bite, brush, catch, comb, curl, cut, dance, dress, drink, iron, kiss, light, orange, pin, powder, rain, ride, sleep, slide, soap, spank, stick, swing, tickle, walk.

I looked carefully at Sarah's utterances in the sections where those words were used. Often she made no response to an utterance that contained one of those words, and often she responded in a manner that from our viewpoint is irrelevant. However, there were many times when she did respond and use the word. In no case was there any evidence of her adopting adult flexibility—using the same word of an object and of an activity—before the 30th session when she was almost 2½ years old. By that I mean that nowhere in the scripts, not just on the occasions when her mother did, did she violate the semantic category boundary. Even more explicitly, she did not, for example, in session 6, use *brush* of the object and in session 24 use it of the activity of brushing. Even after the 30th session Sarah used only the following of objects and actions:

brush, comb, dress, drink and *soap*

Here are some examples from the transcripts of adult (A) expressions addressed to Sarah (S), indexed for Sarah's age in months:

31: A. Want me to give you a *brush* so you can *brush* your baby's hair?

32½: S. . . . go *brush* her hair. A. Gonna *brush* her hair? S. Where's a *brush*? A. Did you have a *brush*?

31: S. Get a *comb*. A. Don't put it in your mouth. . . . S. You *comb* it. You *comb* it. A. Yeah. You *comb* it all up.

24½: A. I want her to have *curls*. It looks all right when I *curl* it.

31: A. You like to wear my *dress* too? We spent all the other day *dressing* all your dollies.

24½: A. You're not supposed to break your *iron*. How you gonna *iron* your clothes?

22½: A. That's the *ride*. You got a *ride* like that, huh.

23: S. I *ride*—(on my horse)—*Ride* horsie. A. Well you know how to *ride* it.

27: A. Do you like a *slide*? S. Nods. A. Do you like two *slides*? S. Two *slides*. A. Do you *slide* out in the backyard? S. Goes to back door. A. You *slide* on the *slide* down at dancing school.

31: A. *Soap*. Look at the *soap*. Wash the *soap* off. S. Irrelevant response . . . S. I *soap* my hair. A. You *soaping* your hair? S. Yeah. . . . A. Where's the *soap*? S. Yeah.

23½: A. Make her (doll) *walk*. See. She *walks*. She doesn't *walk* very

good. One-, two-, three-, four-, Hold baby's hand and go for a
walk . . . go slow or dollie won't *walk*. S. *Walk*. A. *Walk*. S. *Walk*.
A. Yeah, you got to *walk* her feet . . . She *walks*. S. *Walk*.

I have given these examples to underline how natural it is for an
adult to use the same word in two grammatical categories. Indeed
I wonder if an adult English speaker could avoid doing so. The
switch is usually accompanied by a semantic switch; we have seen
several switches from object to activity. It follows that if the child
does not switch likewise, he, not his parents, is the source of the
restriction.

Summary

This chapter has been devoted to building up a number of conclusions related to grammatical categories and their learning. Since
they have been long, it will help to list them:

1. Grammatical categories are linguistic universals in this sense—that
   across all languages in which a category occurs, the category has the
   same inductive basis, namely a semantic one. This means that each language selects from a set of universal categories. In particular "noun" is
   inductively based on the concept, object word—object being that
   which calls for a sortal term.

2. Mature grammatical categories can be defined only in lingusitic terms
   (morphology and syntax). The child's initial learning of such categories
   is not guided by either morphology or syntax. Rather his initial learning of morphology and syntax depends on some prior classifications of
   his vocabulary.

3. The child's semantic categories of words play a role in his early learning of morphology and sentence structure.

4. The child's strategies in learning grammatical categories and grammar
   are not forced on him, and may not even be facilitated, by his parents'
   style of talking to him.

How general are these findings, based on the speech of two children, of children as a whole? The weakest part of the conclusion,
fortunately the least important, is the age at which the child takes
different steps. Some children advance more rapidly than others.
Sarah seemed to relax the constraint that a single word could not
serve as object and action word at the age of about 2½. Others
may do it earlier or later; but in psychological theory age is of no
consequence unless it serves as evidence that learning occurs in a
certain order and the order is critical to the theory. For the rest,
I suspect that the findings of this chapter are quite general. In

nearly all the child vocabularies that have been published, researchers have felt obliged to divide the words into object words, action words, modifiers, and perhaps others. Without doing the analysis we have done, the researchers were motivated by the same insight, that the early categories are semantic. Braine (1976) and Bowerman (1973a, 1973b, 1978a) have argued cogently that the rules for early word combinations are best stated in terms of semantic categories of words. Their conclusions support my claim that my theory is generalizable, at least to English-speaking children: children form semantic categories of words to begin with, and these categories play a part in early morphological rules and in the early rules for word combinations. There may, however, be much variability in detail, such as whether a particular child uses pronouns at an early stage or whether he restricts word combinations to certain lexical items. Interesting though the variations are, they do not seriously detract from the main theory of the chapter.

8.

Names as Nouns

Mögen andere kommen
und es besser machen
—Ludwig Wittgenstein

On the basis of the data just presented I would like to describe how the child learns that certain words are nouns. This demands a description of the child at the beginning of the process of learning, at the end of the process, and a description of the means he used to effect the change. Afterwards I will attempt to extend my conclusions to three subdivisions of noun, found in many of the world's languages. Throughout what follows I will, to avoid tedium, omit the qualifications that sanity demands and speak with a boldness and specificity that the matter does not at all warrant.

I assume that at least by the time he begins to speak, a child's perceptual and conceptual systems present the world to him in certain semantic categories. Among these are object, attribute, action, and many others. The category, object, receives much attention in Chapter 11, and I have written about it elsewhere (Macnamara, 1981), so I will not dwell on it here. It appears to be an innate category. All learning about the physical world presupposes it, and the defining characteristics (see Chapter 11) are not given in the sensory array.

Attribute, as Aristotle observed in the *Metaphysics,* is dependent for its existence on an object. The attributes that we are interested in are mostly given in the sensory array, though their inherence in an object isn't. Some, such as possession, if young children really have that notion, are not given directly in perception. Attributes are of a different logical structure than action descriptions. Action descriptions have one, two, or three argument slots, even in Kieran's speech. Attribute words modify object words. In the standard action word and object word combinations there is no attempt to describe a transient event in which the object is causally involved. Examples of such combinations from Kieran in his 20th month are *best dog, good cake, new truck, dead horse* (Appendix 3).

I did not make divisions among action descriptions, but it seems likely that Kieran distinguishes transitive from intransitive ones. He never added a word that looked like a direct object to such words as *crying, coughing, talking.* Even in his 20th month he regularly included such words with transitive action words; such as *kick, find, wear, catch,* and *push.* Although this conclusion is probably true, we must remember that Kieran did not always place a direct object where adult grammar would demand it of him. We must also remember Melissa Bowerman's (1978c) evidence about children using noncausative verbs as causatives. An example from Kieran's later speech is *let's smile him up,* meaning "cause him to smile." The absence of such examples at the early stages is not evidence that he did not distinguish between semantically transitive and sematically intransitive actions. It seems more likely that at the early stages the child is highly conservative and attempts to model his speech closely on what he hears. It seems improbable that children should fail to know that one cannot *cough* an object in the sense that one can *find* one.

I am not sure how much of the foregoing needs to be innate, but it seems to be operative by the time the child begins to speak. I have suggested that the grammatical category, noun, is not innate, but that the rules for constructing it are. Just to recall the main argument: nouns can be defined only in terms of morphology and phrase structure and languages vary both in morphology and in phrase-structure rules for nouns. It follows that the notion noun varies. On the other hand the category, noun, is not given in the sensory array. Nouns are not, for example, all and only the two syllable words, or anything like that. They cannot be induced by any process that is confined to the physical properties of the sound wave.

Before going on to see how the category, noun, might be learned, let us take a closer look at adult tests for noun status and see why they could not serve the child. An adult can use a number of phrases with blanks in them and say that any word that can fill the blank is a noun. For example, (*the.* . .) could be used to pick out a great many nouns in English, but notice the conditions under which it will do so. The person who is judging whether a word will fill the slot must have a sufficient intuition of phrase structure to judge correctly that the word is the structural keystone of the clause. So, *the man* yields *man* as noun; but *the big* is also a legitimate sequence, and yet *big* is not a noun. Nouns are the structural keystones in noun phrases; and so I can employ phrase structure to identify nouns only if I have a grasp of the structure of noun phrases and know that it is precisely that, the structure of noun phrases. This is clearly getting nowhere. The trouble is that one can only specify the grammatically permissible phrases for English in terms of the grammatical categories. Phrase structure presupposes the grammatical categories, and that includes the category noun.

Moreover, parents do not make any effort to help children discover that certain words are nouns. Imagine a child who called a worm a *caterpillar.* How very odd it would be if his mother were to say: "I'm pleased to see that you used the right category of word in your attempt to name the creature, but you used the wrong member of the category. You should have called it a *worm."* There is no such feedback that tells a child he is or is not assigning words to the correct grammatical category.

What is innate about the grammatical category noun is that the initial rules for inducing it are expressed in specific semantic terms. The general schema for noun, proper and common, is something like this: noun is that grammatical category, eventually distinguished in terms of morphological rules and phrase structure functions, that is initially induced on the basis of a semantic word category, i.e., word that names an object (proper) or word for a kind of object, natural or artificial (common).

I am not sure whether the child starts with two quite separate semantic categories, proper name and sortal, and later collapses them for certain purposes, or whether he starts out with a disjoint category, as I have stated it in the last paragraph. In our present state of ignorance, groping for the outlines of grammatical learning, not much hangs on the difference. The category, name of an object, is clear enough. In describing the basic sortal category I sacrificed explicitness to brevity. A full statement would include the following elements: (1) The category presupposes that the child can distinguish in his environment objects in the sense already described. (2) It presupposes that he has established kinds of objects, some natural, some artificial. (3) The class of words that functions as sortals has a meaning. (4) That meaning when predicated of objects is either true of them or not true of them. What is innate in this is not, of course, knowledge of particular objects or classes of object, but the ability to perceive objects as such, and to categorize them in that basic way that is associated with sortals. Innate, too, is the preparedness to take a conventional symbol as expressing a meaning—that is, as we shall see in Chapter 12, taking a symbol as a name which designates a concept.

In the last chapter we saw some data that suggest how the semantic base comes to bear. The child imposes on himself constraints in the use of words to match the semantic categories. He does not use object words to signify actions, or action words to signify objects. His parents do not observe these constraints; they do not model them for him. Ultimately the contrast between his own constraints and his parents' freedom must be a source of change for the child. Most revealing of all, when he first learns to add bound morphemes to words, he is guided by the same semantic categories, which thus reveal their psychological reality and their relevance to language. In addition, his early rules for word combinations are guided by the semantic categories.

To see what happens we will take a closer look at the possessive. The child's initial rule seems to be proper name + s. It soon becomes: proper name + s + inanimate object word. A little later some of the constraints on what can be the final element are relaxed. In Kieran's data, stage 2 (Appendix 3), the final element was no longer confined to inanimate object words; it could be part of an animate object or even a whole animate object:

Daddy's sandal

Freddie's nose

Peggy Anne's Daddy

Ko's Mammy

The process of generalizing will continue and he will hear his parents speak of such things as:

Kieran's age

Your temper

For pity's sake

Daddy's music lesson

Mammy's knitting

In due course he will find that the list of what can be the final element in the construction has become long and unwieldy. The generalization can be captured in a different way, however. Kieran will have to advert to other linguistic properties that all those final elements have: they can all take determiners (e.g., *an age, the sake*); they can all take modifiers (e.g., *a great age, a violent temper, for old sake's sake*); they can form plurals (e.g., *ages, tempers*) if they are countable. They can also serve the same functions in the greater structure of a sentence, as we shall see in a minute.

Some friends who have followed me this far have asked what impels the child to express the generalization in terms of a linguistic category, noun, rather than some such semantic one as "abstract object?" In reply I point out that the notion "abstract object" is shrouded in thick mist. In fact no one has any idea what it might mean; in Chapter 12 we shall see that *abstraction* is a treacherous term and in a combination with *object* it can do nothing but confuse our intuitions about a valuable construct. However, all this is quite academic, since what the child needs is a category that will do the linguistic work that nouns do. And we have seen that such a category cannot be expressed in semantic terms. The work it does is expressed in morphology and in phrase structure. The child needs the linguistic category noun—*pace* I. M. Schlesinger (1977).

Processes similar to those that are at work in connection with the final element in the possessive are also at work in many other structures. The child begins with some simple structures, characterized semantically. I specified several of such that were common in Kieran's speech by the end of stage three. The list was only partial and omitted such sentences as:

Wear my shoe

Dadda is reading book

Dadda fix the music (from record player)

Mamma give it you

No like it

Mémère gave you.

Yet all of these occur in Kieran's speech. Notice that shoes are not affected in the same way by wearing as books are by reading. That makes it difficult to capture in semantic terms the relations between verb and direct object in these sentences. Consider further such sentences as:

Mammy get the juice

Mammy make the coffee

Freddie loves you

I want a bagel

How can we specify the semantic relations into which enter the final elements in these basic sentences? Sometimes the final element is an object that is made, sometimes one that is found, sometimes one that is wanted or loved or worn or read. The list could be extended greatly even for Kieran at stage three. What such a semantic list misses is that in every such sentence the final element is a noun phrase that is the direct object of the verb. I do not want to delay on the structure, direct object, since it lies well outside the limits I have set myself; my purpose in mentioning it is to point out that there is no possibility of specifying it without having recourse to the linguistic category, noun phrase. And noun phrase itself cannot be specified for any language without the notion, noun. It follows that the child's attempts to discover the rules of grammar for a sentence lead him in the same direction as his attempts to discover the rule for the possessive. Both lead him to abandon semantic categories in favor of linguistic ones, in particular noun.

One final example from Kieran. By the end of stage three Kieran had placed *a* and *the* only before names for objects, sometimes with intervening modifiers—*a dog; the big bus.* Sooner or later he will realize that the final element in such phrases need not be an object name. He will hear *a good spanking, the time, the weather,* and *the reason.* Semantics will have guided him to a basic linguistic structure that at first he characterized as:

$$\left.\begin{array}{l} a \\ the \end{array}\right\} \pm \text{ modifier} + \text{object word.}$$

That characterization will not hold up and, in particular, the communality across final elements will have to be captured in some other way—eventually as noun. I do not know the details of how and when children switch to linguistic categories, even in English. That must be left for futher research. But I hope that what I have given is a reasonable introductory sketch.

Quite simply, I have argued that the child climbs to grammar on a semantic ladder and then kicks the ladder away. Though semantics gets him off the ground, it cannot carry him all the way. Ultimately linguistic rules must take over the initial sortings of words, bound morphemes, and phrase structures, and finish the task of assigning words to grammatical categories.

Recently, Maratsos and Chalkley (1980) have argued that there is never a stage where the child's word classes are distinguished solely on a semantic basis. They argue that such distinctions are always based on co-occurrence restrictions as well as on semantic rules. The main force of their argument is that in adult language the correlation between grammatical category and semantic category is quite weak. This is, of course, true, but it may have little bearing on the early stages of language learning. They bring forward one other argument against the position I am taking here. It has to do with the absence of errors of a certain sort.

The types of error they predict for a theory such as mine relate mainly to stative verbs (e.g., *remember, want, know*) and "action-like adjectives" (e.g., *naughty, snoopy, active,* and *noisy*). The relevance of these categories is that where I have spoken of Kieran's verbs as action demands and action descriptions, stative verbs describe states, not actions; and whereas I have spoken of Kieran's adjectives as modifiers or attribute words, action-like adjectives seem to describe actions (e.g., being naughty, snooping about). Maratsos and Chalkley claim that a purely semantic classification would place the stative verbs with the attribute words and the action-like adjectives with the action words. Since they do not find errors of the appropriate kinds, they conclude that the categories are not purely semantic ones.

The argument is logical, though the examples of appropriate errors given by Maratsos and Chalkley are confusing. Two examples they suggest for stative verbs are *he is see the book and *he isn't remember the movie* (p. 181). These are, presumably, by analogy with *he is happy* and *he isn't tired,* adjectives that describe states. But, of course, the presence of direct objects for *see* and *remember* would mark those words as semantically different from *happy* and *tired,* which never can have direct objects. More important, however, Kieran did not have true statives during the stages described. At stage one, his *see* meant *"look at,"* his *want* meant "give me," his *sleep,* as I argued earlier, seemed to mean "put your head to one side on your hands." At stages two and three his *like* meant "do something" or "give me something," his *no like* meant "stop." Maratsos and Chalkley recognize this possibility: "It might be the case . . . that children do not semantically view these stative verbs as denoting states, but instead believe them to denote processes or actions" (p. 147). But they do not think it likely. Why, they query, do we find *I am running* and not **I am knowing it* (p. 147)? But Kieran had not used the word *know* by the end of stage three. Maratsos and Chalkley seem to have a much later stage in mind, for they say that children "know a great deal . . . about the complex semantics of the mental verbs *think* and *know* by the age four" (pp. 147-48). By that age I imagine the categories are purely syntactic. Incidentally, Maratsos and Chalkley mark the imperative of *think* as ungrammatical, though we commonly hear such expressions as *"think what you like"* and *"think that, if you must."*

Similar remarks apply with even greater force to Maratsos and Chalkley's observations about action-like adjectives. None such appear in Kieran's vocabulary by the end of stage three. Maratsos and Chalkley become simply confused, I fear, when they cite Nelson (1976) for the point "that children's earlier adjectives denote many [such] brief nonenduring qualities as . . . *hot,* or *wet*; brevity is a semantic characteristic of many verbs." Change-ability is one of the main bases for distinguishing sortals, like *dog,* from attributes, like *black* and *hot.* A dog's color and tem-perature can change while it remains the same thing (see below, Chapter 11). Action is not distinguished from attribute on the basis of duration. Some attributes are short lived; some actions, such as writing a book on child language, can last for years.

I conclude, then, that Maratsos and Chalkley do not present serious objections to the semantic theory of early word categories. This is not surprising, since they did not have access to the evi-dence I here present for the first time. This does not detract from the value of their paper, for it can be seen as making valuable sug-gestions about the combined rolls of syntax and semantics in lead-ing the child at a later stage to the adult grammatical categories.

SUBDIVISIONS OF NOUNS

The child's work is not yet done because most languages make subdivisions of nouns that he must cope with. In this section I will discuss by way of illustration three such divisions: gender in Indo-European languages; classifiers (of nouns) as found in a great many languages; count and mass nouns as found in English and in many languages all over the world. Not very much is known about acquisition in these connections, yet a book like this can best serve its purpose by drawing attention to phenomena that are intimately related to naming. (A fourth distinction, between proper and common nouns, was dealt with in Chapter 2).

A. *Gender.* Many Indo-European languages—French, Spanish, and Irish—divide their nouns into two classes, masculine and feminine. To these classes many, like Latin and German, add a third, neuter. Whatever the origin of these distinctions in Proto Indo-European, they are almost entirely linguistic divisions today. That is, over most of their semantic domain they do not relate in any convenient manner to any known cognitive or perceptual divisions of objects. Certainly the notions of masculinity and feminity will not carry the learner far. In French, for example, *homme* (man) is masculine and *femme* (woman) is feminine. But then *personne* (person), which can apply to either sex, is itself feminine. When we enter the asexual world of most objects, the terms masculine and feminine seem to be irrelevant. *Pied* (foot) is masculine, whereas *main* (hand) is feminine. *Roc* (outcrop of rock) is masculine, and *roche* (rock) is feminine. To make matters worse, in German *fraülein* (young woman) and *mädchen* (girl) are both neuter. And as though it were the ultimate in perversion, in Irish, *cailín* (girl) is masculine. In the last three examples, the true nature of the distinction is revealed. In German all words that end in *-lein* or in *-chen,* diminutive suffixes, are neuter, while in Irish all words that end in *-ín,* also a diminutive suffix, are masculine. The objects referred to mostly make no difference.

The learner of such genders must rely on what linguistic clues he can and for the rest commit a prodigious amount of detail to memory. Tucker, Lambert, & Rigault (1977) study the manner in which native French speakers set about the task. They composed a set of nonsense words that meet the phonological rules of French but do not exist as French words. To these they affixed examples of all the common endings of French words. They asked young native speakers of French to tell them whether these words were masculine or feminine (by indicating whether they should be preceded by *le* or *la*). They found that their subjects had a very accurate appreciation of the correlation between ending and gender. Apparently French children note carefully the regular covariations. When the ending is no help, they must simply learn, one by one, which words belong to which gender. Throughout, their task is complicated by the fact that before a vowel several of the cues fail: *le* and *la* lose their vowels by elision, and the masculine form of the possessive pronoun is used. Then the child must note the form of the indefinite article, *un* or *une,* and the form of any accompanying adjectives.

Just one speculative suggestion about a very general semantic clue! Our conceptual system individuates experience on the basis of objects, not on the basis of actions or attributes. It seems to me plausible that this plays a part in the section of grammar we are dealing with. The conclusion depends on their being special links between nouns and objects, between adjectives and attributes, and between verbs and actions. If there are, and there seem to be both in early learning and in frequency of grammatical-semantic pairings at the adult level, then it is not difficult to see why gender is governed by nouns and not adjectives or articles. My suggestion is that because his perceptual-conceptual system individuates reality in terms of objects, the child expects that the control of gender (and number) will reside in nouns and not in adjectives or articles.

B. *Classifiers.* Many languages require nouns (and sometimes verbs) to be marked with classifiers. The general idea can be illustrated by:

three *pieces* of cake

three *cakes* of soap

We are obliged to place some word in such structures immediately after the quantifier, and there are constraints on what can be used. The following are not allowed:

*three *cakes* of cake

*three *cakes* of stone

Many languages have much more elaborate classifier systems than English. Friedrich (1970) speaks of one type that is to be found among many unrelated languages, and he suggests that the major factor in determining choice of classifier is the dimensionality of the object named—whether the object is significantly extended in one, two, or three dimensions—not its overall shape. Peter Denny (1979) has made an interesting study of the matter, and I will give an outline of what he has to say. One reason for going into the matter is my suspicion that dimensionality also plays a part in the count-mass distinction that we come to next—indeed, that it and the system of classifiers we are looking at have a close semantic affinity.

First, a few examples. Denny gives this one from Ojibway, an Algonquian language: *makkakkōnss akāči - minak - at,* which he glosses as "the box, it - three dimensional - is small." There the classifier is *minak,* which means significantly extended in three dimensions. Another example from the same language is *napak-āpīk - at,* an expression referring to anything like a ribbon, which he glosses as "flat - two dimensional and flexible - it is."

Denny (1976) claims to find classifiers indicating dimensionality in a wide variety of languages: Eskimo; the Athabascan languages, Chiricahua–Apache and Western Apache, Chipewayan and Koyukon; the Algonquian languages, Ojibway and Cree; Tzeltal (Mayan); Tarascan (Mexican); Bantu (African); Ponapean, Gilbertese and Trukese (Pacific); Burmese; Malay; Iban, and Australian. If he is right, this is impressive evidence of a tendency for language to code dimensionality by means of some obligatory devices. That in turn suggests that perceptual objects are coded in terms of such dimensions. Presumably, the child, in learning dimensionality markers, is aided by the salience of these dimensions in perception. All this seems obvious if the linguistic facts are as Denny claims, though even then one is puzzled that color, surely an all-pervasive and salient aspect of visual perception, is coded lexically and not by means of obligatory markers in all languages. Perhaps color is not as important as form in the classification of objects.

C. *Mass-Count.* A very common distinction among nouns across the world's languages is that between mass and count. English has it, and so it is easy to illustrate. Words like *cup, spoon,* and *hand* are commonly called count nouns; we say *a cup, several cups, ten cups.* Words like *milk* and *porridge* are called mass nouns; one does not usually speak about *a porridge* or *ten porridges.* At first sight, then, it seems that the distinction can be made on syntactic grounds. As a first approximation one might say that nouns that occur in the plural are count; those that do not are mass. However, there are such words as *oats,* which is plural; but it gives evidence of being mass, because it does not normally permit of the singular. Contrast it with *wheat,* which does not normally permit of the plural. *Oats* is one of those special forms that are called *pluralia tantum* (plural only). On the other hand, we find that even the clearest examples of mass nouns can be used in the plural in special circumstances. One can imagine a waiter telling the kitchen, "three milks and two porridges." The same is true of every mass noun in the language. The opposite is true of words that pass as strong count nouns. Take *books* and *shelves*; when used in the plural they are clearly count nouns. Yet one can imagine a philistine discussing their respective merit as fuel for a fire and saying, "You should always mix a little shelf with book." And the same is true of all the count nouns in the language. Indeed Gleason (1965, p. 135) makes just this point. He goes on to argue that the basis for the distinction is not semantic. He instances *gravel* (mass) as opposed to *pebbles* (count). "Pebbles are no more countable than gravel . . . It is simply a convention of English that *pebble* is a count noun, usually plural, whereas *gravel* is a mass noun."

I would like to argue that the distinction is mainly semantic, that count nouns name things that have a characteristic form, and mass nouns do not. If a substance is referred to in such a manner that it is given a characteristic form, its name becomes a count noun. Hence, *milks* and *porridges* because they mean *glasses of milk* and *bowls of porridge*.

Another way of putting the idea is that when substances are named that usually coalesce when placed together, the name is a mass noun. When you pour two glasses of milk into a jug, they do not visually remain two but become one larger body of milk. When you put two potatoes in a bag, they do not become one large one. Presumably the basis for this is that milk does not have a shape that is independent of the container and potatoes do. When objects are described in such a manner that their characteristic shape, or refusal to coalesce, is either irrelevant or misleading, their names become count nouns. Hence, when used of fuel, one can easily see *shelf* and *book* functioning as mass nouns. They all merge in the flames. Gleason's counter examples can easily be seen to fit the rule. Gravel consists of pebbles; but gravel has no characteristic form, and two bodies of gravel coalesce. Pebbles have such a form and do not coalesce. However, one can easily imagine a truckdriver saying: "I delivered a gravel to McGill this morning and two gravels to the University of Montreal," meaning loads of gravel. Rather similar notions, applying more generally to several grammatical categories, are developed in Talmy (1978). On the other hand, one could imagine a man who ground rocks for some chemical enterprise saying: "Slate does not yield as good a product as pebble."

"Nothing is perfect," says the philosopher in the *Crock of Gold*, "the porridge has lumps in it." So it is with the thesis I am propounding. The thesis seems to fit most uses. Yet certain words that are normally mass nouns can be turned to count nouns, though no characteristic form is intended. If a scientist speaks of *wheats*, he most probably means varieties of wheat. But that is not a very large lump. It merely means that an appropriate rider should be attached to the general rule to the effect that the plural of a mass noun signifies variety when no characteristic form or container is intended. There are other words that look like mass nouns but are called abstract nouns by teachers: *justice, honor, love, truth*, etc. I see no reason to refuse them the status of mass nouns; the abstract objects of which they may be used have no characteristic shape. However, *justice*(s) also means officers of the law, *love*(s) can mean persons loved, and *truth*(s) can refer to statements that are true: all of these have characteristic forms.[1]

From this it seems that the mass-count distinction is basically a semantic one, and rather similar to the dimensionality distinctions of which Denny (1976, 1979) speaks. Denny's dimensionality classifiers, if he is right, make subdivisions of characteristic shapes; the count-mass distinction indicates whether there is a characteristic shape (or form if it is sound). Grammatical distinctions that map onto semantic ones are relatively easy for a child to learn— probably. The two systems support each other.

There is a study of Roger Brown's (1957) that shows that young children spot the covariation of semantics and linguistics related to count and mass nouns. He tested 16 children in preschool between the ages four and six. He showed each child several sets of pictures. In one set the first picture showed a pair of hands kneading (action) a formless substance like spaghetti (mass) in a colored vessel (count). Each of the other three pictures in that set showed one of the three features, hands kneading, spaghetti-like substance, or the container; it did not show the other two features. Brown selected some nonsense words with which to describe the pictures. He then said to a child, for example: "Do you know what it is to sib? In this picture (no. 1) you see sibbing. Now show me another picture of sibbing." If the test was for a count noun, he said; "Do you know what a sib is" and went on appropriately. For a mass noun he began: "Have you ever seen any sib?" and went on appropriately. Of course a child was not tested twice with the same nonsense word.

The contrast between noun and verb was quite evident. Of the 15 responses for verbs, 10 revealed that the child had fastened on the action; of the 29 responses for noun, 28 indicated that the child had picked an object rather than an action. The contrast between count and mass nouns was just as marked. With a count-noun probe 11 of the 14 responses selected the appropriate picture; with a mass-noun probe 12 of the 15 responses did. There were a few "no responses." The differences in response frequencies were statistically significant.

These results showed that the children were sensitive to the semantic differences between verbs, count nouns, and mass nouns. They were relatively senior children, the youngest being four. I suspect that at a much earlier age they had noticed the differences and used them to learn the appropriate syntactic signaling. We can glean a little more information from Katherine Nelson's (1973b) study. She studied the first 50 words used by 18 children, and in her Table 2.9 she lists all the different "nominals" they used. She describes them as "nominals" because they are words that later will function primarily as nouns. I attempted to divide them into count and mass nouns, or rather into words that refer to substances that have a characteristic form and ones that do not. By those criteria I found 94 count nouns, 16 mass nouns, and 4 ambiguous. The ambiguity arises with words like *cake*, which is a count noun when it refers to an entire piece of confectionary and a mass noun when it refers to a serving. However, there is no need to be scrupulous. The great majority of Nelson's nominals will end up functioning primarily as count nouns. Yet there are some very common words in baby talk, like *water, butter,* and *meat,* that will end up functioning primarily as mass nouns. So the child is familiar with objects and words for them that will lead him to the count/mass distinction from his earliest beginnings in language. I believe that his knowledge of the objects referred to will help to guide him to the associated linguistic rules. And Brown (1957) has shown how the syntactic and semantic systems can go hand in hand.

Summary

My general strategy in this and in the preceding chapter has been to look for semantic correlates of grammatical categories in the belief that these could be the child's key to grammatical categories. He needs a nonlinguistic key because the mature grammatical categories can be given circular definitions only—nouns are those words that perform noun functions in phrase structure and take the noun bound morphemes. In order to break into the linguistic circle, the child needs rules that are nonlinguistic, and I adduced evidence in favor of particular semantic rules stated in terms of such semantic categories as "object," "action," and "attribute."

We analyzed the speech of two children and came to the conclusion that they employed semantic categories of words, not grammatical ones, at least until about the age of 2½ years. Evidence for this was inflexibility in the use of words across the boundaries of the semantic categories they formed, but not within them. Furthermore, combinations of words were confined to certain of the same semantic categories, and the addition of inflections was to certain of the same categories. Our study of one mother's speech to her daughter strongly suggested that the constraints the child observed were not modeled by her mother but came from the child herself.

An adequate account of learning describes those abilities of the learner that are relevant to learning, describes that which is learned, and describes the learning itself in which the learner's abilities are put to work to master that which is learned. We have described grammatical categories as learnable on the basis of innate semantic abilities. The most important of these abilities cluster around the semantic notion "object" (as that to which a sortal may be applied), the relation "true of," and that attribute of symbols that will be described in Chapter 12, meaning. The mature grammatical category noun and its subdivisions, which principally concerned us, is a linguistic category of words, not a semantic one; it is distinguished from others by the particular phrase structure and morphological rules of the language. The learning begins on the semantic basis. This yields a division of bound morphemes and of sentence structures. Subsequently, for linguistic purposes, the child abandons the semantic description of the divisions while holding onto the divisions. He does so, for example, because he finds adults do not confine the possessive to names for persons, or even names for objects; he finds expressions like *the week's beginning*. The generalization can then be made only in linguistic terms. He abandons the characterization of one of his sentence types—proper name / action word / object word— because he finds sentences like *This key opens the door.* Again a new, linguistic classification is pressed upon him.

We looked at three subdivisions of nouns and argued that a semantic classification will serve the child well in learning two of them, certain classifiers and the mass-count distinction. Semantics will not serve him so well to learn gender subdivisions, though even here it seems that the role of object in individuating attributes and actions will give the child the direction of control in his language. He will expect the gender of adjectives to be controlled by the noun's gender and not the other way about.

9.
A and *The*

The *owl and* the *pussy-cat went to sea*
In a *beautiful pea-green boat.*
They took some *money and* plenty of *honey*
Wrapped up in a *five-pound note.*
— *Edward Lear*

Edward Lear avoids the business of introducing his main charac-
ters by assuming that they are well known to his listeners. He does
it by beginning with the words: "*The* owl and *the* pussy-cat." He
does not assume that of the boat, "*a* beautiful pea-green" one, or
of the wrapping, "*a* five-pound note." He uses a convention of English to set his scene: one introduces a new character or object
with the article *a*; once introduced it becomes *the*.

In this chapter we will study children's grasp of the contrasting
functions of *a* and *the* with singular nouns. Of course, English
determiners, as they are now called, are far more complicated than
these remarks might suggest. For example *the,* but not *a,* can be
used with plurals; *the dogs* is all right, but not *a dogs. The* can be
freely combined with both count and mass nouns, but not *a* with
mass nouns: *the cat* and *the milk* are right, but *a milk* is right only
if it means *a glass of milk.* Lear gives two other determiners—"*some*
money" and "*plenty of* honey." There are others, too, but we will
not be concerned with them here. We will find plenty to occupy
us with *a* and *the* in combination with singular count nouns. Even
then we must exclude the use of *the* with proper names, as *The
Hague, The Thames,* and *The Connecticut.*

As a first approximation, *the* has the force of suggesting that everyone in the conversation knows precisely what is being referred to, while *a* with a referring noun suggests patience to the listener. So if I were to say to my wife, "*A* friend of yours was asking for you," I am teasing her and making her ask who it was. But I could use a similar construction even if I did not know the referent: e.g., *A* car splashed me as I was coming home." I am, referring to a particular car, the one that splashed me. But I may not be able to identify it or say who owns it. Sometimes the referent may lack even the identity criterion I was able to give the car. If I ask for *an* apple, when there is a basket in the kitchen, I would be happy with any one of them. My request for *an apple* seems really to refer to the whole basket of apples, yet indicate that one, any one, is what I would like.

The use of *a* and *the* is complicated by the fact, used by Lear, that one must take account of the listener's intentions as well as his own. Only when an object has somehow been identified for both listener and speaker is *the* appropriate. I can begin a story with the words, "I met *a* man and *a* woman this morning" and continue with "and *the* man was rude to her." Now that he has been introduced, the particular man I met this morning may be called *the man*.

Roger Brown (1973, pp. 340 ff.), to whom I owe much of what I have to say in this chapter, lists eight circumstances in which a speaker with a particular referent in mind may assume that the listener will know what object he is referring to:

1. The object is unique for everyone, e.g., *the* sun, *the* moon.

2. The object is unique in the setting, e.g., There is a spot on *the* ceiling. *The* car is out of order.

3. The object is unique for a particular social group, e.g., *The* captain wants you.

4. The object has been made specific by pointing or some equivalent action.

5. The object has become specific by some event, e.g., Did you see *the* car crash into the railing?

6. The object is specific because it is entailed by something else that has been mentioned, e.g., I drove home with Harry and *the* safety belt wouldn't work (i.e., the safety belt for the seat in which I sat when I was in Harry's car on the occasion when Harry drove me home).

7. The object has been specified by a definition, e.g., *The* page that you are reading now.

8. The object has been specified previously, e.g., The money was wrapped
    up in *a* five-pound note. *The* note was stolen.

Brown notes only one exception to the general rule. If a speaker
is telling the class to which an object belongs he uses *a* even if
both speaker and listerner are looking at the object. For example,
if a parent and child are looking at a picture together and the child
asks "What's that?", an appropriate answer would be "a rabbit."
But now notice, as Geach (1972) argues many times over, *rabbit*
does not refer either to the creature being spoken about or to the
class of rabbits in general. So Brown's rules pertain only to terms
in referring position, and then his exception need not be appended.

   The syntax of the English sentence does not determine the
choice of *a* and *the* with singular count nouns in referring position.
Even rules 7 and 8 of Brown's list, which specify discourse constraints, are nonsyntactic in character. It seems that the factor
governing choice is semantic. In Chapter 11 we shall see what the
general semantic rule is. A sortal in referring position refers to a
class of objects; *a* and *the* before the sortal both specify that the
predicate is claimed true of only one member of the class. When
the speaker can assume that the listener is able to pick out the
particular member of the class, *the* is appropriate; otherwise *a*
is. *The* with a plural in referring position indicates that the predicate is claimed true of a particular subset of the class named—a
subset, that is, that can be identified without further aid by the
listener.

   This is not the whole story. If a gunman says, "I'll shoot the
first person that moves" (*person* is in referring position), *the*
is appropriate; yet neither the gunman nor his listeners can
pick out any one person as referred to. This is not covered by
Brown's rules either. It seems really to be a conditional: "if *a*
person moves, I will shoot *the* person that will thus be specified."
Another exception is illustrated by Hilaire Belloc's opening of
the cautionary verse on the bison: "The bison is vain . . .". He is
not on the face of things referring to a particular bison (though
at another level he may have been referring to an acquaintance
nicknamed *The Bison*), but to the whole species. However, these
are complications that do not arise in the data we are about
to discuss and, common though they be, we simply have to
ignore them.

Comprehension

The study of what sense children make of all this has advanced along two fronts. Michael Maratsos (1976) gave tests to see if children understood the force of *a* and *the,* thus focusing on comprehension. He also tested their ability to use *a* and *the* in various circumstances. Roger Brown (1973) studied the use of *a* and *the* in their spontaneous utterances. The two sets of studies complement each other, and in keeping with our general orientation I will begin with comprehension.

Maratsos' comprehension test consisted of three stories that he told to three- and four-years-olds who then had to act them out with toys. The idea is more easily illustrated than explained. The toys for one story were four dogs, four chairs, a wooden boy and a toy table. After some preliminary play, Maratsos said, "Now this boy came and sat down in one of the chairs, and just as he sat down, suddenly (a, the) chair fell over." As he spoke he seated the wooden boy in one of the chairs, and the child had to tip over a chair. If Maratsos had said, "the chair," the child should have tipped over the one the boy sat in; if he had said "a chair," he was expected to tip over another chair. After this, all was set to right again and Maratsos continued: "Now one of the dogs jumped onto the table. The boy looked at him, but he just barked, 'woof, woof.' And now (the, a) dog ran under the table." The child had to put a dog under the table, the one from on top of the table if had heard "the dog," any other one if he had heard "a dog."

For the second test four dogs, four cars, and the wooden boy were used. In the story the boy goes and talks to one of the dogs and Maratsos shows him doing it. The crucial sentence, which the child has to act out, is: "while they were talking, suddenly (a, the) dog drove away." The child had to act out this event, and interest focused on whether he chose the dog being spoken to or another one.

The toys for the third test were a lion, a tiger, and four rabbits. The crucial part of the story runs: "One of the bunnies went over to the tiger. He said hello to the tiger. Now (a, the) bunny went over to the lion." The child had to act out the event and of course the interesting thing was which of the bunnies he moved.

The children who took part were from the area around Cambridge, Massachussets, and they fall into two groups, which for convenience we can call the three-year-olds and the four-year olds. The three-year-olds ranged in age from 32 to 42 months, with a median age of 39 months (a little over three); the four-year-olds ranged from 48 to 59 months, with a median age of 55 months (just over four and a half). In each group there were 20 children—10 boys and 10 girls.

The results did not differ significantly with age or sex. Overall the children chose the correct referent for tests of the form *the X* 94 percent of the time. That is as near to a perfect performance as one is likely to get with young children.

It is more difficult to say what the correct response is to tests of the form *a X*. The child might interpret the expression as referring to any *X* other than the one to which Maratsos had already drawn attention. Or equally valid, though a little surprising, he might interpret it as referring to any of the class of objects mentioned, including the one to which attention had previously been drawn. Since the expression is ambiguous, we cannot be sure what to make of the children's responses. In fact, they chose a new object, not the one to which attention had previously been drawn, 76 percent of the time; 24 percent of the time they chose the old one. This result reveals a significant tendency for the child to change to a new object. For the rest we must in fairness to the children count all responses as correct. All the same we should bear in mind that we are giving them the benefit of the doubt—not ruling out the doubt.

Even on a less generous interpretation the evidence is that most of the children, even the younger ones, grasped the force of the contrast between *a X* and *the X*. In all the tests the rule being examined was the one that we listed above as No. 8: *the* is used when the object has previously been specified. Since none of the other conditions for *the* was satisfied in the stories, *a X* was appropriate when the object had not previously been mentioned.

Maratsos' tests of production

The high level of performance that we have just seen is not really surprising, because we noted in Chapter 2 that children aged only 1½ years showed a tendency to respond to the presence or absence of an article. Maratsos found that children aged three can respond to the difference between *a* and *the*. In several other tests he probed their ability to say *a* or *the* as the context demanded. Since these were all tests of production, I will describe them more briefly. The children he tested were those whom I have already spoken about.

With a set of 12 stories Maratsos studied the children's grasp of several of the rules that choose between *a* and *the*. One purpose was to see if they could supply the article when several objects had been mentioned in a general way and then one was singled out. For example, one story told of a lady who had lots of boys and girls. The lady asked them to be quiet and went to bed. One of them started laughing and giggling. Who was it? The child was expected to answer *a boy* or *a girl*. Another purpose was to see if Maratsos' subjects could supply the article *the* when only one object of each kind had been mentioned. The same story, slightly modified, served. The lady had a boy and a girl. One of them was noisy. Who? The expected answer was *the boy* or *the girl*. Altogether there were five stories aimed at these two rules.

Analysis of the results showed a certain group of the four-year olds answering both questions correctly all the time. Other four-year-olds and the three-year-olds showed confusion. In particular the three-year-olds tended to choose at random, or what could be interpreted as at random, between *a* and *the* in contexts that demanded *the*. In contexts that demanded *a* they responded correctly 83 percent of the time.

This is not a correct estimate of their knowledge, however. Very wisely, Maratsos gave the three-year-olds another and more subtle test. He asked them to repreat the stories after him and at the key point he omitted the article (*a* or *the*), hoping that the child would supply it. The ruse proved successful. In 26 cases a child did supply an article, and every child did so on at least one occasion. They supplied an article 13 times in contexts that demand an *a*, and that is what the child gave on 11 of those occasions. They supplied the correct article 84 percent of the time, and that matches closely the 83 percent of correct responses to the corresponding sections of the earlier testing. However, when the context demanded *the,* that is what the children supplied 13 times out of 13. A perfect performance.

It is difficult at this point to avoid moralizing about the need for circumspection in interpreting negative test results. Roger Brown is reported as saying that there is only one universal of child psychology: children can do better than they do on tests. Hence the wisdom of several tests to make sure one is seeing them at their best. It is only at their best that we see what they are really capable of. Any performance less than their best can reasonably be attributed to such nuisances as boredom, inattention, tiredness or the artificiality of the test. Everyone can do badly, but only the skilled can do well in performance that demands skill.

Maratsos' final test consisted of two games, one called *Down the hill*, the other *Feed the dragon*. For expository purposes I will use the second. Each child wore a puppet dragon on one hand, and the game was to feed animals to the dragon who made as though to eat them. The child chose the animals one by one. There were two conditions. In one Maratsos kept the animals out of sight and told the child about them. In the other, the child could see the ones being spoken about. Sometimes Maratsos asked the child to choose between, say, a frog and a mouse. Then the child should have said *the* frog or *the* mouse. Other times he indicated several of each sort and the child should have said *a* frog or *a* mouse. The idea of sometimes hiding and sometimes not relates to the main purpose of the experiment. In choosing one of two objects, the child had to single out one in his own mind and tell the tester which. When there was only one of each kind no effect of seeing the toys was anticipated. In choosing from several of a kind, the child might well single out one in his own mind, but short of pointing, which was disallowed, or using an elaborate phrase such as *the second from the left*, he could not indicate to the tester which one he had in mind. The children were not tempted to employ elaborate descriptive phrases. Even if they had a particular object in mind, then, since the tester could not know which, the appropriate response was of the form *a X*. Maratsos wondered whether the temptation to say *the X* would not be greater when the child could see the objects. Then he could single one out in his mind by looking at it. It would have been far more difficult to do that when the objects were hidden.

The results proved Maratsos' suspicions right. For the most part children's responses in contexts that demanded *the* did not vary with whether or not they could see the objects. However, when the context demanded *a*,—that is, where there were several objects of a kind to choose from—visibility proved treacherous. The results computed from Maratsos' data, are summarized in Table 9.1.

Table 9.1   Percentage of Correct Choices of *a* by Age and Condition.

	Objects visible	*Objects Invisible*
Four year olds	54	66
Three year olds	89	93

Note—After Maratsos (1976).

Oddly enough, the performance of the four-year-olds is poorer than that of the three-year-olds, and that in itself causes some misgivings. However, the main result is clear. Frequently when the children could see the objects, their responses did not take account of the fact that the tester could not have known which object they intended. When the objects were hidden from sight, most of their responses were appropriate. In the psychological theory of Jean Piaget, failure to take account of another person's knowledge or experience is termed *egocentric.* Certainly the children can be interpreted as responding in an egocentric manner.

At this point Maratsos took another wise precaution. He tested groups of adults with tests very similar to those just described and found that as many of the adults were egocentric in their responses. Since adult performance in such simple liguistic matters must be taken as close to perfect, this raises a problem. The children's performance, matching that of the adults, must also be taken as correct. We will leave the matter for the moment and turn to another set of findings.

Children's spontaneous utterances

In his book *A First Language,* Roger Brown devotes a good deal of attention to the use of *a* and *the* by children in their spontaneous utterances. In general he found that they had mastered correct usage shortly after their third birthday (age three). Moreover, he found examples of correct usage in conformity with all the eight rules listed above. There was abundant evidence that when an object was specified for the child speaker and for the listener, no matter how it came to be so, the child used *the.* When the object was not specified either for the child speaker or for the listener, they had learned by the age of 3½ to use *a* appropriately. Many of the examples cited by Brown could have been learned as phrases by the children, e.g. *the floor, the sky.* However, other instances show a child changing article appropriately: "This was *a* big rabbit. And scared *the* rabbit." Brown draws particular attention to instances where a child employed the definite article appropriately because the object had been specified by entailment (rule 6). One child in speaking of a boat went on to refer to "*the* motor." Another referred to "*the* sticky of the bandage." The last example is especially interesting in that it is unlikely that the child had ever heard the phrase *the sticky,* used by an adult, and so must herself have been following the rule that gives correct usage. It is instructive to observe the child's easy mastery of the subtle rule of implication as specified in rule 6. The data suggest a greater power of logic than most child psychologists are willing to allow the three-year-old.

Separately, Brown (1973, p. 354) lists all the errors that the three children made in choice of article. The list contains 27 errors, a very small number. Children seem for the most part either to omit articles altogether or to use them correctly. Furthermore, there were no erroneous uses of *the* when an object was not specified for speaker and listener. The errors were equally divided: the inappropriate use of *a* when the object was specified for both speaker and listener (14 cases); and the inappropriate use of *the* when an object was specified for the child but not for the listener (13 cases).

Brown suggests that errors of the second category can be taken as fairly reliable evidence of egocentric speech (in Jean Piaget's sense) on the part of these children. To buttress this interpretation he observes that in 8 of the 13 cases the mother did not know to which specific object the child was referring and asked the child about it. Before saying any more about this, let us recall that Michael Maratsos found that, so far as the inappropriate use of *the* goes, the adults he tested were almost as egocentric as children. There can be no objection to calling adults egocentric; but we must hesitate to call children egocentric on the evidence before us if by that term we mean a childish weakness or incompetence that they gradually overcome. The matter is further complicated because we do not know whether the errors that Brown reports are due to ignorance of the rule, to the mistaken impression that the listener knew which object was being referred to, or to carelessness and inattention. If the children did not know the rule, there can be no charge of egocentricity. And Brown himself notes that there were not many examples of correct usage of *a* when an object was specified for the speaker but not for the listener. This argues for the view that they were ignorant of the rule, and consequently Brown may be inconsistent (or egocentric, in not considering matters from the children's point of view) in accusing them of egocentricity. The fact that the mother frequently had to ask which object her child was referring to is compatible with any of the three interpretations: ignorance, a mistake, or inattention. Moreover, even a mistaken impression that the listener knows to which specific object one is referring is hardly to be called egocentric unless the mistake is due to carelessness or inattention. It follows that Brown cannot make the charge of egocentricity stick.

The truth of the matter is that neither in Maratsos' work nor in Brown's is there any persuasive evidence of egocentric thought à la Piaget. On the other hand, in both there is abundant evidence

that by the age of 3½ years most children have mastered the
articles both in comprehension and production. Brown (1973, p.
351) notes that there was no indication that the children learned
one article before the other. This he takes as suggesting that the
two, at least as used with singular nouns, are learned as a systematically related pair. Indeed, I have the impression in reviewing this
work that children's comprehension of the contrast between *a*
and *the* has only begun to be explored. Maratsos (1976, p. 96)
says that careful investigation will probably reveal surprising
semantic skill and acuity on the part of children much younger
than those he tested. That is most reasonable, because even the
performance of the 3-year-olds showed near-perfect adherence to
certain rules for definite and indefinite articles, and there was
no very convincing evidence that they did not know any of the
rules. It follows that learning must have begun and been carried
far before the age of three.

Learning

But that raises the questions, which neither Brown nor Maratsos
tackles very vigorously, of how such learning occurs. To stake out
what and how much has been learned, and even the order in which
details are mastered, is a first step, but no more. The time has come
for a little boldness.

What the child has to learn linguistically about the articles in
combination with singular nouns in English is relatively simple.
There are two articles. They precede the noun and are nearly
always the first element in a noun's phrase; so *the man* and *a big
man* (though we also have *so big a man*). They are not used with
proper names. *The* can be used with both count and mass nouns, *a*
only with count nouns. Admittedly the categories noun and noun
phrase are not empirically given. Neither are they manifest in any
simple manner in the empirical array. This matter we dealt with
insofar as we were able in Chapters 7 and 8. Besides, the child
needs to learn the categories noun and noun phrase in order to
determine the structure of a sentence in English. Since here we
are studying special cases of the category, noun phrase, I shall say
no more about the general problem. Before passing on, however,
note that among the errors listed by Brown there is no instance of
an erroneous combination of article and proper name. There is
just one that at first seems like an erroneous combination of an
article and mass noun: *"the sticky* of the bandage" (1973, p. 325).
But even this would not be an error if the child meant "the sticky

portion of the bandage." So there is ample evidence that Brown's subjects obey the relevant rules.

The semantic side of the correspondence (language and meaning) seems more complicated. Apart from the restrictions of which I just spoke, the child's task is to match each article with the appropriate set of semantic descriptors. If we can suppose that the child is able to grasp the semantic descriptors without benefit of language, and indeed that he does so with ease because his mind is so constructed, we would have grounds for believing that semantic factors would aid his linguistic learning.

Probably Brown's eight rules, which say when an object is specified, do not have to be learned. All the child needs is a marker to index when he has picked out a particular object. Brown's rules are merely cases in which a person is almost certain to so mark an object. What the child has to learn, then, in order to comprehend the force of *a* and *the*, is when the speaker has picked out an object and is referring to it in language. If he can somehow determine when that is the case and when it is not, he has automatically satisfied the conditions that relate to the mind of the listener. He must understand, though, that the conditions relating to the listener have to be stated obliquely: they relate to the understanding of the listener as assessed by the speaker. It is when the speaker attends to a particular object and can reasonably suppose that the listener without further help can be induced to attend to the same object that *the* is appropriate.

How might the child learn what the speaker is attending to? The problem has been a recurrent one for us. If we grant that he can successfully determine when the speaker is attending to an object as a whole, and not to some of its attributes (in a manner to be discussed in Chapter 11), we will have little difficulty granting that he can discover the force of *a* and *the*. Several teaching links for the special cases suggest themselves. If there is only one object in view of the kind mentioned, the child can assume that it only is being referred to. If there are several objects of the same kind and the speaker singles out one either by a gesture or by a descriptive term (*the big stick*), the child can assume that it is being referred to.

When there are several objects of a kind present and none has been singled out, the child can assume that none in particular is being spoken about. Subsequently the speaker may specify one. For example, he may say "Let's pick *a* flower." All this might well act as a clue to the child that before an object has been specified for both, *a* is appropriate, whereas when one has been specified, *the* is.

In other circumstances the adult may ask for an object, and if the child can assume that he would be satisfied with any of a number of objects, he can also assume that the adult did not designate a particular one. This is helpful in many circumstances: the adult asked for *a spoon, a slice of bread, a card, a block,* and so forth. Noting when a particular object has been specified and when it has not, he also has to notice which article is employed. Presumably all this must occur at the outset in the presence of the objects spoken about; later the rules so learned can be extended to objects that are not present to the speakers.

We have been speaking as if *the* goes only with singulars, whereas we noted earlier that *the* can go with a plural: *the spoons, the cards,* etc. In none of the research has this complication been looked at. However, to get the articles right the child must not tie both unyieldingly to a single individual, since he sometimes needs *the* in connection with particular subsets of a category named. I will continue to focus on single individuals, partly because the singular-plural distinction has the next chapter to itself.

Summary

There really is no way to avoid attributing to the child the forms of thought that we find in adults over a wide domain of operations. By the age of three or soon afterward he has mastered in his own speech the complex set of semantic rules that guide our use of the articles *a* and *the*. In addition we have examined several experiments on children's production and one or two on their comprehension. We found no very persuasive evidence that three-year-olds function at a level much inferior to adults. There were indications that if the testing could be focused on the articles in such a way as to draw out the children's competence, they would have been shown in an even better light. Moreover, when adults were subjected to the same tests, they sometimes, but not always, performed as poorly as the poorest performance of the three-year-olds. Perhaps the sanest conclusion at present is that more work needs to be done with both adults and children. When it is, if we may extrapolate from the findings to date, the surprise is likely to be how well the children perform.

We defended the three-year-olds against a charge of egocentricity and returned a verdict of "non-proven." We felt all the more confident in that the whole business of talking, if it is not a soliloquy, involves in an essential manner the monitoring of another's mental state. Clearly some are better at it than others, and clearly some have more art than others to communicate in a manner that is based on a just assessment of another's mental processes. Nevertheless, we all can monitor each other to some degree, and it seems misleading to label some as egocentric unless by that we mean not a lack of capacity but a momentary carelessness or inattention. This is one of the conclusions that prolonged attention to children's normal language forces upon us. We would be likely to miss it if we based ourselves completely on tests, however astute, of other cognitive capacities.

We emphasized the peculiar subtlety demanded of the child. He must assess when the speaker has specified an object in his own (the speaker's) mind and assess further that the speaker expects the child to identify that object. The child must correlate the results of these observations with the speaker's choice of article. Learning a language, then, demands an adroitness in spotting linguistic regularities, and ability to deal with objects and ideas, and a considerable sophistication in human psychology. The child must assess the speaker's intentions and the speaker's assessment of his own (the child's) intentions.

10.
The One and the Many
(Singular/Plural)

*We are not asserting the unity of soul in the sense of a
complete negation of multiplicity . . . we are thinking of soul as simultaneously one and many, participant
in the nature which becomes divided among bodies,
but at the same time a unity by virtue of belonging to
that order which 'suffers no division.'*
—*Plotinus,* The Enneads

English, like most European languages, has singular and plural
forms for its nouns, and those, together with their signification, an
English-speaking child must learn. Later we will come to the linguistic rules; I will begin by a brief exploration of the semantic
force of the singular and plural morphemes in the least controversial terms.

Quite early in his linguistic career a child will begin to talk
about a *dog* and *dogs,* about *shoe* and *shoes,* about *foot* and
feet. He may not always get all of them right. He may for a time
call all quadrupeds *dogs.* For the moment we can afford to neglect
such inaccuracies and appreciate that a singular form usually has
a special relation to one of a kind, and a plural to many of a kind.
A child will not use *dogs* of a shoe and a dog, even though he may
call four cows *dogs,* or a horse and two cows *dogs.* However he
manages it, he has made groupings in his environment that he
considers similar in some important respects and different from
other groups of objects.

What does it mean to say the child has grouped together objects
of a *kind?* It means among other things, that certain objects fall
under a concept or that the concept is true of them. It also means

that he has developed perceptual tests that enable him for most purposes, to tell members of the kind. But the key thing, the raison d'être for the perceptual tests, is the concept. To put this another way (to be discussed in Chapter 12), the objects of a natural kind share the same nature. But what philosophical sea-weed hangs thereby!

The key to practically the whole of Greek and medieval philos-ophy is an appreciation of the problem of the one and the many. What makes things similar and what makes them different? Sheep, notoriously similar, are said to share the nature of sheep, or sheep-ness. That is what makes them similar to one another. But how can there be two or more sheep? Obviously for an explanation we cannot appeal to what makes them similar. We need some prin-ciple to make them distinct from one another. Aristotles's answer, later developed by St. Thomas Aquinas, was that the principle of individuation was a special type of matter, called first matter.

Now it is highly unlikely that the child concerns himself with all this. But the reason he does not and need not is that his mind is at home in a world built on some plan that permits of the one and the many. His mind is undisturbed by the fact that there is a plurality of objects, and it sets to work to reduce them to intelli-gible groupings. To continue with our example, a sheep grows wool to keep it warm; its legs lead it to pasture and away from danger; its mouth enables it to eat the grass it needs, etc. The child probably gains the ensemble of insights one at a time in relation to many sheep, and the insights as a bunch apply to every sheep. It seems that with many classes he begins with the fact of the many and proceeds to construct the one, i.e., the shared nature. But sometimes it may be the other way about. He may have identified the nature of dogs in the family pet. Having begun with the one, he had to proceed to the many; i.e., the fact that the same nature is shared by many creatures.

English

One reason for going into this was to jolt us into an awareness of what semantical assumptions underly the simplest seeming linguistic regularities. The child learns common names, like *sheep, cat* and *apple,* for classes of objects. He is supposed to use a plural form only when he is talking about several objects that fall under a single concept—except for words like *scissors* and *trousers* that occur only in the plural form. This is not to say that the singular form can refer only to individuals. *Canadian* in the sentence "The Canadian is a friendly person" is used to make a claim about all Canadians. Nevertheless, singular words generally refer to individuals and plurals to several individuals.

We must not think that the English system of nouns is the only possible one. Japanese has no plural. Sanskrit and old Irish have, in addition to a singular and plural, a dual number. The dual is for cases where there are just two of a kind. Actually, Irish has separate sets of numerals for counting people and nonhuman objects. Fijian has a four-way division; singular, dual, paucal (a few) and multiple (many) (see Hockett, 1958, p. 234). Even in English the system is less straightforward than I indicated. There are nouns like *sheep* whose plural and singular forms are the same. It is optional whether to say *fish* or *fishes* as plural of *fish*. Then we can speak of a brace of *pheasant,* though most of us would speak about *pheasants.* Furthermore, we speak about a *three-foot rule* and a *sixteen-foot boat*; we do not in that context say *feet.* However, the main system of plurals in English is relatively straightforward, the main complication being certain irregular forms, *man–men, child–children, foot–feet,* etc.

But English, as we noted at the end of Chapter 8, does not allow plurals of words used as mass nouns. *Porridge, milk,* and *rice* are usually mass nouns, and I have argued that they can be used in the plural only when they have been given, at least conceptually, a characteristic form. Yet *rice* and *milk* are no less natural kinds than *dogs* and *cats,* and they are no less capable of being individuated. Yet *milk* and *dogs* differ in at least one relevant way. Take a spoonful of milk from a jug and it is milk just as much as that in the jug. Cut a puppy's tail off, and the tail is not still a dog. Gather several dogs together and they remain several; they do not coalesce into a single large dog. Gather several glass-fuls of milk and they do coalesce; they form a single jugful of milk. Hence the lack of a plural.

This gives us a clue to a cognitive conclusion that a child must reach in order to use the plural correctly. He must have noticed the difference just mentioned, between milk and dogs. Quine (1960, p. 93) suggests that at an early stage a child might take a plural, like *apples,* as a mass noun meaning a heap of apples, just as *rice,* a mass noun, means a heap of rice. In that way the child would take apples as a quantity of *apple* and not see it as denoting multiplicity. The apples need not even be in a heap to permit of such an interpretation. We use *milk* to speak of the two bottles in the fridge and the jug on the table. Quine is undoubtedly right, though it is very unlikely by the time the child begins to talk that he has not made the necessary observations. Put in the terms I have been using, the relevant observations are: (a) some objects have characteristic forms (recognizable through numerous transformations) (b) they retain those forms and can easily be discriminated when they are placed together. Now it is incredible that a fifteen-month-old should not have met those requirements in his play with wooden blocks, toy cars, people, and many other classes of object. The ability to recognize individuals demands even closer attention to characteristic form across transformations than the ability to recognize mulitplicity (see Strawson, 1959). We have seen in Chapter 2 that by 1½ years many children, when suitably guided, can in the space of a few minutes learn to treat a doll as an individual. In addition, Huttenlocher (1974) has collected evidence that children usually learn proper names for familiar individual objects, like *Freddie* the family pet, before they learn common names like *dog* or *animal.* Taking one thing with another, one can discount Quine's scruples when speaking of a child who is old enough to begin to talk.

The Child's Understanding

I have allowed myself this long introduction to the subject of plurals because beneath the grammatical regularities of English lurk surprising complications. An awareness of them sometimes helps us to assess the literature more critically. Take Jean Piaget's (1964, pp. 239-240) records of some conversations with his daughter when she was 2½. He interprets her as failing to cope with individuality and plurality. The following passage is well known, but I will translate it in full:

> But at about 2½ she also denoted by the term "the slug" the slugs that we used to see every morning on a certain path. She cries "there it is!" when she sees one; ten paces further on we see another and she says: "The slug again." I reply: "But isn't this another one?" She then retraces her steps to see the first one: "Well, then, is it the same?" "Yes" she replies. "A different slug?" "Yes" again she replies. "A different one or the same one?" But obviously the questions have no meaning for her.

Piaget concludes that for his daughter there is only one slug that reappears in different places. He takes the child's responses as an indication that she lacks a grasp of general classes as well as of true individuality, a position we discussed in Chapter 4.

The child's replies and Piaget's interpretation remind one of

Whorf's conclusion that the Hopi Indians consider each day a reinstantiation of the last on the grounds that their linguistic forms for counting days permit of such an interpretation. I mention this merely as a warning that one jumps from a child's language to his understanding at one's own risk. Little can be concluded from the child's use of the definite article, *the slug*. She might have been misusing it. Or, realizing that the slug was the only one visible to her father and herself, she might have used the definite article correctly. The same frame of mind might have led her to say, a little more unusually, "there it is" when she came upon a new one. But what of the reckless responses to the question whether it was the same or different?

Donaldson & Wales (1970) and Clark (1977) carried out tests of children's understanding of the words *same* and *different*. Their results support Piaget indirectly. They found that 3½-year olds seemed to confuse the two words and take *different* as synonymous with *same*. On the other hand, Glucksberg, Hay, & Danks (1976) have pointed out, as Plato did, that the words are ambiguous. They constructed new tests, designed to remove the ambiguity, which they gave to six children between the ages of two years and eight months and three years and three months. They asked the children to find another bead of the *same color* as one they held up to the child; sometimes they asked for one of a *different color*. In other words they specified in what respect the beads should be the same or different. They found that all the children, even the youngest, responded correctly to the new questions.

Interestingly, Glucksberg et al. gave the Donaldson & Wales tests to young adults and obtained results very similar to those Donaldson & Wales had obtained. One could hardly say that young adults confuse the words' meanings. So let us return to the slugs. Each new slug is the same as the previous one, but also different from it. It is the same in color and shape, different in numerical identity and location. Unless we assume that the child does not realize this–and that is what we want to find out– we should not be surprised to learn that a 2½-year-old refused to respond to the question whether the slug was the same or different. Piaget concluded that the question made no sense to his daughter, and that may have been quite true, though for reasons more profound than he supposed.

If we cast about in the child's experience for examples of individuals and pluralities, we do not have far to seek. His shoes go on one at a time, but there are two of them. There is the family car as well as all the other cars that go by on the road. There is his chair and other chairs. There are many cups, at any one time he drinks from only one. We could go on; it seems inescapable that by the age of 2½ every child will have had the problem of the one and the many borne in upon him and learned to handle it.

Developmental Studies of the Plural

Roger Brown (1973) is in agreement with the foregoing. He notes that from the earliest stages of speech, children obviously know individual objects, and they frequently have expressions to mark a new member of a single class. For that purpose they frequently use 'nother or more. The three children he studied also used the word two to mark plurality. They never used it of only one object, though they did not always confine it to two. They did all this before they mastered the plural morpheme in their own speech.

Brown (1973, p. 331) gave tests of comprehension to the three children to be studied intensely and was surprised to find that their production seemed to be ahead of their comprehension. He gave them instructions like Give me the pencil and Give me the pencils. To respond correctly a child had to attend to and interpret correctly the presence or absence of the plural morpheme. Brown was disappointed in their responses and wondered why. He reflected on the difficulty of getting the best from children in such controlled testing. He also wondered whether the difficulty was that children are used to hearing the plural marked twice: e.g. give me some pencils (or those, or two, or all the).

Another possible explanation is one to which Chapter 9 should have made us more sensitive. The critical words in the test were the pencil or the pencils. To say the pencil without prior introduction is to presuppose that there is only one. Since of necessity several pencils were visible, the instruction may have confused the children.

In production Brown's (1973, p. 271) three children mastered the plural morpheme quite early. His criterion of mastery is correct usage 90 percent of the time in six consecutive hours of recording. Adam reached that level at about the age of 2½ years, Sarah at just under 3 years, and Eve at 2 years. This was not rote learning because they used the same word correctly in the singular and in the plural. Brown's finding and conclusions have the support of a study carried out by de Villiers & de Villiers (1972) of the speech of 21 children.

The Form of the Plural Morpheme

Though our main interest is the growing development of meaning and word, it happens that we have a very authoritative study of the pluralization rule that children learn. It would be a pity not to summarize the results. Derwing & Baker (1977) administered tests of ten English morphological rules, but we will concentrate on the plural morpheme. They tested 112 children, all native speakers of English, ranging in age from 3 through 9 years, 8 boys and 8 girls at each yearly level. Derwing & Baker had constructed nonsense syllables that conformed to the rules of English phonology. In particular every ending of English nouns in the singular was represented. The use of nonsense syllables, though in itself a little upsetting for children, does not disturb the study of the form of the rule. Besides it ensures that we are not just examining the results of rote learning. After all, it is strictly possible that each English-speaking child learns by rote the related singular and plural forms of every noun.

The regularities can be stated simply. If a noun ends with a vowel or a voiced consonant, the plural is formed by adding $/-z/$; e.g. *bid*—*bids, bag*—*bags.* If a noun ends in an unvoiced consonant add $/-s/$; e.g. *shop*—*shops.* If a word ends in one of these, $/s, z, s, z, c, j /$, add $/-iz/$; e.g. *glass*—*glasses, box*—*boxes, watch* —*watches.*

The results prove conclusively that children do not just learn singular and plural forms by rote. They recognized the regularities of English in their choice of plural forms for nonsense syllables. Since they had never encountered those forms previously, their plurals could not be the result of rote learning. So the children had learned some form of rule, but which?

Could it be that the children formed the plurals on the basis of rhyming analogy? The idea is that children might have learned by rote some such pair as *bag-bags,* and when confronted with a nonsense word, *dag,* assimilated it to the familiar *bag,* and derived the plural as analogous. Nonsense words aside, children might have learned by rote one prototype for each ending and derived all other plurals by analogy. So, for example, having learned the pair *bag-bags,* they might form by reference to it the plural of all such words as *fag, gag, bag, lag, nag, rag, sag, tag, wag,* and *zag,* and such more complicated words as *stag* and *nametag.* The answer is no. About half of Derwing & Baker's list of nonsense words had no real-word rhymes at all, yet that did not appreciably affect performance. This indicates that it is not the final syllable, but only the final segment of the word that guides the choice of plural.

Berko (1958) who had conducted a similar study, though more limited in scope, thought that children learn the plurals for each final segment one at at time. For example, she claimed that children learn separately how to form the plurals of words ending in /-b/, /-d/ and /-g/, though all three are voiced consonants. Derwing & Baker's results make that unlikely. Children tended to learn the correct plural for all segments of the relevantly similar sort as a set. So, for example, they either gave the correct plural for all nonsense words ending in a voiced consonant, or they tended to get them all wrong. This suggests that it is not so much the final segment as a whole that guides the selection of a plural form as some of the segment's distinctive features, e.g. whether the segment is voiced or unvoiced, whether it is a consonant or not.

The data do not permit Derwing & Baker to decide between two other hypotheses. Most phonologists today would say that one of the three allomorphs, say /iz/, is the underlying form of the plural, and it surfaces as /s/, /z/, /iz/ depending on certain distinctive features in the final segment. Derwing & Baker prefer a rule based on "phonotatic" principles, i.e., rules that simply state the regularities of the language. For example, one such rule might be that when two consonants occur side by side, they are both voiced or both unvoiced. Ultimately such a rule might be based on physiological ones; in other words, in some absolute sense, it might be easier to pronounce two adjacent consonants if they were alike in being voiced or unvoiced. If this were the case it would not only explain the phonotactic rule but indicate that the child did not have to learn it; he just does not attempt to overcome the inertia of his articulatory system.

Actually, the derivational rules of generative phonology and phonotactic rules may be just notational variants, from the standpoint of physiology. If we take the generative phonologist's formulation as a characterization of abstract competence, we then need further specifications to say how those rules are realized in some device that will put them into operation. That is what the physiological rules would do for the human articulatory system. Abstract competence would then be restated in terms of ease of articulation for a human being. However, we must not expect physiology to explain too many of the regularities of English morphology. At root, morphology and physiology are distinct systems; physiology just describes the mechanisms that must put the morphology to work.

Summary

We began by noting that the plural in English usually signifies multiplicity of some particular kind. This we related to the common-sense belief that several objects can share the same nature, and that, we claimed, is the baby's instinctive way of handling the problem of the one and the many. We concluded, Piaget notwithstanding, that children by the time they come to talk have learned to discriminate among the individuals of many classes of object and event. The grounds for this are common observation and in addition the fact that children often learn proper names for certain individuals before they learn common names. To learn a proper name and apply it correctly, we argued, presupposes all the discriminations necessary for a correct use of the plural.

We reviewed two types of developmental studies. One was of children's use of singular and plural forms. Brown showed that before the age of three the three whom he studied used the plural correctly 90 percent of the time. The second study was of the rule by which children learn to form the plural of nouns. Derwing and Baker were able to rule out other hypotheses and conclude that the important conditioning of the rule was whether or not the final segment of the noun was voiced, and whether or not it was a fricative. But that is a highly abstract characterization of the rule, and they settled for a phonotactic interpretation of it, which may ultimately be grounded in ease of articulation.

PART III
MATTERS MAINLY PHILOSOPHICAL

11.
Reference, Names, and Objects

*"The world was so recent that many things lacked
names, and in order to indicate them it was necessary
to point."*
—*Gabriel Garcia Marquez,* One hundred years of solitude

Speech is not the only sound that an infant hears his parents emit. Some people whistle while they work, hum while they do the crossword, and grunt when they bring in the groceries. How does the child know when they are talking about things as distinct from making soothing sounds? Even a lot of speech is not *about* things; the man who in hanging a picture says, "let me see," is not talking about the picture, probably not even about himself. When he meets his child and says, "Well, hello there," he is not talking about the child; he is not referring to him. So the child has the problem of determining when an expression refers as distinct from something else, like salutes, or amuses, or soothes.

Of course we are confronted with the same problem when we ask ourselves if a child is using a certain word "with meaning." That is one way in which psychology differs radically from other sciences, like physics and biology. A physicist, for example, may hypothesize the existence of a subatomic particle and then track it down. He does not attribute to the particle the ability to discover and describe particles; that belongs to him. A psychologist who claims to know what a child learned when he learned a word is in a very different position. The psychologist who claims to

know what the word meant to the child really claims he has discovered what the child thought the word meant to his parents. Of
course the psychologist will attempt to be explicit about many
factors that guide the child implicitly. But if he is fully aware and
honest, the psychologist must realize that the same factors guide
his interpretation of the child. The grounds for expecting success
are simple: if the child uses a word in a manner that agrees in
general with the way adults use it, he is credited with adult command of that word. I believe there is much anthropomorphizing
here; how much is brought home to us when we come up against a
word-using chimpanzee and we have to ask ourselves if the chimpanzee means the same by it as we do. However, anthropomorphizing may not be so pernicious when dealing with children; after
all, a child is an anthropos.

In this chapter we will examine three general problems; (1) how
does the child know what it is to refer and when someone is referring; (2) how does he learn the reference of words; (3) how does
he know when reference is to an object as a whole and not just to
an attribute or quality? My answer to the first question will be
that various communicative intentions, including referring, are
given intuitively to the child. In some important way he does not
learn what reference is or what it is to refer. Instead, his grasp of
them guides his learning of names. This means that his main task
is to identify acts of referring as such; classify them under his intuitively given category. My hypothesis is that, at least when he is
beginning to learn the language, not all intentions occur to him in
all contexts. More to the point, in certain contexts the intention,
referring, occurs to him without rival contenders.

The answer to the second question is that reference is learned
through the correct interpretation of acts of referring.

The answer to question three will be similar to that given to
question one. I will claim that interpretations of what is referred
to occur to the child in a certain order. He first takes a word as a
name for an object as a whole. Other interpretations occur to him
only later.

1.1 Acts of referring

Imagine a child who came to the task of learning a language
with no more cognitive machinery than Mill's canons of covariation. Imagine that he has good eyes and ears, but that all he looks
for and notices is patterns of co-occurrence of vocal sounds with
objects. We have to skip over for the moment several problems:

what is an object? What is the same object? What is the same kind of object? What is the same name? Imagine all that as given and ask what the child can discover. He can discover that words like *Hi!* are addressed to many but not all people. In fact *Hi!* may be addressed to just those people that his parent goes on to speak to. To be true to our task, we should not say *addressed* or *speak to* because these refer to intentions, and we are pretending the child knows nothing about them. It would be better to use more neutral terms, like the child experiences *Hi!* only in connection with a class of people who in the company of his mother give rise to the experience of continuous speaking. Other sounds he hears only in connection with particular individuals: *Freddie* in connection with a certain dog; *Harry* in connection with a certain boy; and so forth. Yet other sounds are associated with certain classes of objects: *dog* with a certain type of animal and *cat* with another. Will such regularities give the child the notion of an act of referring?

To answer, we must continue with associations a little further. In order for the learner to pick out Freddie, the dog, and Harry, his little friend, there must be something distinctive about each. Let us suppose Freddie has a white spot over his eye that distinguishes him from all other dogs in the neighborhood. Only when the child meets Freddie does he see the white spot. If he has also regularly heard the dog called *Freddie,* he has two distinctive features that mark the experience of meeting Freddie. What would enable him to mark one a name and the other not? Perhaps he might be looking for sounds emitted by humans in association with objects. Very well, let us suppose that his parents whistle only to Freddie. How could the child know that one sound expresses an intention to refer and the other does not? Notice that each may occur in more elaborate sequences: parents whistle whole tunes and utter whole sentences.

The trouble is that the two are distinguished basically in the intention of the speaker. As physical signs they might be exchanged so that the whistle was the name and *Freddie* was an order that meant "come here." Furthermore, it is both obvious and well known (see Anscombe, 1957; Taylor 1964; Wright, 1971) that no behaviorist account of intentionality is adequate. There is all the difference in the world between meaning what you say and just saying it; and it would be hopeless if the child took speech as nothing more than noisy behavior.

We did not fit the child out with enough cognitive equipment. We gave him the skill to notice covariation but not to use it for anything else. Should we say that the child uses the occurrence of sounds in certain contexts as grounds for inferring that the utterer had an intention to refer? The model here would be that the child has, privately, the experience of intending to refer when he utters some sounds, and infers that his parent has a similar experience? That would be odd at the very beginning of language learning, because it would have the child himself referring before he had ever noticed that his parents did. That is not impossible, but the whole model must be ruled out on other grounds.

In *Philosophical Investigations* (part 1, paragraph 293), Wittgenstein makes fun of the whole idea. He is talking about how a child might learn the word *pain*, and the general model he is attacking is the inferential one. Pain is a purely private affair, the argument runs, but it is often accompanied by external signs, such as groans and grimaces. Each one learns which signs usually signal which pains, e.g. I groan and hold my jaw when I have a toothache. When I see someone else do the same, I infer that he has the same private experience as I had. In particular I can tell when a child has a toothache and thus teach him the word. Wittgenstein asks us to suppose that everyone has a little box into which he alone can look. Each person says his box contains a beetle, but the only way he has of learning what a beetle is is by looking in his own box. The point is that each box might contain something different, one a hair, another a pebble, and another a snail. It would follow that the word *beetle* would mean different things for each person. But that is absurd, for if we are to communicate successfully as we seem to, words must generally mean the same, or very nearly the same, to us all.

There is no guarantee that subjective experience is the same from person to person, so there is something wrong with the model of inferring on the basis of purely private experiences. This applies, with suitable changes, to the model of inferring, from private experiences of referring, that another person is referring. Wittgenstein, as I understand him, would conclude that the word *referring* means referring behavior and nothing else, where behavior means something observable. This is too much behaviorism for me. In keeping with the thesis to be proposed and supported in Chapter 12, I suggest that "referring" is our explanation for referring behavior; it is that which gives rise to the behavior. But that is not a private experience. "Referring" is an explanatory construct innately given. It occurs to a human being in certain circumstances, in part because of what he observes, and in part because of the structure of his mind. He is on the lookout for acts that fall under that concept. The problem to be solved then is: what are the rules that lead a child to place the construction "referring" on an event? We will come back to these, but it follows from Wittgenstein's observation that the child's knowledge of his own acts of referring is on exactly the same footing as his knowledge of anyone else's. In both cases, "referring" is an explanatory construct. Moreover, positing such a construct is a cognitive act performed on the basis of evidence. It is not a process that just happens to him, as does conditioning. We turn now from referring to reference.

THREE PRELIMINARIES [1]

Before we go any further into how children learn the reference of names, we must be more specific about what reference is. This means that we must settle three questions:

1. Are there different sorts of reference? It might appear at first sight that there are, seeing that the same expression may refer to either one or many objects. Compare

1. The dog is loose again.
2. The dogs are hungry.

(1) will usually refer to some dog known to speaker and listener, say Fido; (2) probably refers to a few dogs, say Rover and Towser. But that does not prove that there are two modes of reference, singular and plural. That can easily be represented by some such formula as R (X, Y) where R expresses the relation of reference and X is a variable that ranges over sets of names and Y ranges over sets of objects, which can be one or many. I doubt that anyone would want to claim that reference was many-moded on those grounds.

Consider the following example, where so easy an escape is not available:

3. Some dog bit my child.

At first sight it might seem that *some dog* referred to an indefinite dog. But there is no such creature; every dog is a definite, particular one. That might prompt one to distinguish two modes of reference: definite, as in (1), and indefinite as in (3). That at least would take the indefiniteness out of the dog, where it cannot be left, and place it in the reference, where it might find a home. Indeed that is what certain medieval logicians did by distinguishing *confused* and *definite* reference. However, Geach (1962, especially chapter 7) argues strongly, with the support of Aquinas and

Frege, for the view that the definiteness and indefiniteness attach not to the reference but to the predicate. The clue is that if we could list all the dogs in the neighborhood, we would, by (3), claim that one of the following is true: Fido bit my son; or Towser hit my son; or Rover bit my son; or . . . ; or . . . The act of referring is to the particular dog that bit him. The reference of *dog* is to the dogs on the list. Not knowing which he was, I said *some dog*. *Some* or *a* indicate how the predicate is to be interpreted. The effect is to say that one and only one of the statements that can be made by placing a dog's name before *bit my son* will be true.

If instead of (3) I had said, *The dog hit my son,* the predicate would still be true of only one dog. The force of *the* in such a context is to indicate that both speaker and listener know which dog it is. They might know him for any of a number of reasons, such as that he had been mentioned previously in the conversation or he belonged to the speaker. The general effect of *the* in the sentence is: "that dog that you can identify without more ado bit my son." Once again *dog* refers to all those objects that are dogs.

Does the word *dog* always refer to objects that are dogs? Geach (1972, sec. 1, chap. 5) gives a resounding no for answer. In *Fido is a dog*, it does not, because *dog* is in predicate position. The argument is subtle, but since it touches the heart of what a child must learn, I will outline it briefly, replacing some of Geach's points with, I believe, stronger ones.

a. The standard interpretation of a sentence like *Fido is a dog* is that *Fido* picks out an object and *is a dog* is claimed true of that object. For this to happen *Fido* must refer, but *dog* need not.

b. And *dog* in that context does not seem to refer. Reference is a relation between words and objects. Wherever there is genuine reference some form of the question "Which one?" is legitimate. If, following our analysis of *a dog* in referring position, the sentence meant "Fido is one of the objects referred to by *dog*," it would be quite in order to ask which one? But my intuition is that that question is odd: "Which dog is the dog that Fido is?" It indicates that *dog* in predicate position does not refer. *Dog* there just describes him.

c. Whenever an object has been specified for speaker and listener, the definite article, *the,* is used. Now *Fido* in our sentence specifies the dog and so if *dog* referred, the sentence ought to be, *Fido is the dog.* That sentence always means something like: "Fido is the dog that did so and so" or "that we were talking about"—something quite different in meaning from *Fido is a dog*

on its own. The impossibility of using *the* in place of *a* here argues
that *dog* does not refer at all.[2]

The psychological relevance of the distinction between the use
of a sortal (a word for a sort or kind) in referring and in predicate
positions will be raised in section three of this chapter.

It may be well to state succinctly the position we have reached
and indicate some residual questions. One way of referring to particular objects is by means of a proper name. Proper names are the
prototypes of referring terms. Common names in referring position refer to a class of objects. Besides referring, they describe.
The two semantic functions are involved in certain standard inferences. For example, from *All dogs are animals* and *Freddie is a
dog,* we infer, *Freddie is an animal.* Notice that by our account
dog in the first premise refers and describes; in the second it only
describes. If it only referred in the first and only described in the
second, there would be no explaining the validity of the inference.
Roughly the inference can be construed: all creatures of whom the
description "dog" is true are animals; Freddie is a creature of
whom the description "dog" is true; therefore Freddie is an animal. The third position we reached is that common names in
predicate position do not refer; they only describe.

Certain residual questions need to be mentioned. *Cinderella*
functions in every way like a proper name, but it refers to no
physically real person. Since we are taking reference as a relation
between word and object, we can ask (a) whether *Cinderella* is
a name at all, since it picks out no physical object; (b) whether we
should allow the existence of nonphysical objects, in particular of
fictional ones, and say that *Cinderella* refers to one such. The matter is clearly relevant to child language. It seems that we ought to
allow the reality of such objects, for it is implicated in much of
our thinking. For example, we can count the number of daughters
in Cinderella's family—Cinderella plus two ugly sisters makes
three. A count makes sense only if applied to individuated entities
that continue in existence at least from the beginning to the end
of the count. If the first object one counted ceased to exist before
one finished counting, one's total would be wrong. It follows that
Cinderella and her two sisters must be allowed individuality and
continuing identity. Note that Cinderella is not an object of any
sort in my head. When you talk of Cinderella, you do not refer to
anything, imaginary or otherwise, in my head; nor when I so talk
do I refer to anything in yours. All this urges on us that Cinderella
is a certain sort of object and that the name *Cinderella* refers.

This means that all proper names refer. From certain points of view that simplifies the child's task.

A second residual question is whether common names in referring position refer to past and future members of the class. For example, does *dog* in referring position embrace dead dogs and possible future dogs? While it is not in principle impossible that all dogs past and present be counted, it does seem in principle impossible to count all possible ones. Perhaps a Lamarkian angel could count all the dogs that have been, all that are, and all that will actually come to be. What he could not count is all that might have been, might now be, and might, but will not, come to be. The criterion of countability would give us all those that our Lamarkian angel could count. Though the matter is not without deep psychological interest for the development of language, we can afford to skim over it with little more than raising it as we have done. The young child probably must learn the reference sense of such words as *dog* in connection with physical objects that have been present to the senses. Possible dogs are almost certainly in a back seat. We can, I hope, afford to leave them there.

2. The second preliminary issue is whether reference can be defined—in such a manner as to help us to understand how children come to refer. The only definition of reference that I know was suggested by Tarski (1956, chap. 8). He claimed that the notion, at least for certain formal languages, could be defined in terms of a more basic motion, satisfaction.

> The concept just defined [satisfaction] is of the greatest importance for investigations into the semantics of language. With its help the meaning of a whole series of concepts in this field can easily be defined, e.g., the concept of denotation [reference], definability, and truth.   (p. 193-194)

We will have a look at what satisfaction is, how Tarski justifies his claim, the applicability of his method to natural languages, and its implications for a theory of name learning. Since proper names are the prototypes of referring terms, we will make them the focus of our inquiry.

The secret of Tarski's success lies in his manner of setting up the semantics for formal language. To begin, one chooses a domain of objects about which to speak. We shall choose persons. To each we must assign an ordinal number unique to itself. And to each we assign a proper name, also unique to itself. Then we set up a sentence schema, x_i *is N*, where the subscript on x can be supplied by one of the ordinal numbers for objects, and N by one of the names in quotes. This will give rise to numerous sentences of the form, *Object₁ is Tom,* and *Object₂ is Jane.* Some of the pairings of object and name will conform to the semantics. When they do, the pairing will satisfy the sentence schema. That is how *satisfaction* is to be interpreted. There can never be any confusion because the semantics rules out such double pairings as Object₁ with "Tom" and with "Jane"; it also rules out the pairing of Object₁ and Object₂ with "Tom."

All this enables Tarski to define reference with formal correctness. The idea, if not the formal correctness, can be suggested thus:

> Any name, "*N,*" refers to the object x_i, if and only if that name and that ordinal satisfy the schema "x_i *is N.*"

Notice that the word *refer* does not occur after the *if and only if;* this is formally required. The meaning of *satisfy* has been fully specified in the semantics. The result is that even if the word *refer* is eliminated from the formal language, its names will not fail to refer.[3]

How applicable is this to a language like English? The answer, as Tarski well knew, is that it does not apply well at all. One important problem is that Tarski depends on a unique pairing of words and objects. We must remind ourselves that such a pairing does not ensure that an English word is a name. Let us suppose that a farmer has a single chicken and that he calls it to feed by saying "Chuck! Chuck!" Let us suppose too that he calls no other animals in this way. We now have a unique pairing of chicken and "Chuck! Chuck!" Yet for all that "Chuck! Chuck!" is not a name. Of course this sort of thing will not happen in a Tarski formal language. But there is nothing to prevent it in English. The point to stress is that a child coming to English with the expectation that a unique pairing of object and word established the word as a name would be sometimes misled.

There are other problems too. Leave aside the complications that in English there are not enough names to go round; and many of us are, for example, called *John.* That may not trouble the child in the early stages of language learning. The child may find, however, that although he is mostly called *Harry,* he is sometimes called *Henry.* In other words there is not a one-to-one correspondence between names and objects, even in his own experience. To save him from pitfalls he must have the notion of identity, and be able to apply it in relation to names. He must appreciate that *Harry* = *Henry* in the sense that the person picked out by *Harry* is identical to the person picked out by *Henry*. The one-to-one correspondence fails at the other end, too. *Cinderella*, for example, does not refer to a real person. It follows that the child must not take the physically real as the domain of names. Or if he does, he must appreciate that words that in every other respect behave like names do not have any physical object assigned to them.

An even greater source of uneasiness is that in speech, from which the child must learn, there is nothing equivalent to inverted commas, or to the italics that we have been using to distinguish talk about linguistic objects from talk about people. Shifts in what is intended are frequent and rapid in the child's world. If he should happen to meet someone called William, he is likely to be told *This is William*. If he does not pronounce the name correctly, he is very likely to be told, say *William*. In the first the word *William* refers to the person, in the second to the person's name. The absence in speech of special devices to distinguish talk about language suggests that Tarski's system cannot readily be applied to the child language learner. Of course Tarski was not thinking of the child. He defined the semantic notions of truth, reference, and satisfaction for such domains as mathematics, where the difficulties just mentioned need not arise.

Suppose, however, that Tarski's system could be somehow supplemented so that it could handle the foregoing problems for the language learner of a natural language; there would remain other considerations that make one wonder what one gained in doing so. Tarski's definition enables one to use the notion of reference without mentioning it. It could not be used, however, to convey the notion of reference to someone who had no idea what reference was. In fact the definition of reference twice uses the notion in its sentence schema, x_i *is* N. The x_i refers to an object through its subscript, and N is to be replaced by a name that also refers to the same object. This should make us quite uneasy about the applicability of the definition in developmental psychology. The reason is easily seen if we allow the imagination a little scope. Just for the moment indulge the fancy that Tarski was allowed to design a child's mind and that he planned to build into it his semantics and definitions. Tarski's child would never come to understand the definition of reference unless Tarski also supplied the notion of reference—so that the child could understand the definition of reference. But then Tarski would have had to supply the central notion that we are exploring. Tarski does not analyze the notion or provide a frame-work that illuminates how it might be learnt. Similar points, though with different objects in mind, have been made by Hartry Field (1972) and Hilary Putnam (1975b).

3. What about defining reference in terms of the psychological act of referring? The idea would be that reference would be that relation between words and objects that is established by acts of referring. Whether one chooses to do so depends on which one takes as basic, reference or referring. I know of no conclusive argument in favor of one rather than the other. There is a strong argument, from parsimony, for defining one in terms of the other. Arbitrarily, then, I choose to make the psychological act the more basic and use it to define reference.

Before leaving the act of referring, it is well to dwell on the im-plications of the decision to treat it as an undefined primitive. It means that we give up the search for elements out of which it might be constructed. Ideally a definition gives internal specifi-cations that constitute necessary and sufficient conditions for something to be in the defined class. For example H_2O specifies the ingredients and their proportions for something to be water. Failure to define referring satisfactorily means among other things failure to find its ingredients. Lacking knowledge of the ingredi-ents, if such there be, we cannot hope for any account of how the child forms the notion of referring. This is tantamount to taking the notion as unlearned, or innate.

It does not follow, however, that we abandon the search for necessary and sufficient conditions for when the act of referring occurs. These would be extrinsic conditions. For example, re-ferring might be the interpretation that a child automatically im-poses on a certain event because of characteristics of the event. For example, he may be so constituted as automatically to impose the category, referring, when his parents use a word when drawing attention to an object for which he has hitherto learned no name. The relevant characteristics of the event might not reveal what the event is, just that it is different from other events and that it is assigned to the category, referring.

How are we to understand how children come to refer if they do not learn the notion, referring. My suggestion is that they are endowed with an intentionality space akin to Quine's quality space (of which more presently) that favors the attribution of one intention rather than another granted certain events. Evidence for this hypothesis would be indications that children systematically misinterpret attribute words or positional ones before they know a name for an object as a whole. Once they know such a name, another word is unlikely to refer to the object. But we are anticipating our discussion of Professor Quine's position.

2.1 Reference and referring

Since we have taken referring as primitive, the question arises of how the child learns reference. We have set him up so that he correctly (almost always) judges that the speaker is referring; how does he then learn that certain words have reference to certain objects? To do so he must detect which words in an utterance are doing the work of referring and which objects are being referred to, then represent the words as having reference to those objects. In the next section we will consider how the child knows what is being referred to; here we will confine ourselves to the two other tasks.

The business of detecting the referring words is probably aided by the child's own limitation: he can say only one word at a time and frequently that is a name. Parents, too, often single out the name, saying something like: *This is Bill; Bill.* That is probably an important way of emphasizing a referring word, though it may also serve to emphasize a predicate: This is a *caterpillar; caterpillar.* Chapter 2 dealt with how the child can tell the difference between a common and a proper name, and we will not repeat its findings here. What about the distinction between a noun used as a (non-referring) predicate and the same noun used as a name? The first thing to note is that all the words we are discussing are what some logicians call sortals. Sortals place an object in some natural kind, like dog, or some artificial kind, like brush. We have laid aside true attribute words, like *red* and *hot.* Now all sortals move freely from predicate status to subject status, the main semantic effect of the change being the acquisition of reference. See sentences 6 and 7 in which *caterpillar* is so changed:

6. That is a *caterpillar.*
7. *Caterpillars* are hairy.

Furthermore, such interchangeability is, I believe, a linguistic universal.

I have studied my son Kieran's early use of sortals, which are included in Appendix 3. Admittedly, one's grasp of whether he used a sortal as a predicate or as a name is tenuous. Nonetheless, if we apply adult intuition to his most complete utterances to the end of his 20th month, we find many sortals in referring position, several in predicate position, and a few that switch roles. Here are some examples:

Referring Position	Predicate Position
See a *bus*	Here's a *boy*
See a *car*	You're a *girl*
See the *ball*	It's a *cover*
Look the *watch*	It's a *car*

Notice that *car* occurs in both lists. In addition Kieran clearly distinguished sortals from proper names. He used *a, the,* and numerals only with sortals, never with proper names. He never, mistakenly, used a proper name of many people as though it were a sortal; he never showed any hesitation about using a sortal of many objects.

From all this I conclude, tentatively, that by the age of 20 months Kieran had already formed a category of sortals (see fuller discussion in chapters 2, 7 and 8) and was already using them, sometimes interchangeably, as predicates and as names. This is really making just two claims. (1) When he first formed full sentences he already knew and used the basic form of a proposition: refer to something and say some description is true of it. (2) He knew, implicitly, that any sortal could be used to refer and also to give a description of an object.

I have already pressed the claim that the notion of referring is a primitive of cognitive psychology and unlearned. In chapter 12 I will argue that the notion, true of, is also a primitive and unlearned. Granted that, and the ability to detect which words are performing which functions, the child is in a position to learn that any sortal can be used to refer or to predicate. That is a generalization over adult usage.

But we must not allow our original question to slip away: how does the child know which words do the work of referring, as distinct, say, from predicating? Position in the sentence is not much help. In *John shoved Mary* both *John* and *Mary* refer. The distinction between common and proper names, which a very young child has, might well help. Proper nouns can never be used to predicate; their function is so focally to refer that even if they have an associate sense, that sense cannot be predicated by means of the proper name. If we grant that the child grasps the semantic force of proper names, he is then in a position to learn that a sortal often performs the function of a proper name. Sentences 8 and 9 are examples that might easily be paired in a child's experience:

8. Freddie is sick.
9. The dog is sick.

Another clue might be the set of attribute words which cannot without complication be made to refer and will seldom be made to do so in talking to children. In Chapters 7 and 8 we saw that Kieran's earliest speech gave evidence of a category of attribute words which he kept distinct from all other categories. If we allow that its members had the semantic force of describing objects, not referring to them, we can imagine the child learning that words that can occupy the same linguistic slot as attribute words do not refer either. So in 10 *a sick dog* fills the same linguistic slot as *sick* in 8 and 9, and might well perform the same semantic function.

10. Freddie is a sick dog.

This is meant to be no more than conjectural because I have not any convincing evidence to offer, I have simplified considerably and not drawn attention to such sentences as 11 and 12:

11. This is Harry.
12. That is gold.

Harry in 11 is used to name, and presumably the child, if he is to learn as suggested above, will have to distinguish its semantic function from that of *sick* in 8 and 9—despite the similarity of syntactic environment. *Gold*, too, in 12 would usually be taken as a name; the sentence means something like "that stuff is called gold," whereas neither *a sick dog* in 10 nor *sick* in 8 and 9 names anything. Presumably, the child has to learn the vehicles of naming, like 11 and 12, very early.

At any rate what I am basically arguing is scarcely controvertible: clear cases of names, such as proper names, guide the child to the set of names, which includes sortals in referring position; clear cases of descriptors that do not name, like attribute words, guide him to the set of descriptors, which includes sortals in predicate position.

Because certain words have been singled out as doing the work of referring, the child concludes that they are apt for that task. They retain that aptness over time and so can be used to perform the same function. That is, names acquire permanent reference from the fact that they have been used to refer in acts of referring.

And reference is defined as conventionally agreed aptness for performing particular acts of referring. The principle would serve the child well in nearly all his name learning, but its application, if wooden-minded, would lead to errors. The personal pronouns *I* and *you* have permanent reference only if we take account of the roles, speaker and listener. They have had a special chapter to themselves, Chapter 3. Demonstratives like *that* in example 12, above, refer to whatever object has become salient. Other apparent exceptions may not be real ones. Father may call the child's mother *Betty*, but both parents may object to the child's doing so. However, that does not mean that *Betty* loses its reference; just that the child may not avail himself of it.

At this juncture a disclaimer. In suggesting that reference can be defined in terms of referring, I do not claim to have greatly illuminated either term. Whatever opacity pertains to the one pertains to the other. The motivation for defining one in terms of the other is merely a (I hope laudable) parsimony in positing primitives.

3.1 Professor Quine

Noticing that someone is referring presupposes the notion of something referred to. How does the child know what is referred to? Occasionally the matter is settled because the child invents the word himself. Presumably he then knows what it means, and it is the adult's task to find out. Roles are reversed. I once knew a little girl aged six who invented a useful technical term for the sort of slimy scum which formed on her glasses and made vision difficult. She called it "broo." "There is an awful lot of *broo* on my glasses. They are all brooey." It was our task to find out what the word meant; presumably she knew.

Most names, however, children do not invent, but learn. Yet even some of these they use in a new sense, and the adult must try to follow rather than lead. Eve Clark (1973) has gone through a number of diaries which parents kept on children's speech and singled out the "overextensions." These, if Clark is right, are mostly what in adult language would be called metaphors. For example, one child called a doorknob by the word he had learned for an apple. We have already seen several such examples in the speech of Melissa Bowerman's (1978b) daughter, Eva. Yet we cannot always be sure that the child is not simply confused. The child who calls all quadrupeds *bow wow* may either be extending the term metaphorically or failing to distinguish between dogs and other quadrupeds, or using *bow wow* as synonymous with *animal*.

It is not our purpose here to follow him, but rather to point out that a child often uses words differently from adults, and the adults' task is to grasp the significance (if any) of the innovation.

Professor W. V. O. Quine (1960) poses the main question that interests us in a very general form. The chapter is entitled "Translation and Meaning" and there he asks, how do we decide what a name means? He supposes that a linguist finds himself in a land where the language is not cognate with any that he knows, and things proceed pretty much as follows, though I have taken the liberty of questioning even some of Quine's very modest assumptions.

The linguist somehow persuades a native to teach him, and lessons begin when a rabbit runs by and the native says "gavagai." A linguist in such circumstances would normally make some such entry in his notebook as, *gavagai = rabbit*. A skeptical linguist, and this is the point, might ask does the term mean "animal." He could perhaps find out by pointing to a cat, saying "gavagai" and watching the native's reaction. If the native laughs or gesticulates wildly, he can assume that *gavagai* should not be used of a cat. But why not? Perhaps the native wanted to give the word for cat as distinct from that for animal. If the native gives no sign of dissent when *gavagai* is said of a cat, he may be merely polite, or he may take it that the linguist is using the term metaphorically (as Eve Clark thinks children often do). It seems impossible to provide conclusive evidence to satisfy a scrupulous linguist that *gavagai* is not equivalent to *animal*. Nevertheless, suppose the linguist can somehow settle that matter and rule out "animal," a host of other conjectures will trouble him. Could it be that *gavagai* means "rabbit ears," or "paws," or "fur" or "skin?" If he has devised means for ruling out "animal," he may find some to rule out these; for example by producing rabbit's ears without the rabbit and saying "gavagai." Of course there will be trouble in interpreting the informant's reactions. If the informant takes the ears as signs for the rabbit, he may assent to the use of *gavagai* in their connection. However, suppose the linguist wonders whether the word means "rabbit shape" as distinct from "rabbit," how is he to proceed? If he draws the outline of a rabbit and says "gavagai," how on earth can he determine whether the native understands the term of the shape rather than the object as a whole? There seems to be no way of discriminating satisfactorily. But if the linguist wonders whether his informant has a normal human intelligence and wonders, too, whether he forms ideas of objects that endure through time and local motion, the linguist is likely to give up in despair. That last question suggests itself because of Piaget's claim that young babies do not represent objects as continuing to exist once they are no longer in sensory contact with them. Piaget's babies seem to resemble Bishop Berkeley in the stance that *esse est percipi* (To be is to be perceived). Surely if the informant was of the same kidney, misunderstandings would be bound to arise between him and the linguist, and they could not all be removed.

Quine's conclusion, and I concur, is that the linguist can never determine that *gavagai* means the same as *rabbit*. But, Quine goes on, leaving me for one behind, the hypothesis that they do is in worse case than hypotheses in science; and scientific hypotheses are notoriously underdetermined by the evidence (see Quine, 1969). Although science is gradually approaching a true representation of reality, attempts to determine meanings for the words of ordinary language, he believes, wander aimlessly.

The arguments Quine makes about translation apply equally to communication within a single language group. How do we know that other people mean the same by *rabbit* as we do? Quine's answer is that the only possible grounds are in the sensory stimulation occasioned by the rabbit. He refuses to speak about concepts or ideas, eschewing all such abstract entities. He opts for stimulus meaning; the set of stimulus events when we would be disposed to accept the term *rabbit* is the same as that when the informant agrees to accept *gavagai*. This, according to Quine, is all there is; it is useless to ask further whether the informant's concept of a gavagai is the same as the linguist's of a rabbit.

At this point I resolutely part company with Quine, basing myself on the conviction that the very least I generally know is when English speakers are referring to an object as a whole rather than to just one of its properties. As we shall see later in this chapter, the notion object is a construct, but that should not deter us. Quine (1969) himself speaks about scientific constructs, such as electrons, that are related only indirectly—and with the aid of much scientific theory—to sensory stimulation. A track in a cloud chamber may be the observable grounds for proposing the existence of electrons; but the track is not in any sense the meaning (stimulus or otherwise) of the word *electron*. Physics affords an elaborate description of electrons, referring to many properties such as mass, charge, and velocity, but nowhere does it claim that being a track in a cloud chamber is one of their properties. Indeed Quine (1975, pp. 312-313) speaks of such acts as the positing of electrons as "a *creative* decision." Were it not that Quine has so repeatedly declared himself an empiricist and behaviorist and rejected such constructs as meanings, I would assume that we were in the same camp. For all his protestations, I believe that he cannot be too far in spirit from my position.

The child, according to Quine, learns names for objects by being rewarded for uttering the appropriate word on some stimulus occasion and not being rewarded for its inappropriate utterance. So the child may say "Mamma" when his mother is present and be enthusiastically acclaimed. However, he may on that occasion have felt a breeze. If subsequently he says "Mamma" merely on feeling a breeze, he will not be rewarded; the presence of his mother is a necessary condition for being rewarded for using the word. Unrewarded behavior becomes "extinguished." To me it seems that Quine has misunderstood the behaviorist enterprise to which he clings. He refers several times to the "creativity" of the language learner (1969, p. 4; 1975, pp. 312-313). He likens the child, or jungle linguist, to the scientist who forms hypotheses, examines data, reaches conclusions. This is all very remote from a behaviorist account, in which all that is formed is habits; there is no place in behaviorism for creativity, hypotheses, or conclusions. Perhaps what Quine meant is that the child looks for signs of assent or dissent from his parents. Hintikka (1975) points out that the notions of assent and dissent—even called by those names—are basic in Quine's theory. Quine's position loses nothing if it drops all talk of rewards and confines itself to signs of assent and dissent. These are much more in keeping with hypotheses formation, confirmation and rejection.

At any rate my theory is that situations suggest to a child particular interpretations of what a name refers to. He tests out the names on well-disposed adults who, by some signs, say *yes* or *no*. But this returns us to our initial question; how does the child know that the adult's assent relates to the name's being applied to an object as a whole and not some of its qualities, and for that matter how do adults know what the child meant by the word and that they are giving assent to the right thing?

Quine's answer to a closely related question seems right, though it does not go far enough. He believes that child and adult reach agreement because they are biased by nature to do so. He proposes that the child is endowed with "a prelinguistic quality space" (1960, p. 83) which is "innate" (1969, p. 123). This the child shares with adults, and it guides his hypothesis-forming about stimulus equivalence in the domain of qualities.

It is odd, but Quine does not seem to have proposed an innate structure that relates to the characterization of certain stimulus events as individual objects. Yet the linguist who saw a rabbit and heard "gavagai" would be most inclined to conclude that the word referred to an object and not just a quality. Quine speaks of objects. He called his book *Word and Object.* In his epistemology "middle-sized, middle-distanced objects" (1960, p. 10) are the basic stuff of experience. Elsewhere (1969, p. 10) he allows that "Mamma" refers to a "cohesive spatiotemporal convexity" and "an integrated spatiotemporal thing." Now the object, Mamma, is not just an amalgam of qualities somehow held together; she is not just a tissue of pink, and grey, and soft, and slow moving, and noise emitting. She is an object which is all those other things (see Kripke, 1972, p. 272).

3.2 NOTION OF OBJECT

The notion of object is closely associated with the sort of names we are discussing. *Mother* names an object; *person* and *woman,* when in referring position, name sets of objects. Words like *pink* and *soft* do not name objects. Their normal function is to describe the attributes of some object that has been referred to by a proper name or sortal. This indicates a sharp semantic distinction between sortals and attribute words, a distinction incidentally that Gupta (1980) makes basic in modal logic. The distinction is also basic in the business of name learning, and we will pursue it for a time here.

The notion "object" is not, I suspect, the top element in a conceptual hierarchy related to "animal" and "plant," for example, as "plant" is related to "wisteria." Gupta (1980) argues that the word *object* is best viewed as a "prosortal." His reason is that the principle of identity functions best in association with such sortals as *man* and *animal,* not with *object.* We are reasonably sure that a live cat and its subsequently dead body are neither the same cat nor the same animal. We are puzzled when asked whether they are the same object. It seems that *object* affords no criterion of identity distinct from that which is afforded by *cat* and *animal;* and since the principle of identity is essential to a true sortal, *object* is not a true sortal. I will use *object* in the sense of prosortal; the concept "object" is that which is common to all sortals. But I also use *object* to denote that external thing that may be referred to by a name, or of which a sortal may (or may not) be true.

Our common sense and common speech distinguish between object and attribute. We do not treat an object as a mere set of attributes. The very terms are complementary: an attribute is attributed to something; an object is not so attributed to anything, and to it attributes are attributed. It's not that attributes are unreal or that we cannot talk about them. The central point is that reference is primarily to objects; it is to attributes only as grounded in an object. The distinction is so central to our theme that we ought, briefly, to explore further its role in commonsense judgements.

We individuate our environment, basically, in terms of objects, not attributes. We do not say *I encountered two softs,* or *I encountered three warms.* We do talk about two soft objects and three warm ones. When we seem to disobey this principle, we are really doing something quite different. *Two different reds* means two different shades of red; *two different heights* means something like two different points on the vertical scale. To recognize the distinction at issue, philosophers speak of a *principle of application* as well as a *principle of identity.* Color and weight have a principle of application; they have no principle of identity of their own. What identity they enjoy derives from the objects to which they belong. *Person* and *dog* have associated principles of identity and application. When we ask, *is that the same person?* we primarily wish the principle of identity to be exercised; that the principle of application (that he is a person) holds good is presupposed. When we ask *Is that the same red?* we wish only the principle of application to be exercised.

The principle of identity is especially relevant to proper names. *John Macnamara* used on the same occasion of someone in Dublin and someone in Montreal is used correctly only if it is the same someone. It is used correctly of someone on two different occasions but again only if he is the same someone. To identify over time and local motion is the traditional function of "object" in psychology, but there is more to it than that.

Aristotle (*Metaphysics,* 7.12) was fond of pointing out the distinction between compatible and incompatible predications. We can say of a single horse that he is black and white at the same time; not that he is a horse and a cow. *Horse* applies to an object in its entirety; *black* and *white* can apply to different parts. Objects can, of course, be composite: a horse can have four legs. But *horse* applies to the composite as a whole and *leg* to the member as a whole.

We can say of the same cat that he is sick at one time and healthy at another; we cannot say he is a cat at one time and a pumpkin at another (fairy tales apart). If he dies and disintegrates, the composite object we called *cat* has ceased to exist (presumably).

Object, too, plays an important part in our representations of causality. If I awkwardly bump into you in the corridor, it is not my weight that must apologize, but me. You attribute the carelessness to me, not to my mass and momentum. Actions are individuated partly in terms of objects. If in a movie the hero dives into a river, is what you see one dive or two? That depends first and foremost on whether the man you saw leaping from the cliff was the same one as you saw entering the water. Now obviously the hero can do two dives, but only one person can do one dive. It is irrelevant that eleven men can win a soccer match; that merely shows that we do not regard the gaining of such a victory as a single act. Only one player can perform the action of kicking the ball once.

The mature use of sortals involves the general characteristics of sortals that we have been discussing. Where is the child to discover those general characteristics? They are not given in sensory stimulation from the environment; rather, they are imposed on the interpretation of such sensation. Kant claimed that the general notion of an object was a synthetic a priori of mind, in the sense that the mind was so formed as to apply it automatically, granted certain sorts of sensory input. This may well be correct, if only for the humble reason that no one has any better explanation. However, we need not necessarily accept the related claim of Kant (at least on the usual reading) that because "object" is imposed by the mind, it has no external validity. I do not doubt the reality of causality, though neither is it given in the sensory array.

Certain puzzles about the principle of identity associated with names I have not dealt with. The number of passengers that Canadian National Railways claims to have carried in 1978 may be far larger than the number of persons they actually carried. The same person may have been a passenger hundreds of times and been so counted. *Book,* too, is a difficult word. It is possible to have two copies of two different books. I have not dealt with these because they do not, so far as I can see, arise in the vocabularies of children at the age we are studying.[4]

The notion "object" has more particular roles to play in language learning than the one just outlined—providing the child with targets for his acts of referring. In Chapters 7 and 8 I argued that it plays a central role in the process of learning that certain words are nouns. I also argued that it leads the child to expect that the rules of agreement, in number and gender, are based on nouns rather than on adjectives and articles.

Summary

The general thesis of this chapter is that children naturally represent their environment as occupied by objects. When they first hear a word in the presence of a salient object, they automatically take the word as applying to the object as a whole. Objects can reliably be made salient for the child by nonverbal gestures, particularly pointing. The child, too, can indicate that some object is salient for him by the same gestures. An adult then knows that the time may be ripe for teaching a name for the object (see Macnamara, 1977a).

I have argued that *referring* is best taken as a primitive of cognitive psychology. That is tantamount to saying that it is not learned. I am assuming that referring is basic and that reference is learned in terms of it. The child assumes that words that have been used to refer can be used to do so again; they retain their reference. This works except for deictic terms like *I* and *you*, and they form a special class in which reference depends on conversational roles.

Normally when adults say for a young child a word that refers, they intend to refer to the object as a whole. To convince yourself of the force of this, imagine yourself in a foreign-language classroom. The language is Irish; the teacher points to a stick and says *faid*. Later you will have grounds for complaint when you learn that that is not the word for stick but the word for length. The teacher ought to have known that you would have guessed stick. Interestingly, the illustration shows that the teacher, to succeed, must be able to guess correctly what the student's interpretation will be. Similarly, the parent must be able to guess the child's interpretation. That suggests that parents retain the interpretation biases of their childhood. That in turn suggests that imagining oneself in a foreign-language classroom is a good thought experiment for getting at the child's word-learning strategies.

Interpretations other than the whole-object are not ruled out altogether for the child; they are just ranked as less probable. Sooner or later the child must learn words for attributes. Occasionally, an adult uses an attribute word too soon and misleads a child. Hoffman (1968) records how one child gave evidence of believing that *hot* was a name for the kitchen stove. Apparently his mother had warned him in some such words as:

Don't touch that.
That's hot.

The child took *hot* as a name for the forbidden object.

We can accept Professor Quine's argument that there never are full empirical grounds for taking a word in one sense rather than another. At the same time we need not reduce meaning to "stimulus meaning," supplemented by "analytic hypotheses" that are ultimately based on sensory stimulation. That, on the face of it, leaves little room for imaginary, past, present, future, and possible states of affairs. Furthermore, I do not share Quine's belief that an infant's language learning can be explained by behaviorist learning theories. Instead, I believe, in keeping with what I hope is the spirit of Quine's philosophy, that the child forms hypotheses about a speaker's intentions—not just speaker-originated stimulation—and looks for signs of assent or dissent. Indeed his interpretation of language relates far more directly to perception than stimulation, stimulation itself being only a hypothesis to explain perception. This is all quite different from the set of processes envisaged by learning theorists of a behaviorist persuasion.

An important element in Quine's discussion is an innate quality space that leads the child to attend to qualities in a particular order. I go beyond Quine and appeal to the notion of an object, closely associated with sortals, that is not reducible to a quality or set of qualities. The notion is needed to explain how sensations from several modalities are integrated into a whole; it serves to explain the constancy of sensations over time and over spatial movement; most of all it helps to explain how we individuate the elements of our experience and to ground the criterion of identity so essential to naming.

12.
Meaning

*You have done me the honour of inviting me to give
your academy an account of the life I formerly led
as an ape.*
    —*Franz Kafka: A report to an academy*

Chapters 2, 4, and 5 explored the child's manner of coping with
three sorts of words that relate to a single object: proper, specific,
and general names. In this chapter we will pursue in greater depth
what it is to learn the sense or meaning of such words. The ground
upon which we enter is embattled. No side has had a clear victory,
though there have been some conclusive defeats. In the spirit of
the book as a whole, yet within the scope of a single chapter, we
will try to work out some conditions that a theory of meaning
must meet. With this we may be able to catch a glimpse of what a
satisfactory theory would be like. That glimpse suggests something
rather different from any theory that has standing at the present
time in either psychology or philosophy.

Unfortunately it will not be possible to present more than a
glimpse together with pointers to writings that I find illuminating.
At a later date I plan to write a detailed account of my views.

To keep a check on ambition the discussion will confine itself to
the main issue that Chapters 4 and 5 dealt with, the meaning of
hierarchically related terms as they apply to a single object. It will,
however, be necessary to go beyond the evidence that was set out
in those chapters.

This chapter begins with a critique of several theories of meaning that are widely accepted in psychology, followed by a critique of two widely accepted theories in philosophy. After this will come a set of desiderata for a theory of meaning. That will lead to a brief sketch of my own theory. The chapter concludes with an account of how children learn meanings. Though we will confine ourselves to names for things one could bump into, and though we will focus on hierarchically related names, I believe that the theory sketched here can be extended to other words.

Psychological Theories

1. THE TRADITIONAL THEORY: ABSTRACTION

The most popular accounts of meaning and concept in psychology—which does not generally distinguish between the two—are all based on some form of abstraction. The traditional view of abstraction is that it is a singling out of some proper subset of features in the sensory array. For example, Walter Kintsch (1977, p. 484) defines "concept learning" as "learning to classify a set of objects into categories on the basis of relevant attributes." On page 386 we find that the "relevant attributes" are values on "stimulus dimensions." That is how we pass from individual to concept. The next citation, where *attributes* is still to be read, in the last analysis, as sensory attributes, refers to levels of concepts:

> The concept of fruit is presumably an abstraction of the attributes that are shared by specific instances of fruit; one must abstract certain attributes that are common to both bananas and oranges, for example, to arrive at the more abstract concept of fruit. Note that of the total set of attributes that define a specific instance, such as banana, only a small subset are relevant to defining fruit. Not all fruit are crescent-shaped or have the consistency or taste of the banana.   Saltz (1973, p. 37)

The core of Humean empiricism, from which the traditional psychological theory stems, is that the form of knowledge is the form of the sensory input. Associations among sensory traces aside, what we know are the impressions our senses receive from the environment. Modern psychology has emphasized that these traces are modified in various ways: for example, by the processes that create the perceptual constancies and by certain rules to which Gestalt psychologists drew attention. But none of these processes or rules change the basic language of sensory experience. Sensory and perceptual form, for example, can be expressed in a single medium. So from the standpoint of our present analysis such perceptual processes are irrelevant.

Consider now that *dog* and *animal* can be true of the same individual—say, Towser. The only way the traditional psychological theory can handle this is by making a distinction in Towser phenomena. *Dog*, the theory claims, is true of him in virtue of one set of attributes; *animal* in virtue of another (though there may be overlap between the two sets, and indeed the animal set may be a proper subset of the dog one). That distinction we shall now see cannot be maintained.

A supporter of the distinction might argue that there are peculiarly canine features common to dogs but not to other animals. As a suitably subtle example of such a feature take ratio of length to height of head seen from the side. Let us suppose that we have calculated a mean value for this ratio and also a standard deviation so that we now have a typical canine head together with a measure of allowable variability. This, if one is kind enough to go along with the example, is a feature distinctive of dogs, or perhaps it just gives us a probability that some creature is a dog. It is not entered in the meaning of *animal,* though it is entered in the meaning of *dog.* Now what might serve as a feature common to all animals? Not number of legs, since worms are legless animals. Not covering, since some animals have feathers or scales instead of hair. Such a feature cannot be color or shape or texture or weight, since all these are variable. It cannot even be movement, since the movements of a bird, a dog, a fish, and a snake are very different. The trouble with the traditional theory is that there aren't any sensory or perceptual features that are common to all animals. This has the unfortunate consequence of making *animal* meaningless. And since parallel arguments would make *plant* and *furniture* meaningless, it should follow that *animal, plant,* and *furniture* mean the same, since they all mean nothing at all. Obviously, something has gone radically wrong—precisely the attempt to maintain a distinction among sensory attributes between canine ones and animal ones.

Perhaps the traditional theorist would respond that whereas we have been looking for sets of attributes in Towser, the physical object, he would have been looking for them in mental representations of *dog* and *animal.* This will not, I fear, serve the theorist's purpose. The basic reason is that the only type of representation he envisages is a sensory or a perceptual record. What we have just seen is that there cannot be a record of sensory features common to animals, because there aren't any such features.

Yet *dog* and *animal* differ in meaning. It follows that the difference cannot be attributed to sensory or perceptual processes of the type envisaged. It must be due to some other cognitive processes. It matters not for present purposes that we would never have coined two terms with different meanings if the only animals that existed were dogs.

That removes nothing from the interest of the fact that *dog* and *animal* are true of a single creature. The following illustration, inspired by Cassirer (1923-1953), whose lead I follow here, will help to clarify what is going on.

Cassirer noted that mathematicians move from specific to generic expressions not by jettisoning symbols but by replacing them with ones of a higher order. Consider the formula for a straight line of slope .5: it is $y = .5x + c$. The formula for straight lines in general is not reached by omitting the .5 entirely. In the general formula the particular slope is replaced by a parameter that can vary over some range of values. It is $y = bx + c$, where b is the parameter. Applied to our purpose, it suggests that we form two abstract representations of the same thing, one more specific than the other. Just as $y = .5x + c$ and $y = bx + c$ can each represent a single line, including its slope, "animal" can represent a single creature and leave out nothing in him that "dog" represents.

One of the lessons we should draw can also be illustrated by the mathematical example. The formula $y = bx + c$ does not represent a straight line in virtue of physical similarities between the formula and the line. Any such similarities that exist are accidental. Similarly the failure to find distinct sets of sensory attributes for dog and animal indicates that the meanings of these words are not representations of the creature in virtue of physical similarities between the meanings and the creature. In other words meanings are abstract with respect to the sensory array.

Fodor (1975) makes the same point with a different argument. He begins with the simple fact that a child must learn, in some sense, to classify the things he finds in the environment. Presumably he must try out various sortings of objects until he hits on "satisfactory" ones. Now either we visualize the process somewhat as predetermined mental photographs developing in the child's mind on contact with the environment, and that is not learning at all; or we visualize the child as playing a more active part and trying out the sortings. If the latter, the process is basically one of hypothesis formation and testing. But to form a hypothesis about experience and test it presupposes a medium in which to express the hypothesis and the results of the testing. Here a few points need to be added to Fodor's argument. While it is logically conceivable that the predicates in the child's hypotheses could be expressed in sensory terms, an entire hypothesis could not. Logical, nonempirical, connectives may be involved, such as *or* and *not*. Predication itself (claiming some descriptor *true of* an object) is not empirical. And the evaluation of the hypothesis involves the predicates *true* and *false,* which are certainly not empirical. Thus at least some of the language of mind is nonempirical. There is an argument from parsimony that it all is.

Miller and Johnson-Laird (1976) note that we can talk about things we see, so there is need of a connecting medium between speech and vision. We can also talk about the things we hear, smell, touch, or contact through any of the sensory systems. In addition we know when what we see is also what we touch, smell, or hear. So information from one sensory system can relate to information from another. Suppose the number of interconnecting systems is N, and suppose there is no language of mind common to all, then the number of interfaces is N $(N-1)$. Remember that the connection from vision to speech is not the same from speech to vision. On the other hand, if we allow an abstract language of mind, all we need is N interfaces. (The parsimony argument I owe to Steve Pinker.) The parsimony argument is interesting, but in my view it is not as strong as the argument based earlier on the application of hierarchies of predicates to a single individual.

2. PROTOTYPE THEORY

A new line of research promises to improve our understanding of sensory tests for category membership. We must look at it because it sometimes gives rise to confusion between such tests and meaning. The research is aimed at prototypes of categories. In ordinary language a prototype is the original after which copies are fashioned, and that is very much the sense in which the term is mostly used by Rosch (1977) and her collaborators. There is another sense, now common in the psychological literature, that amounts to some type of average computed over category members.

The two senses, though distinct, are useful and well grounded in psychological research. Rosch has made particularly good use of hers in explaining how people judge one object as more typical of a category than another. For example, most people judge a robin to be a more typical bird than a penguin or a chicken. Moreover, if asked to imagine a bird or name one, they are far more likely to imagine or name a robin than less typical ones. There is now a whole range of observations that show a robin to be more accessible under the description *bird* than penguins and chickens. Rosch argues that the reason is that children learn a word, like *bird,* as applied to the more typical exemplars; she and Anglin (1977) have published some evidence that they do. Children build their tests of category membership, the argument continues, on the perceptual data in the exemplars used to teach them. Little wonder, then, if the most typical exemplars fit the tests best. For example, if we suppose that the angle of inclination of a standing robin's body is taken by the child as a good index to the category *bird,* then penguins are more difficult to classify as birds because they stand completely upright.

The other tendency in the prototype literature presents the learner as averaging across instances and forming for himself a pattern or prototype that he has never seen. Rosch (1977) sometimes writes in that vein: "The most cognitively economical code for a category is, in fact, a concrete image of an average category member." Posner (1973) summarizes several studies that support the notion. He explains how he and his colleagues made several distinct patterns, and then prepared sets of random distortions of these patterns, one set for each pattern. They then presented the distorted patterns (not the basic patterns themselves) to learners and taught them to discriminate among the types. Then came a test period in which the learner saw for the first time the basic patterns and some new distortions as well as the original set on which he had learned. He was not told anything of the basic patterns. His job was once again to identify the pattern types. The interesting finding was that learners performed most accurately on the basic patterns. It was as though without seeing it, they had constructed the basic pattern of each type. In further studies they showed that learners also obtained some measure of the variability of each type. Experiments with similar results were conducted by Franks and Bransford (1971) on geometric shapes.

Central to this line of research is the belief that learning to recognize members of most categories involves learning to compute their similarity, along physical dimensions, to stored information. This seems eminently sensible and indeed inescapable since we all manage to assign objects to appropriate categories on the basis of observable physical properties. The extraordinary thing is how well children can do this after seeing one or two exemplars—see Miller's (1977) calculation that children learn about one word per waking hour up to the age of six.

The enormous value of prototypes must not lead us to mistake them for meanings. Posner certainly does, calling his prototypes "iconic concepts"—in my view a contradiction in terms. Posner, I take it, considers *meaning* and *concept* equivalent terms in the discussion of language. Rosch is generally more circumspect and uses the word *category* instead of *meaning*. But she does not distinguish between means for distinguishing category members and the mental representation of a category. Moreover, expressions like "semantic noun categories" sometimes escape her, in which "semantic" strongly suggests the confusion. However, little is to be gained from drawing up a schedule of errors; what is important is to avoid the confusion, or, if one insists on confounding things, to deal with the issues clearly.

Two further points about categories, both highly relevant to our present purpose: Prototypes seem suitable for discriminating among members of low-level categories, e.g., among dogs, cats, and cows. They seem less suited to deal with superordinate ones, like animal. Rosch (1977) found that people take much longer to form images when instructed to imagine an animal, say, than a dog, and in a number of ways the difference between superordinate and subordinate levels revealed empirical differences. Rosch (1977) is quite willing to accept the idea that at the superordinate level images or prototypes will not serve in categorizing because at that level the "categories . . . possess few attributes common to members of the category." The situation is worse; they possess none. Indeed I have great difficulty, in the spirit of Berkeley, in conceiving how a single image of a chair can serve in the recognition of all chairs. Perhaps one should really speak of prototypes for individual types of chairs.

It is clear that a robin is a more typical bird than a chicken. This is probably because our perceptual tests for "birdiness" work better on robins than on chickens. Yet everyone allows that *a chicken IS a bird.* They do not say, *a chicken is LIKE a bird.* Implicitly they are saying that a chicken has all that anything needs to be a bird. Being a bird is not a matter of appearances. It makes no difference that chickens don't look much like the image we typically form for a bird.

The purpose of these observations is to show that what a child learns when he learns common names is more than a prototype. Rosch conceded that the meaning of *animal* cannot be an image. Neither can the meaning of *bird*. Prototypes may serve in perceptual tests, but they are not meaning.

3. NETWORKS AND FEATURES

Information processing, so fascinated by language, has made several attempts to represent meaning. Quillian (1967, 1968, 1969) began with a theory of the form of word meanings that kept close to the model of dictionary definitions. His work has been adapted and supplemented by several other workers, e.g., Lindsay and Norman (1972, chaps. 10 and 11), Smith, Shoben and Rips (1974), and Anderson (1976).

Now we undoubtedly have much information that serves important psychological functions, but not everything that is relevant to the interpretation of a word or a sentence should be represented as the meaning of the words. The fact that fathers sometimes dote on their children is not part of the meaning of *father*. If it were it would be uninformative to tell some one that fathers sometimes dote on children; that would be true in virtue of the meaning of *father*.

The models run into serious trouble of this type. Take the network that expresses the meaning of *fascist* in Lindsay and Norman (1972, p. 425). It says *fascist* is ugly, cruel, short, radical, and fat; and fascist is a person. Pass over niceties about use and mention and there remains the trouble that *fascist* means none of those things except, probably, person. It matters not that the stereotype of fascists may include cruel, ugly, radical, and other such elements. In other words it is not a contradiction in terms to say that some fascist is not cruel, as it is a contradiction to say a bachelor is married. Moreover, the model owes us an account of the meaning of *person.*

The argument extends to numerous theories that take meaning to be a set of semantic features. For example, several theories propose that "yellow" and "sings" are part of the meaning of *canary.* That would rule out the possibility of an albino canary. It would say that a plucked canary was not a canary at all. Such theories are equivalent to the network theories without the network of logical relations.

Some theoreticians attempt to avoid such difficulties by loosening the connection between semantic features and truth. One such approach is sometimes called the cluster theory of meaning, more commonly heard from philosophers (e.g., Strawson, 1959, and Searle, 1969) than psychologists. The theory denies that any particular feature is essential to the correct use of a predicate; all that is needed is a weighted sum of features true of the object being described. The theory as applied to reference has received a drubbing from Kripke (1972). Kripke's arguments, suitably modified, go through for the cluster theory of meaning. There simply is no set at all of semantic features, of the type envisaged, that must be true of a creature for *canary* to be true of it: it could be a canary even if it had been plucked, lost a leg, couldn't sing, couldn't fly, etc. Such features are not the right sort of thing for meaning.

Much of the information that such semantic networks seek to represent is really not part of the word's meaning but what others call "collateral information." Later, when we have discussed the relation between meaning and truth, we will define collateral information. In the meantime we can draw the distinction between it and meaning by asking whether some item of information is *necessarily* true of creatures that fall under a category name. If it is not, it is collateral and not part of meaning.

4. DEFINITIONS

One of the standard ways to decide whether someone knows the meaning of a word is to ask for a definition. In the Stanford Binet test of intelligence there is a vocabulary item that does just that, and many people take satisfactory answers to such questions as statements of meaning. Among the "correct" answers to the Stanford Binet request to say what an orange is are: "it's round"; "it's yellow"; "an orange is something to eat." It seems clear that what children do when asked what an orange is, is to answer one of two different questions: (1) how can you tell an orange from other things? (b) what does one normally want an orange for, or what does one normally do with one? Such translations are perfectly sensible, but the responses to them must not be taken as expressions of meaning. An orange would still be an orange even if the whole human race lost its taste for oranges; and an orange is an orange even when it's green. The theory now being discussed is generally not explicit, unlike some of the others. It must be mentioned here because it is very common; perhaps because it is implicit in the construction of dictionaries. Dictionaries, if I am right, answer the question how to tell X's from other things, and what to do with them. They also have a shot at the related concept —i.e., at the set of necessary and sufficient conditions for belonging to the relevant category. Such statements must not be taken as meanings. If they were, it would follow that anyone who did not know the definition of the concept would not know the meaning of the word. For example, if H_2O specifies necessary and sufficient conditions for some stuff to be water, we don't want to say that no one knew the meaning of *water* before A.D. 1800.

STOCKTAKING

Our critique of psychological theories employed certain principles and it may help to make them explicit. We also reached negative conclusions about meaning and we will briefly list them.

Language picks out objects for consideration. The function of picking out objects we call reference and that we discussed in Chapter 11. Language also describes objects and states of affairs. The function of describing, taking that term broadly, is a large part of what we intend by meaning. We are not directly aware of the form of meanings; we are aware of our words and of what they describe. Meaning has to be inferred on the basis of some skill. The skill we have been canvassing is common sense judgment about the truth or falsehood of statements. For example, we all share the judgment (or intuition) that *a chicken is a bird*. From that we concluded that our judgment implies that a chicken has all that is necessary to be a bird. That in turn led to the conclusion that the meaning of *bird* cannot be an image of a typical bird, because a chicken differs in obvious ways from a typical bird, such as a robin.

The whole argument is an exploration of that which is implicit in a common judgment. The judgment itself is a conclusion that a proposition is true. Judging true, then, is an important clue to underlying representation. Notice, however, that in judging *a chicken is a bird* we do not reveal that "bird" is part of the meaning of *chicken*. "Chicken" and "bird" might for example be related by some such logical connective as *implies* ($\supset$).

On the other hand if some feature really were a component of a word's meaning, that feature would be implied by predicating that word of some creature. For example, if "yellow" really were part of the meaning of *canary,* we would infer that if any creature is a canary, it must be yellow. The fact that common sense does not rule out the possibility of an albino or of a plucked (not yellow) canary reveals that "yellow" is not part of the meaning of canary.

This method of arguing presupposes a close tie between meaning and belief in our judgments that a proposition is true or false. I think the argument is sound, though we shall see it challenged in the next section. Notice, however, that we have so far used our intuitions of truth to rule out theories of meaning, not to support them.

Our main negative conclusion was to reject traditional psychological empiricism, the doctrine that the form of knowledge is basically the form of the sensory input. We did so mainly on grounds that relate to the matter of the foregoing chapters. Empiricism cannot satisfactorily handle the fact that a single creature is both dog and animal. In particular, abstraction as understood by traditional theorists does not work. Abstraction depends on our finding a distinction between those sensory properties that make him an animal. Actually we found that there is no set of sensory attributes in virtue of which he is an animal as distinct from those in virtue of which he is a dog.

We concluded that meaning is not expressed in the form of an image, or of an average of sensory impressions, or indeed in the language of the sensory array.

Philosophical Theories

Most philosophical discussion of meaning has hinged one way or another on truth. That there is some connection between meaning and truth is not difficult to see. For example, if I ask you whether you think the following sentence true,

Mol an óige agus tiochfaid sí[1].

you will say that depends on what it means. So truth depends on meaning. Does meaning depend on truth? Is truth the key to meaning? We will begin with a philosopher who answers no.

PUTNAM

Hilary Putnam (1975a, 1978) mounts a powerful argument against the view that the meanings people carry in their heads determine the truth or falsehood of sentences. He points out that most people do not know what determines whether something is gold or water or a dog. He is not talking about how we tell whether something is gold. The problem is that many do not know what gold is. What are the necessary and sufficient conditions for something to be gold? Of course we have some idea: a precious metal, yellow in color, used in jewelry and dentistry. That serves well enough most of the time. We know, however, that other metals can look like gold, and when some importance attaches to the matter we have recourse to an expert. He is supposed to be able to go beyond appearances and tell us for a fact whether some sample really is gold.

Why are the expert's tests considered better? Not merely because of his authority. Unlike an umpire who decides how a play will be interpreted, whatever the facts, the expert is supposed to establish the facts. The reason the expert prevails is that his tests have a basis in science, and he can show that. On the assumption that he has discovered the nature of gold he has the appropriate concept (leaving aside his tests) and the layman does not.

How then, according to Putnam, do laymen manage to converse and reach mutual understanding, if they do not know the concepts related to the words they use? (I am using concept in a technical sense solely to mean necessary and sufficient conditions for category membership. In that sense, if chemists have done their work well, H_2O specifies the concept water.) Putnam's answer is that they manage to communicate because they share stereotypes —i.e., "standardized sets of beliefs" (Putnam, 1978, p. 115). He also says that a stereotype is all that the layman has in his head (Putnam, 1975a, p. 169). The layman, however, may lack even the stereotype. Putnam says that he himself lacks the stereotypes for *elm* and *beech* and could not tell the trees apart. Even in the matter of stereotypes there is a "division of linguistic labor." Only the expert may know the stereotype. The stereotype, Putnam holds, guarantees that reference will usually be correct. The community can allow the concept to be whatever it turns out to be. That, for Putnam, is what science ultimately makes of it. Though even here Putnam, like Quine, is something of a skeptic in that he believes that the work of science can never be immune from revision.

I have not given Putnam's case in its full force, but I have said enough to show that it undermines some popular views of how meaning relates to truth. Since on his view meaning in people's heads is stereotype, and since stereotypes may be false, one cannot go from truth to such meaning or from such meaning to truth.

The strong part of Putnam's position is the argument that meaning in the head does not normally provide necessary and sufficient conditions for category membership. Most people don't know such conditions for most common categories, and no one at all knows them for such ones as dog and cow.

The weak part of his theory is the claim that meaning in the head is stereotype. A stereotype is described as a standardized belief in the truth of some proposition. But there are difficulties, as Putnam well knows, in describing the logical status of such beliefs.

Having four legs is part of the stereotype of dog. Yet people do not hesitate to call a creature a dog just because it lost a leg. Being yellow is part of the canary's stereotype. But people do not rule out the possibility of an albino canary. Being liquid is part of the stereotype of water, yet even young children are told that ice and snow are really water. There is little to be gained by appealing to a similarity metric. It seems inconceivable that any such metric could reveal enough similarities at the sensory level (the only relevant one) to warrant calling snow water. From these examples if follows that stereotypes will not explain our everyday use of names.

While keeping Putnam's observation that meaning (that people carry about in their heads) does not generally furnish necessary and sufficient conditions for category membership, we must reject the proposal that such meaning is merely stereotype. Since *concept* as I use it involves necessary and sufficient conditions for category membership, it follows that we must establish a distinction between the meaning people have, as competent speakers, and concept. In refusing to accept meaning as stereotype I am preparing to reestablish the link between meaning and truth. But first some other theories.

VERIFICATION/FALSIFICATION

Remember what we are looking for, a theory of the meanings people know for the names of physical objects; a theory that will handle such facts as that a dog is an animal. Because dog is not a category for which at present anyone can state necessary and sufficient conditions, it follows that the meaning of *dog* cannot be such conditions.

Can we, nevertheless, make a connection between meaning and truth? Suppose, for example, we wanted to be sure in general which things are dogs and which are not, a set of necessary and sufficient conditions is exactly what we need. That the meaning of a word (as generally known), does not supply.

Nonetheless, most of us believe that everything either is a dog or is not. Nothing is in between. Implicitly we believe that necessary and sufficient conditions for being a dog exist. And it's not just that we don't know them, though in most cases we certainly don't; and it's not that we trust science inevitably to reveal them to us, for many of us share Putnam's skepticism about science, nor is it that implicit in our ordinary thinking is the belief that scientist and layman alike are oriented toward a real set of necessary and sufficient conditions for category membership. In this, common sense is, technically, realist. In this chapter I maintain a realist stance.

Talk of necessary and sufficient conditions puts people in mind of Wittgenstein's analysis of the word *game* in his *Philosophical*

Investigations. He showed that there don't seem to be necessary and sufficient conditions for something to be a game. The notion is vague. This seems right, but it does not follow that natural-kind terms, like *dog,* are. In fact, common intuition is on the side that they are not vague.

In this connection, too, people mention fuzzy sets, i.e., sets in which membership is not a matter of all or none. They are prompted to do so by the observation that it is difficult to establish boundaries for species. Are wolves and foxes really distinct from dogs? Now vagueness can arise in at least two ways. The category might indeed be vague, as a fuzzy set is vague. But one's test for category membership might also be vague. For example, the birdwatcher peering at a little brown bird at the far side of the bush has little doubt about the distinctions among species. He has grave doubts about assigning this particular bird to one species. My own tests for whether something is water are vague, though serviceable. It does not follow that the category water is vague.

What happens is that our sensory system gives us a useful first division of objects. The division is tested for its contribution to intelligibility. Adjustments are made. At one time seals and whales were treated as fish, but we were persuaded that it made more sense, because they were air-breathing milk-giving creatures, to place them with the mammals.

What has this to do with the layman's language? It is a backdrop to all his thinking, hence to his use of language. That is why the layman yields to the expert who says something is or is not gold. That is why we cease to call seals fish. Notice, too, that the layman and the expert's vocabulary overlap. *Gold* is both a layman's word and an expert's. The same word. Even more basic, the layman and expert are both people. And the expert's ideal of understanding is the layman's, though the layman may make less use of it.

All this is a preamble to a sympathetic analysis of theories that tie meaning and truth. We can see words like *dog* linked not to a set of necessary and sufficient conditions that people know, but to a set that they believe exists in those creatures they call dog. It may, of course, be necessary to extend *dog* to some creatures that are not now called *dog,* or to exclude some that now are. It is inconceivable, however, that terriers, spaniels, setters, poodles, and collies should be excluded, so central are they to our application of the name *dog.*

Before going on, a word of caution about terms that really are vague. Not only is *game* vague, but so is *tall.* Society does not establish precise points at which *tall* is applicable. Closely akin are *stream* and *puddle*. *Stream, brook, river* are vague regions on the continuum that measures quantity of running water. *Puddle, pond, lake* are vague regions on the continuum that measures quantities of still water. *Mound, knoll, hill, mountain* are vague regions on the continuum that measures quantities of earth raised about the plane. These are a different kind of term from *dog* and *cow*, and it is necessary to keep them distinct.

Michael Dummett (1978) has revitalized an approach to meaning that was made popular between the world wars by logical positivism. While avoiding much of the empiricism of the logical positivists, he argues that the key to meaning is in our ability to verify or falsify statements. Since to verify or falsify is to establish a truth value for a statement, his approach depends on a connection between meaning, psychologically real meaning, and truth. Dummett does not, however, subscribe to the connection I have just sketched between meaning, ideal concepts, and truth.

Dummett makes several valuable points that I think we should adopt. He insists that the speaker's grasp of meaning must be manifest in some "practical ability" (pp. 69 and 74). He demands, then, that a theory of meaning include an account of such an ability and of how it relates to the "understanding" of sentences. In addition, the theory should explain how the meaning of a sentence is built from the meanings of its component words. Furthermore, he distinguishes, with Frege, not only between sense and reference but also between these and force. *Force* denotes a range of intentional attitudes toward an utterance. It includes stating, questioning, commanding. While there may be linguistic differences between statements, questions, and commands, a single sentence may also be employed with different forces (p. 13). Storytellers use statement forms without intending their utterances to be taken as true.

Dummett's own choice of a practical ability to serve as the key to meaning seems unfortunate. He chooses the ability to verify or falsify a statement. (For utterances like commands he would, it seems, accept some other ability, such as compliance, p. 73). To verify or to falsify is to establish a truth value. Meaning, on this account is the means employed for assigning a truth value.

Consider the child who is learning such words as *dog, cat,* and *bird.* He hears his parents say such things as *That is a cat; Freddie is a dog;* and *Look at the bird.* The verificationist would have the child discover means for verifying his parents' statements. This

seems odd. The child probably just accepts their word. It is easier
to understand the verificationist approach when one thinks of the
child's own efforts to use the words. He predicates them of
various objects and watches his parents' reaction to see if he has
used them correctly or not. Notice, however, that what the child
is doing is neither verifying nor falsifying, as those terms are usually
understood, but conforming to common usage. That must be so,
since his parents do not have necessary and sufficient conditions
for the application of *bird, dog,* and *cat.*

The verificationist is aware of this and several moves are open
to him that save his overall position. One is to present a new
notion of truth. Another is to give up the idea that natural-kind
terms have sharp boundaries. He may have independent reasons for
coming to those conclusions. I do not propose to go into all the
related issues. I prefer myself to see if a theory of meaning can be
worked out with the conventional notions of truth and natural
kinds. The theory I want would maintain a link between meaning
and truth as truth has been understood in realist philosophy.
Verificationism cannot provide that.

The rest of this section should not be read as a survey of the
philosophical literature. It is much more like a foray into philosophical territory in the hope of carrying off some useful ideas.

TRUTH CONDITIONS

In the second chapter of her excellent book on *Semantics,* Janet
Fodor (1977) discusses a variety of theories that can broadly be
characterized by the claim that meaning is a set of truth conditions. Truth conditions are neither truth nor verification. As their
name suggests, they are conditions that determine the truth of an
assertion. The general idea is this: *Freddie is a dog* is true if and
only if the object picked out by Freddie satisfies certain conditions,
C. The next move is to say that *C* specifies the meaning of *dog.* The
theory can be stated in rather different ways. The most interesting
version is that *C* specifies properties that any creature under any
circumstances must have if he is to be a dog. That is, *C* is a set of
necessary and sufficient conditions for being a dog.

Janet Fodor's critique of this class of theories reveals their
inadequacies and need not be repeated here. From our point of
view the additional observation that needs to be made is that
following Putnam to the extent we do, we realize that the meaning
people have in their heads for *dog* cannot be necessary and sufficient
conditions for being a dog. No one in fact knows such conditions.

What is instructive for us is to note the existence and popularity of such theories. Dummett (1978) says they are the most popular theories of meaning at the present time. What is valuable in them is the determination to relate meaning and truth. What is weak in them is the confounding of meaning with necessary and sufficient conditions. In the terminology we have established, they wrongly confound meaning and concept.

MEANING AND USE

The idea that meaning is use is associated with Wittgenstein, particularly in *Philosophical Investigations*. I will not review Wittgenstein's main ideas on meaning—that is well done by Fodor (1977), for one. I want to make a single point suggested by the word *use*. In Wittgenstein's general theory the meaning of a word— say, *kettle*—is its use in some linguistic system. Besides the word there is the object, and it too has uses in the business of cooking. It ought to make sense to speak about the meaning of the object kettle. I think that this much is right, but on Wittgenstein's account the meaning of the word and the meaning of the object will be quite different.

In the theory that I will later adumbrate, I will suggest that objects, too, have meanings. In fact I will suggest that a word and the related objects have the same meaning. Our sensory experience is meaningful; we make sense of it. The notion of meaning is not foreign in the study of perception. Perception, in the world of information processing, is seen as an interpretative process. A percept is the sense we make of experience at one level. We also interpret percepts. The next level of interpretation I would like to call sense or meaning. We will see more of this. It is enough now to give warning that I will suggest that the meaning of the object kettle is the meaning of the word *kettle*. Of course I am not suggesting that the object functions as a symbol in the way the word does. A word is a conventional symbol, and an object is usually not a symbol at all. That difference does not preclude their both accessing a common level of processing. Indeed the non-arbitrary nature of the objects' interpretation is exactly what is needed to guarantee that the arbitrary linguistic symbol is assigned a meaning that is constant to all members of a speech community.

The attraction of the view that word and object have the same meaning is that it suggests an explanation for how we can talk about the things we see. It indicates a path to follow if one wishes to explore one way in which words and objects are related.

Desiderata for a Theory of Meaning

One of the reasons for surveying psychological and philosophical theories of meaning was to find positive and negative criteria for a theory of meaning. The survey also provided an initial processing of the material. We will now go on to take stock of what we found. We will do so in the form of a list of guiding ideas, each followed by a brief comment on its justification and force.

NEGATIVE CONCLUSIONS

1. *We are not directly aware of meanings.* This is commonly held in psychology. We adverted to it when we noted that meaning has to be inferred mainly on the basis of certain intuitions.

2. *Meaning is not given directly in sensory stimuli.* This is a little different from the previous principle. We are not generally aware of sensory stimuli. Hence the need to separate a principle about awareness from one about sensation. Note, however, that percepts are in the language of sensation. Visual percepts involve color, shape, texture, and these are expressible in terms of sensory stimuli.

The principle derives from our analysis of widely held psychological theories of meaning. In rejecting them we rejected the notion that abstraction yields meaning. Abstraction is the singling out in attention of subsets of sensory features. Together with abstraction we reject the notion that meaning is a set of semantic features abstracted from the sensory array. We also rejected the view that meaning is an image of any sort, prototypical or other, or that it is an average computed over sets of sensory data.

The reader familiar with J. J. Gibson's (1979) work will notice a certain similarity between Gibson's position and the one here proposed. Gibson downplayed what we call "the sensory stimulus", and in particular argued that knowledge is not abstracted from the sensory stimulus. I agree with all this. What is difficult to accept is Gibson's equation of knowledge and percept. I hope to deal with the issues elsewhere—(see Macnamara and Niall, in preparation).

3. *Meaning is not use.* This desideratum is stated without proof. Those who seek one will find it in Fodor (1977).

MEANING AND TRUTH

4. *Truth depends on meaning.* This is taken as self-evident. There is, however, a way of taking Putnam's position on stereotypes

that would seem to oppose it. If we take meaning, effectively, to be stereotype, then the truth of sentences will not depend on such meaning. We argued that stereotypes are not meanings.

5. *Truth value does not determine meaning.* This is based on Putnam's point, that most people do not know necessary and sufficient conditions for membership in most of the categories they have names for.

A similar line of argument shows that the means for correctly assigning truth value are not meaning. In particular, means for assigning truth values can hardly be what the language learner is after.

6. *Truth value judgments provide a test of theories of meaning.* A theory of word meaning must not, without grave reasons, run afoul of our common sense judgments. Such reasons have not been given, so far as I know. In particular if a theory claimed that being four-legged was part of the meaning of *dog*, then it would have to maintain that a three-legged creature could not correctly be called *dog* in the literal sense of the word.

Another obvious judgment we must respect is that if Rosy is a cow, necessarily it cannot be a cat. On the other hand if Rosy is a cow, it is also an animal. We noted that one can accept that without making "animal" part of the meaning of *cow*.

DISTINCTIONS

7. *Meaning is distinct from reference.* Informally, reference has to do with designating what one is talking about, and meaning has to do with describing it. Modern logic began with a semantics that related language to objects that actually exist, their relations and properties. Such a semantics is called *extensional.* Modal logicians extend semantics to objects in possible worlds and to their relations and properties. In such semantics, called *intensional, dog* might refer to all possible dogs as well as to the actual ones. In fact *intension* is defined in terms of reference to objects in all possible worlds. Such reference is held in check, ideally, by a set of necessary and sufficient conditions associated with the terms. Hence, modal logic makes a close connection between reference and what I call concept. Even in modal logic, however, a distinction is required between reference and meaning.

8. *Meaning is distinct from force.* *Force* denotes a speaker's intentional act in making an utterance as a whole. Frege distinguishes it from meaning and reference. The necessity of the dis-

tinction is widely, though not universally accepted (see Janet Fodor, 1977, chap. 2).

9. *Meaning and concept are distinct.* The reader will recall that I am using *concept* in a technical sense to signify necessary and sufficient conditions for category membership. I am also using *meaning* to denote something that ordinary people have in their heads. Putnam forced on us the realization that meaning and concept, so defined, must be distinct. For example, if the concept of water really is specified by H_2O, that is not the meaning of *water*. The meaning of *water* did not change when people decided that water is H_2O. It would not change if we found out that it isn't H_2O.

10. *Meaning is distinct from partial concept.* I am here introducing the term *partial concept* to signify the understanding a person has of some object if that understanding is less than ideally adequate necessary and sufficient conditions for membership in the category the word names.

For example, we all have some understanding of the nature of dogs. It explains how they can bark, run about, digest food, and have puppies. Biologists know a great deal more. If they have specialized in dogs, they know all sorts of details about their digestive system, for example. They have a partial understanding of how it works. Of course some current biological beliefs may be wrong. I will use the word *partial concept* of such comprehension as a person has achieved.

I have not proved that meaning and partial concept must be distinct. The argument that proved meaning and concept distinct will not do. Several arguments will come up later, such as that meaning must be attainable without a scientific training, and meaning must be the same for all who use a word to communicate. These are sufficient to prove meaning and partial understanding distinct, but the arguments depend on principles yet to be laid down.

One argument can be made at present. People's theories are frequently erroneous, at least in some details. If we allowed a person's theory (understanding) of dogs to be the meaning of *dog*, we could not explain how he might change his theory. For example, scientists once thought that all combustion involved a substance called phlogiston. One can imagine such scientist believing that the explanation of a dog's muscular contractions involved phlogiston. It turns out that there is no such substance.

If that early biologist's meaning for *dog* was his theory of dogs, it would have included the notion of phlogiston. Being part of the meaning of *dog* (on this account of meaning) it would then be analytically true that dogs had phlogiston. But that is false. Therefore the theory that makes meaning equal to partial concept must be false. The argument runs parallel to that by which we argued that "four-legged" is not part of the meaning of *dog,* not a semantic feature.

11. *Meaning is distinct from collateral information. Collateral information* signifies information that is part neither of a word's meaning nor of the partial concept associated with it. The term is used in the philosophy of language.

Much of the information that psychologists place in semantic features is really collateral. That canaries are generally yellow is collateral information. That fascists tend to be cruel is too. Under that heading falls any information that one may glean about a class of objects that one would not tie by means of logical implication to the object. That may, for all I know, be most of my information about such a category as dogs.

ADDITIONAL DESIDERATA

12. *Meaning is based on publicly observable events.* We must not permit our rejection of empiricism to distract us from Wittgenstein's admonition that there is no private language. What he intended to hammer home is the fact that English (and each natural language) is a public communication system. Children learn it from their parents on the basis of publicly observable objects and events. Meanings that are not tied to the publicly observable are non-communicable and therefore unlearnable. The point did not come up in previous discussion. It is made with sufficient clarity and force in the *Philosophical Investigations.*

13. *Meaning is constant across all members of a speech community.* This is perhaps the basis for the last point. It does not rule out ambiguity. It does not even demand that all members of a speech community know all meanings of an ambiguous term, such as *bank* (money, river). It claims, for example, that any member who knows those two meanings of *bank* enters the very same two meanings as anyone else who knows them. The principle does not rule out historical change of meaning. For example, in Old English *deor* meant animal, while its modern descendant, *deer,* means one species of animal. The introduction of *animal,* ultimately from Latin, dislodged the original meaning of *deer.*

The principle just enunciated states that where such a change in meaning occurs, it must occur in a short time and it must not escape the attention of members of the speech community in which it is occurring. (It may not occur in a particular dialect.)

Meanings must be subject to a very strong constraint if communication is to be as successful as it generally seems to be. Of course partial concepts and collateral information will vary from speaker to speaker.

14. *Meanings exist in ordinary people's heads.* This is merely to formalize a requirement that we have assumed all along. It implies that one can learn meanings without benefit of science. For the most part what science gives us is a partial concept. The distinction between meaning and partial concept helps to solve a problem in the philosophy of science. Do words change their meanings as science advances? Did *electron* mean something different to Maxwell from what it means to a modern physicist? And if so, are Maxwell's writings unintelligible today? The distinction between meaning and partial concept opens the way to a solution. Meaning remains constant while partial concepts change. Modern scientists can understand their predecessors.

15. *The skill that reveals grasp of meaning is categorization.* Dummett warned us that theories of meaning must be grounded in a practical ability. We are dealing only with the meaning of category terms. Dummett's principle has some affinity with Wittgenstein's requirement that meaning should rest on the publicly observable. The appropriate ability to reveal grasp of meaning of the sort we are studying is successful categorization. A child gives good grounds for the belief that he knows the meaning of *dog* if he applies the word to all and only dogs.

In Chapter 5, doubting whether children understood the force of the word *animal,* we gave them a nonverbal test. We asked them to copy us in separating animals from vehicles. The word *animal* was not used. Success indicated that a child knew of the category, animal, even if by other tests he revealed a reluctance to apply the word, *animal,* either to a single animal or to several animals of a single species. We interpreted our results as evidence that children had the meaning of *animal* even if they had not attached it to that word.

Too much confidence should not be placed in our tests for grasp of a meaning. We earlier considered children who might know the word *chopstick* and apply it only to chopsticks, yet not have any idea of what a chopstick is for. Such a child lacks the central ingredient of the meaning of the word *chopstick*. On the other hand, a child who has a meaning may fail to reveal it for any of a number of reasons.

16. *The meaning of the word is the meaning of the object.* Any attempt to define "meaning of an object" must wait until we define "meaning of a word"—for by the principle they are one and the same. Nevertheless, it may help to indicate that meaning will eventually be presented as a theoretical entity whose function it is to designate an object's nature precisely as the explanation for a certain set of phenomena connected with the object.

This principle, which was introduced when we were foraging in Wittgenstein's writings, was employed implicitly in explaining desideratum 15. In using a nonverbal test for grasp of the meaning of *animal* with children who did not apply the word correctly, we were assuming that the adult meaning of the word and the meaning of the object is one and the same.

We cannot make the principle a strict criterion of a theory of meaning. What we can demand of such a theory is that it help to explain how we can talk about the things we perceive. Some words refer to them, but more than reference is involved. Some words describe objects. A general theory of cognitive psychology must explain how language relates to perception, both in the learning of words and in their use. Logically, the relation need not be identity of meaning. Such an identity would, however, greatly simplify psychology.

Besides the argument from simplicity there is another, that comes from Ray Jackendoff (in a lecture given at McGill). I can point to the kettle and say, *That is what I boil water in,* and mean the very same as if I had said, *The kettle is what I boil water in.* In one sentence the listener supplies the appropriate meaning when he hears the word *kettle*; in the other he must supply the same meaning from an inspection of the environment. One might argue that if one inspects the environment, the word *kettle* occurs to the listener and then he attains the meaning. But that is to forget that that cannot be how the child learned the meaning of *kettle* in the first place. When he first heard the word, he had no other course than to determine what it meant by inspecting the object that it designated.

17. *A theory of meaning should specify a connection between meaning and our ability to assign objects to categories.* There is broad agreement that the meaning of *dog* has some connection with the manner in which we distinguish dogs from other creatures.

In principle 15 we used the connection, suggesting categorization as the skill that normally reveals grasp of meaning. At the same time we must distinguish dogs on the basis of sensory attributes, even though we have rejected empiricism, (which makes meaning a set of distinctive sensory features).

The discipline that studies how we distinguish in perception between categories is called pattern recognition. An adequate theory would tell us how sensory features are recognized and how they contribute to category assignment. We should not include such tests in meaning. There can be many ways to determine category membership; there can even be many equally valid ways: yet the meaning of the category is not many. For example one can sometimes determine which element some substance is by atomic weight or by electrical resistance. The meanings of the elements' names do not change with the discovery of new methods for deciding which elements are which. Sometimes the criteria for category decisions can be quite trivial. When I was a child, one knew that if another child wore a ribbon, it was a girl. Since then ribbon wearing has become much less common, yet one does not want to say for that reason that the meaning of *girl* has changed, even for me.

Nonetheless there must be an intimate connection between meaning and concept on the one hand and sensation and perception on the other. We do apply our words to the objects we see and feel, and any success in doing so presupposes a stable relationship between words and objects. It is therefore desirable that our theory explain how words, meaning and concepts relate to our system of assigning objects to categories.

Sketch of Theory of Meaning

Our preparatory work is complete, and we must now look for a theoretical entity that will satisfy the requirements we have just listed. I fear we will not find exactly what we want ready made, but many of the ingredients are in the late writings of Gottlob Frege. We begin with his treatment of thought.

For Frege (1918) a thought is "something for which the question of truth arises." A thought is ascribed a truth value. A thought is itself complex, having as minimal components a reference to some object and a predicate. The reference picks out some object and the predicate bears the relation "true of" or "not true of" to that object. We must focus on the predicate.

Frege (1892) says that the predicate has "a reference" and that reference is a concept. In the *Grundgesetze* (vol. 1, sec. 3) we read that "a concept is a function whose value is always a truth-value." More simply, this means that the predicate itself is not part of the thought, but it designates a concept, which is. The sorts of concepts Frege had in mind were ones with "sharp boundaries"—that is, a concept that would "unambiguously determine, as regards any object, whether or not if falls under the concept (whether or not the predicate is truly assertible of it)" (*Grundgesetze,* vol. 1, sec. 56).

In the essay "On sense and reference" he clearly distinguishes between sense and reference: "It is natural, now, to think of there being connected with a sign . . . besides that to which the sign refers, which may be called the reference of the sign, also what I would like to call the *sense* of the sign, wherein the mode of presentation is contained." It does not seem that Frege applied the distinction to predicates to differentiate between a sense and a reference. In fact, he held that thought and sense are identical. With John Perry (1977), though Perry was working on the problem of indexicals, I believe Frege ought to have distinguished between the sense of a predicate and its referent (a concept). And I believe that it is sense as so distinguished that we are after.

I shall argue, then, for a distinction between meaning (for I shall continue to use that term rather than Frege's *sense*) and concept. Meaning, so distinguished, is the manner in which a concept is presented. The parallel with proper names is exact. Just as *Aristotle* denotes a person and the meaning of *Aristotle* is the manner in which the name presents him, so the predicate *dog* denotes a concept and its meaning is the manner in which it presents the concept. It presents the concept precisely as explanation.

The arguments that Frege gave for distinguishing meaning from reference in connection with proper names will not serve in connection with predicates. What does support the distinction is desideratum 16. It is the one that demands that the meaning of a word and the meaning of the object it named be the same. Let us see how this supports our theory of meaning.

Frege seems to have thought that it was enough to have a linguistic predicate, say *dog*, and the concept it designated. The problem is, how does the child, or anyone for that matter, manage to attach the predicate to the concept? If the child were simply to hear a predicate applied to some object or objects, he would have no way of tying the predicate to a concept, unless something were to guide him. For even if we suppose that he knew enough to appreciate that a predicate claimed some descriptors true of some objects, he still would have to find some way of determining which descriptors. In calling Freddie a dog one cannot be simply saying that all descriptors that are true of Freddie are true of him. Some, for example, are not true of Towser, who is also called a dog. We lately saw that the relevant set of descriptors for the use of *dog* are not given directly in the perceptual array. In fact they are not even known to any person at present. What keeps the child, or anyone else, on course here? What ensures that all English users are claiming the same set of descriptors true of those creatures they call dogs? That the/ should be so doing is expressed by desiderata 13 and 14. I know of no answer that does not appeal to the notions of uniqueness and explanation. Remember, one cannot point to concept as one can point to dogs.

What we need of a concept is that it supply necessary and sufficient conditions for category membership. But that is not enough. It is theoretically possible to have several different sets of necessary and sufficient conditions for a single category. Both logic (Ajdukiewicz, 1969) and science, however, have always aimed at the set of such conditions that has the greatest explanatory power. That is, they value those necessary and sufficient conditions that contribute most to explanations of the phenomena associated with a category. In addition they value statements of such conditions in terms that show the greatest number of interconnections between the category to be defined and other categories that the theory deals with. For example, a definition of measles in terms of a virus has greater explanatory power than one, however exact, in terms of spots on the skin. The one in terms of virus helps to explain how the disease is communicated, the course of its development, and likely approaches to prevention. A definition in terms of spots would not help, directly, with any of this. Moreover, the definition in terms of virus relates measles to all other viral diseases. One in terms of spots would not.

Incidentally, I believe I am well within the spirit of Frege's writing when I use concept not of what people actually have in their heads (partial concept), but of an ideal set of necessary and sufficient conditions for category membership. The concept, in conjuction with the reference (to an object), determines the truth or falsehood of the thought in which it occurs; it has to do only secondarily with what people will assent to or affirm.

Meaning in the sense suggested is closely related to *nature* in one of its common usages. I will give a few examples to show the relation and then show that meaning and nature must be kept distinct. The examples will also serve the function of showing that meaning, as presented, is not in the least recherché.

There is today, I am told, a new breed of poodle so tiny that an adult will fit in a teacup. I have not seen it, but people who have report amazement that a mature dog should be so small. It jolts the stereotype. Why do people agree that it is a dog? I submit that what decides the matter is the fact that the teacup poodle was bred directly from poodles. In the layman's categorizing breeding is a winner. The reason is that parent and offspring are believed to share a nature. In fact if you ask a layman why a dog has pups and not kittens, he is liable to tell you that it's a dog's nature to have pups.

The notion of nature is robust. It is undoubtedly part of the stereotype of dog that a dog has four legs. Yet if a dog loses a leg he does not for that cease to be a dog. The nature, dog, is not identified with surface phenomena; rather, it serves to explain a variety of such phenomena. Similarly a plucked canary remains a canary, at least for a while, though it is no longer yellow.

The layman's belief that water is a natural kind implicitly recognizes a common nature underlying a variety of phenomena. It seems likely that the idea starts off in connection with water in its liquid state. However, water can freeze and form ice and thaw and become liquid again; it can crystallize into snow and return to liquid again. All this is reflected in common speech where one tells a child, for example, *ice is really water.* The *really* there warns him that, despite appearances, ice is water. The interchangeability of states indicates a common nature underlying all the states. And the nature is what explains, ultimately, why water is good to drink and good for plants.

Associated with differences between dog phenomena and cat phenomena in common belief is a difference in nature. The appeal to nature is an appeal to a fundamental explanation for the phenomena that are grouped together. Nature then is a common sense explanatory construct. Before such a construct is invoked, the layman must recognize that a dog, for example, in all his manifestations is a single organism. The phenomena call for a single, though highly complex, explanation. *Nature,* in common speech, is a symbol for that largely unknown explanation.

Nature so used has a close affinity to meaning. A meaning is a symbol for a generally unknown concept; just as nature is a symbol for a generally unknown explanation. There are, however, two reasons for keeping meaning and nature distinct. *Nature* indicates primarily something in an object; whereas *meaning,* as I use it, indicates something in the head. For meaning is in the head. Besides, *nature* denotes the internal organization of an object in all its essential detail. *Meaning* does not suggest anything so detailed. The nature of gold, for example, involves a certain number of electrons; we do not want that number to be part of the meaning of the word *gold.* For these reasons we must distinguish clearly between meaning and nature.

So far, to keep exposition simple, we concentrated on natural kind words, like *dog* and *water.* The theory extends naturally to names for artificial kinds, like *kettle* and *razor.* The main difference between a natural kind word like *iron* and an artificial kind word like *kettle* is that the status of being iron does not depend on human intentions and purposes. That of being a kettle does. A kettle is assigned certain functions, like boiling water. The metal of which it is made remains metal even if it is melted down and is no longer a kettle. It follows that the concept "kettle" must represent the appropriate human intentions as its core. To know the meaning of *kettle* it is sufficient to know that there is a set of functions peculiar to kettles. This in turn depends on having identified kettle shapes and kettle related actions. Knowledge of the corresponding concept depends, ideally, on developments in cognitive psychology parallel to developments in biology that might yield knowledge of the concept "dog."

We must not, of course, expect the distinction between natural and artificial kinds to be unproblematic. Botanists classify onions and garlic with the lilies; cooks don't. It follows that there is a cognitive interaction between two classificatory systems—the botanist's, which is entirely natural kind in orientation, and the cook's, which is in some measure intentional.

THE INDIVIDUATION OF MEANINGS

Meaning might at first seem so vague as to be useless. After all, I said that the meaning of *dog* is the manner of presenting the concept "dog," which I don't know, and the meaning of *cat* is the manner of presenting the concept "cat," which I don't know either. What supports the belief that the two meanings are different? What individuates them? I sound as though I claimed to know two chemical formulas and said the first was H_2O and the second was H_2O too. People would object that on that showing I seemed to know only one. Now it would be fatal to any theory of meaning if it failed to explain how the meaning of *dog* and *cat* might be different.

Two ways exist to differentiate meanings. One is intrinsic, the other extrinsic. For example, H_2O and NaCl are different chemical formulae. They differ in the elements they specify and in the ratios of one element to another. Extrinsic differentiation serves when intrinsic is not available. For example, I can specify two distinct ladies by the expressions *Tom's* wife and *Harry's* wife, though I know nothing whatever of the ladies except their relations to Tom and Harry.

The meanings of *uncle* and *aunt* differ intrinsically. *Uncle* means "male sibling of parent"; *aunt* means "female sibling of parent." Each meaning is complex, of course, and designates a complex of concepts.[2]

The meanings of *dog* and *cat* cannot be differentiated intrinsically, but they can be extrinsically. The extrinsic bases for differentiation are the phenomena. Dog phenomena and cat phenomena are sufficiently distinct to indicate two different categories, each with its own name. Because the categories are distinct, each calls for its own intrinsically distinct concept. Meaning is the link between the phenomena and the concept. But the phenomena are the bases for differences at the levels of meaning and concept.

The phenomena on their own will scarcely do the work required of them. The phenomena are in the environment while meanings or their representations are in the head. To keep meanings in the head distinct requires something in the the head. It is convenient to appeal to the sensory tests that enable us to distinguish dogs from cats and to recognize which is which when we see one on its own.

What about the meaning of *animal,* though? We saw earlier that there are no sensory tests that distinguish animals from non-animals, so we need some other principle of individuation. That is not far to seek, however. "Animal" is a superordinate category that embraces dogs, cats, cows, worms, etc. "Animal" is differentiated from "plant" by the set of subordinate categories. It is not necessary to know all the subordinate categories of any superordinate term, but it is necessary to know some; otherwise there would be no reason to call it superordinate.

I will not go further into the difficult problem of individuation. In passing, though, note that the above principles help to explain some of Eleanor Rosch's findings. Her subjects found difficulty in

imagining creatures designated by superordiante terms like *animal,*
plant, and *musical instrument.* They had little difficulty imagining
a creature designated by subordinate terms, like *dog, rose,* and
guitar. This is exactly what one would predict on the basis of the
principles of individuation that have just been suggested for the
two sorts of meanings.[3]

EVALUATING THE THEORY

It will not surprise anyone that the theory of meaning that has
just been suggested satisfies the criteria we have drawn up. Nevertheless, it will help to go through those criteria briefly, the better
to grasp them and the theory of which they are the test.

The theory satisfies the first three negative criteria. We are not
conscious of meanings as we have described them. They are not
expressed in the language of the sensory array. They are not, for
example, images. They are not the rules for the use of the words
to which they are attached.

Meanings are distinct from all those theoretical entities from
which they should be distinct. Meanings are not referents, concepts, partial concepts, or collateral information. They are clearly
distinct from the force attached to sentences. That is, a single
sentence with a single meaning can be employed with different
forces (or in different speech acts).

Meanings as described also satisfy the different positive criteria.
Meanings rest squarely on publicly observable phenomena. Indeed
the meanings of subordinate category words are individuated on
the basis of differences among such phenomena. That is how they
relate to our ability to categorize objects in the perceptual field.
That is why skill in categorizing is a useful test of whether a person has grasped a meaning.

Because meanings rest on the publicly observable, we begin to
understand why they are the same for all members of a speech
community. I am fully aware, however, that at this point the
theory needs to be supplemented with some principles relating
to sensory tests. The discipline that studies them is called pattern
recognition. I do not intend to discuss it; I simply assume that
some perceptual principles must explain why we see dogs as
different from cats. The principles must be sharp enough to permit
of quite delicate distinctions, yet not so sharp as to impose un-
helpful distinctions. The sort of thing that has to be achieved can
best be illustrated. Let us suppose that owing to differences in
climate, dogs in the southern United States and in Canada were

generally different, though all were called dogs. One would want a southerner's sensory tests to accept Canadian dogs as dogs. Otherwise, by the present theory, the meaning of *dog* would differ from southerners to Canadians. Clearly that would be undesirable. So if the theory is to show how it would avoid that, it needs theories of pattern recognition that are at present unavailable. On the other hand the theory does not, so far as I am aware, run foul of any principles of pattern recognition that are at present available. But ultimately that is not enough.

The theory relates meaning and truth in such a manner as to satisfy the relevant criteria. Truth is not in general a key to meaning. It could only be such a key if we had knowledge of the relevant concept; and that we do not possess.

The link between meaning and truth is concept. A word like *dog* denotes a concept and it does so through its meaning. The concept is true of or false of the object that has been picked out by the subject of the sentence. That is the main way in which simple statements, such as *Freddie is a dog,* are true or false.

The link enables us to employ truth not as the key to meaning but as a test of a theory of meaning. The test rules out theories that either do not link meaning to truth or that lead one to infer a sentence is true when one knows intuitively that it is false. A frequently given example of a theory that is ruled out is any that makes four-legged part of the meaning of *dog.*

Our theory obviously permits the claim that the meaning of the word is the meaning of the object in the sense indicated earlier. The child who sees dogs and succeeds in identifying them from cats and birds attributes dog nature to dog phenomena. The nature thus hypothesized must be sufficient to exclude cat and bird phenomena, but it must permit of that variability to which dogs give rise. The obvious problems in pattern recognition remain unsolved. The important point is that the nature so hypothesized is the physical correlate of the concept. And the concept is primarily specified by an expression in what Fodor (1975) calls the language of mind. That mental expression can be formed before the child learns the word *dog.* And when he does learn the word, the mental expression is entered as the word's meaning. The theory, then, throws some light on how we can talk about the things we see, which was part of desideratum 16 and closely related to desideratum 17.

We see that our theory satisfies all the requirements that we listed for a theory of meaning. I know of nothing else that does.

Learning Meaning

Before attempting an account of learning, one negative! Quine's quality space, the innate propensity to attend to some sensory qualities rather than others, though useful for other purposes cannot be at the root of meaning. Indeed Quine would not wish it to be, inimical as he is to all talk of concepts and meaning. The qualities of which he speaks are sensory ones, and we have seen that meaning is not expressed in the language of sensation. I mention the point because I have frequently, in psychological discussion, heard appeal to Quine's quality space to account for meanings.

Two great principles of cognition are at work in the child as he learns meanings. One is the principle that every event has an adequate cause. Put psychologically, the principle expresses the belief that the world makes sense. For every event there is an adequate explanation. What exists objectively as a cause is represented in cognition by an explanation. Ultimately this all means that we expect the world to conform to our own principles of explanation. We do not need to go into the forms of explanation here. It is sufficient to note that the principle would give the child general specifications for concepts even when he could never hope to attain them in detail. That is what I mean, in describing concepts, by the expression "ideal explanation."

Another closely related principle of cognition is that differences in events are due to differences in underlying causes. The principle is at work in the psychologist's interpretation of chronometric studies. Differences between reaction times are attributed to differences between underlying processes. The principle guides the child's formation of meanings. Because cat phenomena are perceived as different from dog phenomena, they demand different explanations. They therefore demand different meanings to specify the appropriate explanations. Indeed the meanings are individuated by the phenomena, or rather by the sensory tests that identify the phenomena.

Each object belongs in many kinds: Freddie is a pal and male as well as a dog and an animal. How does the child know which of such kinds his parents mean when they say *dog*? Leave aside the problem of how to detect a proper name, because it is more easily solved, and in Chapter 2 we saw in principle how it is solved. A partial answer to the present question is probably a constraint imposed by the child himself. He interprets all common names as applying to the lowest species, the most constrained set of phenomena, that he has identified. So if he had distinguished animals, and among animals, dogs, he will at first take any name applied to a dog as appropriate for the lower level. That avoids confusion. If he makes a mistake and takes *animal* as a word for dog, he will soon find, to his surprise, that his parents use it for cats and cows, and so he abandons it. That seems to be his initial strategy for handling hierarchically related terms.

He learns the next highest term, *animal,* to refer to a group of living creatures that do not as a group fall under any lower level term. Having identified such creatures, he may have the meaning "animal" but not as attached to the word *animal.* Only later does he learn that *animal* can apply to individuals, and in Chapter 5 I suggested some situations that lead him to learn that—namely, all situations in which he hears *animal* used of individuals for whom he already knows a lower-level term.

That is how he learns related names. I suspect the formation of the corresponding meanings takes the opposite direction. The child sets out with the broad observation that some creatures move about of their own accord and others do not. That prompts him to begin the formation of the meaning "animal." Subsequently he notices divisions among these creatures. That prompts him to form meanings related to different types of life—"dog," "cow," "horse," and so forth.

The two-year-olds we studied seem not to have brought these two processes to completion. They had, if we judged them correctly, achieved the meaning "animal" and several of its subordinates. They had learned names for the species, *dog, sheep, horse,* etc., but applied *animal* only to a set consisting of many species of animal. But the meaning "animal" was there awaiting its appropriate symbol, *animal.*

How does the child handle hierarchies, like *dog* and *pal? Pal* is a relational term, so that someone can be a pal of Tom's and not of Dick's. A dog is a dog to everyone. That distinction will provide a clue to the meaning of many terms. Often the discourse area will provide a clue. A single object can be both a penny and copper. *Penny* relates it to the monetary system; *copper* relates it to the system of minerals. A child who can follow the general drift of a conversation may find that helpful in learning such names. But I will go no further with this, as it leads away from the concerns that have been central so far.

PART IV
IMPLICATIONS FOR LEARNING
AND COGNITION

13.
The General Judgment

I'm Alec Bings; I see through things. I can see whatever is inside, behind, around, covered by, or subsequent to anything else. In fact, the only thing I can't see is whatever happens to be right in front of my nose.
—*Norton Juster,* The Phantom Toll Booth

Because we have been concerned with issues, one after the other, the child has to some extent fallen out of focus. In this final chapter I will try to remedy that while drawing together the different issues. Here we shall review what it is about the child's mind that enables him to learn names for things, basing ourselves mainly on what we have seen but sometimes drawing attention to relevant aspects that were not at the center of earlier chapters. We will end with a discussion, promised in Chapter 1, of what all this reveals about the mind of the young child and about the nature of cognitive development.

Semantics

We made the intentional act of referring the basis on which reference is learned. Referring is a three-place predicate: a person uses a word to refer to an object. The child who learns a new name must coordinate all that. He must grasp that the teacher has used the name to refer to an object. I do not think he could learn the name without such a schema. He need not get it all right the first time; he might represent the sound inaccurately and misconstrue the object. But he must be trying to grasp the name and identify the object. Indeed if he is oblivious of any one of the three places of the predicate, it is not the predicate referring that he is tackling, because it is essentially three-place.

Speaker, word, and object do not guarantee that the connecting predicate is referring; they do not even guarantee a connecting predicate. However, I suggested that the infant has an intentional space, akin to Quine's quality space, and that it yields the reading, referring, in case the child hears an adult utter (for the child's benefit) a single word in the presence of a salient object for which he does not already know a name. Independently, I argued that referring is a unitary concept and should be taken as a primitive of cognitive psychology. This means that the child does not learn what referring is, nor does he learn to refer. His problem is to identify which events fall under his primitive concept, and, at least initially, the answer is given him by an ordering that favors the interpretation, referring, in certain circumstances.

No psychological theory of language learning, so far as I am aware, takes referring seriously, and that marks them gravely inadequate. Part of the reason for the neglect has been uneasiness with any notion that cannot be expressed as an association or system of associations. Moreover, psychology has been and still is stoutly positivist and reluctant to employ categories that cannot be defined in terms of sensory attributes. Now referring involves an observable act, but the act expresses an intention. I have proposed that the intention to refer is an explanatory construct; it forms part of the explanation of certain events. Such an intention always involves a purpose, that of referring to an object by means of a symbol. In claiming that a child naturally interprets certain events as acts of referring, I am claiming that he imposes on the observable event the explanation—carried out for the purpose of picking out an object in attention. That in turn implies that he has a mind that deals in those categories and relations.

Reference is a property of certain symbols, one they acquire from acts of referring. What the child needs is the ability to detect which words do the work of referring and attribute to them the permanent capacity to refer that is reference.

Objects played a prominent part in our discussion of referring, because objects are what names refer to. We decided that the notion "object" is really a prosortal, a substitute for a sortal term, like *dog* or *chair*. We continued to use the word *object* as shorthand for "that to which a sortal can primarily be applied." We decided that objects are not equal to a cluster of attributes. Object is a commonsense construct. The word *same* applies to it in a sense that it does not apply to attributes. We can ask is this the *same* dog as we saw yesterday? The dog's shape, however, can change continually. We cannot, then, coherently ask if his shape today is the *same* as his shape yesterday in the sense we can ask about the dog. Shape does not have identity of being over time as dogs do.

Attributes are individuated in terms of objects. The coherence of a set of attributes over time and local motion is explained in terms of the continued existence of the objects they belong to. Actions, too, are individuated in terms of objects, and attributed causally to them. The general notion of an object is not abstracted from the sensory array but imposed upon it. The general notion seems to be unlearned, since it informs all experience. It specifies the semantic work that more precise sortals (*dog* or *chair*) will perform.

A major part of the semantic work that sortals must perform is to explain our intuition that a sentence that employs a sortal in predicate position is true or false. When I say *Freddie is a dog,* by Freddie I pick out a physical object. The predicate claims that "dog" is true of that object. If the predicate is true of the object referred to, the sentence is true; otherwise it is false. In the expectation of truth or falsity there is implicit the belief that *is a dog* invokes a precise description, indeed a set of necessary and sufficient conditions for something to be a dog. Now, Hilary Putnam has pointed out that we do not know necessary and sufficient conditions for membership in most natural kinds. However, it does not follow that we do not know the meanings of natural-kind terms—not if we take meaning as Fregean sense. A concept of dog specifies an explanatory set of necessary and sufficient conditions for being a dog. The meaning of *dog* does not supply them; the meaning helps to denote them by ensuring that a predicate picks out a concept precisely as an explanation. Through its relation with concept, meaning caters for truth and falsity.

Theoretically, several sets of necessary and sufficient conditions are possible for membership in a category. We suggested that concept be identified with the set that has maximum explanatory power. By a set of conditions with such explanatory power is meant the set that, ideally, is invoked to explain the largest number of phenomena related to a category and the set that established the maximum of relations with explanations of other categories. Though the description contains the word explanation which

forms part of that which is to be described, the description is intuitively informative. Ultimately, *explanation* must itself be grounded in principles of cognition, for an adequate explanation is one
that satisfies one's power of understanding.

In proposing meaning as Fregean sense and taking concept as
ideal explanation, I am identifying meaning with a stage in the
process of understanding. I also suggested a single semantic space
for language and the perception of objects. Indeed I suggested
that word and object have a single meaning. This suggests that
we explore the possibility that meaning is a level of interpretation
common to the processing of speech and the processing of perceptual information. Not that the same processes give us meaning
when we listen to speech and when we perceptually examine
objects; but the product is the same.

As a child learns meanings, he simultaneously learns collateral
information and partial concepts. In the first category go all
details of information that are not necessarily connected with
the truth of a sortal predicate. This includes common stereotypes,
such as that dogs are four-legged and canaries are yellow. Since a
three-legged dog is not a contradiction in terms (as is a married
bachelor), "four-legged" is not part of the meaning of *dog*. Clearly
most of what one knows about categories is collateral information.

Partial concepts are more closely related to truth. They are a
person's attempts to achieve concepts, where concepts are ideal
explanations. Concepts are intimately related to truth, and truth
is a test of partial concepts. Our present belief is that H_2O expresses
the concept of water. We test whether it does or not by testing
whether all that we want to call water is H_2O. That is, we test the
truth of the characterization H_2O.

The more numerous the theoretical distinctions, the more
complex the interactions, and somehow children are forgotten
in the whole thing. Yet all the theoretical entities and processes
I am proposing are seen as functioning in children's minds. Meaning, as I see it, is never for the child a set of sensory tests for category membership. Truth and falsehood are the same for children
and adults. Meaning makes the same contribution to truth value
for both. Children have the same ideals of understanding as adults.
They attempt to set up sensory tests for category membership of
the same type as adults. They perform the same types of intentional acts. They accumulate the same types of collateral information.

Sortals, too, are sometimes arranged hierarchically and then their application is regulated by the logical quantifiers *all* and *some*. We saw in Chapter 4 that the well known empirical evidence against the command of those quantifiers in children under six is extremely dubious. We saw some new evidence and some old that certainly three-year-olds comply with the logic of those quantifiers in their use of heirarchically related sortals.

It is forced upon us by this that quite young children command the essentials of the quantified logic of predicates. They do not, of course, know it as a logician knows it, but it is implicit in their categorizing. This, as far as we could see, was true of even two-year-olds, though not always true of their language.

All of this leads to the conclusion that the child has a language of mind, distinct from the language of the sensory array, which is regulated by at least certain parts of logic. Because we dealt only with the most elementary types of names, the logic of relations and the logic of propositions did not arise. We did not go into such terms as *brother* and *father,* so we cannot say anything about the logic to which they relate. And because we did not concentrate on propositions, we cannot say anything about the child's grasp of propositional logic. In another study (Macnamara, 1977b), however, I did explore four-year-olds' ability to draw inferences from propositions, and found that they had at their disposal a powerful propositional logic.

Propositions themselves, as distinct from propositional logic, seemed to cause even the youngest two-year-olds no problem. When we asked them, *Is that an animal?* (pointing) they seemed to understand us and said such things as, *No, it's a dog.* This means that they were able to bring reference and sense into that coordination that we call a proposition. In other words they coordinated the relations, reference, and, true of, in judgment. Like referring, judging is a three-place predicate: a person judges a predicate true of an object. The meaningful learning of common nouns presupposes the capacity to form such judgements.

Linguistics

In Chapter 6, we studied the acuity of the infants' hearing and discussed two problems: how he establishes the phonology of his language and how he segments utterances into words. We say that the problem of identifying which words are which is as formidable as the task of forming categories of objects. That undermined the popular conception, expressed among others by Merleau-Ponty, that common names are the means whereby the child learns cate-

gories of objects. One might as easily argue, and sometimes more
persuasively, that the child's grasp of categories gives him the clue
to important phonological rules. Just as we posit an innate quality
space to sort out categories of objects, we suggested a phonological
similarity metric to regulate the child's construction of phonology.
We suggested the metric when discussing how the child's grasp
of meaning might help with phonology; we were trying to explain
why he does not always attempt to relate, phonologically, words
that have the same meaning. It might also have occurred to us if
we had discussed the role of syntax in the learning of phonology,
because ultimately certain phonological rules refer to syntax. We
did not discuss syntax in this connection, because the scope of the
book ruled out all but the most elementary syntactic considerations.

   In Chapters 7 and 8 we have a long discussion of how children
learn that certain words are nouns. We came to the conclusion that
nature fits the child out with a set of semantic rules that provide
him with a useful sorting of morphological rules and phrase structures. In particular, we concluded that the child's grasp of sortals,
as opposed to attribute words and action descriptions, guides his
early learning of morphology and his early word combinations.
Exactly the same semantic properties that are involved in the intelligent use of sortals, then, guide the formation of the category,
noun. Ultimately the child must replace the initial semantically
based object category with a linguistic one, noun, individuated in
terms of the morphology and phrase structure of his native language.

   Meaning, too, we saw, plays an important part in the learning
of the subdivisions of noun: proper noun (versus common), mass
noun, count noun, and classifier noun type (closely related to
number of salient dimensions). Meaning probably plays a lesser
part in the learning of gender, although even there it probably
guides the child to expect the gender of articles and adjectives
to be governed by that of the noun rather than the other way
about. He represents attributes as dependent on objects, not the
other way about. We also discussed the role of semantics in the
learning of the plural, and of the articles *a* and *the*. In the learning
of the personal pronouns *I* and *you,* we saw the role of both
semantics and of discourse constraints.

   The general strategy was to seek out semantic clues to linguistic
regularities, but that is in no way to detract from the linguistic
acuity of the child. All the semantic clues in the world will not

ultimately yield the rules of phonology or the grammatical categories to which words belong. The child must actively compare, contrast, and arrange his linguistic material with great linguistic skill. Likewise he must by linguistic acuity construct the linguistic rules for forming and using the plural, and for employing the articles appropriately. Indeed I hold an unusually strong version of the thesis that linguistics is independent of semantics. Not only do I believe that linguistic rules should be stated without reference to semantics; I believe that they cannot, generally, be expressed in semantic terms. I mention this merely to guard against the possible charge that I am attempting to explain all linguistic learning in terms of meaning.

Structure of Child Intelligence

At the end of the first chapter there was a promise to review our analysis of learning names to see if it would answer the question, is a child's intelligence structurally equivalent to an adult's? The standard position in psychology is that the two are formally quite different. That is either implicit or explicit in most of the writing I have seen on cognitive development, whether by Piaget and his school or by others. Some exceptions that come to mind are Donaldson (1977), Fodor (1975), and Macnamara (1976b, 1978).

To begin with, the argument that the standard position is more parsimonious is spurious. If the child while learning about the world is also building the mind whereby he knows the world, not only is he in a paradoxical position, but he must be endowed by nature with a program powerful enough to build a mind as a function of experience. That is, he would need to have a mental program whose function it was to construct or restructure mind on the basis of cognitive experience. We simply have no way of knowing whether it is more parsimonious for nature to build into us such a program or to fit us out with a finished mind.

One must not expect an apodictic argument for either side of a discussion so general as that about whether mind comes ready-made or has to be constructed on the job. Strategically, however, the position that it comes ready-made should be adopted. That the mind is ready-made is the null hypothesis: there is no structural difference between the adult and infant mind; therefore, the researcher's task is to reject the hypothesis. That is standard procedure in science and indeed in pyschology. For the rest I am not at all convinced by the evidence so far produced that this null hypothesis is false, and this book has argued for far more mental structure and far more logical capacity in infants than the field generally allows.

The relevant findings were listed in the early part of this chapter, so we can be brief here. Learning to use names meaningfully involves the three-place predicate of referring, with all that implies. To deal with the simplest proposition involves another many-place predicate, judging true of. The proposition, if it contains a referring term, can be grasped only by one who can coordinate both predicates. And the entire proposition is itself evaluated as true or false. To ensure that the young child could manage all this, we had to equip him with several innate conceptual categories, several innate principles, and several innate evaluative devices. The business of constructing meanings, we concluded, strongly resembles part of the process of theory building in science. Moreover, there seems to be ample evidence that three-year-olds, and probably even two-year-olds, are governed in their categorization by the quantificational logic of *all* and *some*.

We are able to defend the young child against a charge of egocentricity à la Piaget—that is, the charge that unlike adults he is unable mentally to take the position of another person. The whole of language learning is taking another person's position; it is finding out what words and expressions mean to another person. The learning of the personal pronouns and of the use of *a* and *the* yield particularly telling evidence against the charge.

Other cognitive conclusions that come from the study of language lie outside the scope of this essay, since they involve propositional inferences. In Macnamara, Baker, & Olson (1976) and in Macnamara (1977b) there is extensive evidence that four-year-olds apply in the interpretation of ordinary language a propositional logic of great power. An attempt is there made to characterize the logic. This undermines the well-entrenched theory, attributed to Inhelder and Piaget (1958), that children cannot employ abstract logic before the age of about twelve. To be fair, Inhelder and Piaget probably mean something different by their "formal logic" than we mean by abstract logic. They seem to mean a logic whose formal structure can be consciously manipulated. If that is what they mean, I fear their claim is senseless, because there is no evidence I am aware of that anyone but a student of logic is able to reflect on such a structure (see Braine, 1978). In any event, I am happy to rest with the claim that four-year-olds (and by unpublished evidence three-year-olds) interpret sentences in accordance with a surprisingly power-ful logic.

On the linguistic side we were obliged to allow the infant not only great auditory acuity, but the capacity to divine the pho-nology of his language. That included an innate similarity metric for sounds. We were also obliged to fit him out with an innate capacity to distinguish objects in the environment (and actions and attributes, etc.) and use them as the basis for setting up a semantic category of object words (as opposed to action words, attribute words, etc.). This category provides him with a sorting of morphological endings and phrase-structure roles that will eventually define the linguistic notion, noun. I know of no theory in psycholinguistics that is the counterpart of Piaget's in cognitive psychology; no psycholinguist, so far as I know, has concluded that the child constructs the linguistic equipment of his mind as he learns his language. To be sure, he learns the words and gram-matical structures of the language; but always in terms of, and by means of, innate categories and processing principles powerful enough to construct his entire language. That looks like a tautol-ogy, and I believe it is one; but it has not always been seen as one.

In McGill one is continually reminded that there is extensive neural development well after the age that has most concerned us, perhaps until the age of twelve. Further, one is reminded that this development is to some considerable degree conditional upon sensory stimulation. While I do not doubt this, I do doubt that the import of such development for cognitive psychology has been sketched even in broad outline. We simply do not know what types of logical reasoning or perceptual categorization are ruled out in the four-year-old for lack of myelination, for example. On the other hand, one expects learning to involve some changes in the brain. So we have no way at present of evaluating the relevance of the observations of developmental neuroanatomy for whether the mind's structure changes after birth.

But further, even if we did know the relevance of neural devel-opment it would still be extraneous to the description of develop-ment from the standpoint of cognitive psychology. Just as it is no part of cognitive psychology to explain how messages in the DNA lead to the construction of a brain and a sensory system in the foetus, it is no part of cognitive psychology to explain the con-tinuation of that construction after birth. Similarly, all develop-ment that is attributed to the control of the genes depends on en-vironmental factors, some of great complexity. It is therefore to be expected that the development of neural tissue should depend on such factors, including the impact of stimulation. Nevertheless, it does not follow that such matters should form an integral part of cognitive psychology. The stage of neural development might place boundary conditions on cognitive psychology. Developmental neuroanatomy might, for example, state that before the age of six the child is generally incapable of calculus. However, the changes that give him the basic capacity to understand calculus, insofar as they could be attributed to prearranged development of neural connections rather than to the learning of arithmetic or the gaining of mathematical insight, are not thereby an intrinsic part of cognitive psychology.

We should be quite clear about what this means. What I have said is no argument for dualism (that is, the doctrine that mind transcends matter, particularly brain matter). It is merely the observation that even if all mind events are brain events, it does not follow that the discipline of cognitive psychology reduces in principle to physiological psychology; any more than the categories of furniture reduce to physics, though every article of furniture consists of physical things. However, this is academic in relation to the main point of this section. We simply do not know if the stages of neural development after birth place boundary conditions on cognitive functioning.

To return to the main point, I know of no evidence that the minds of children and adults differ structurally. In this book we have seen considerable evidence that even to learn names for things, a modest part of what the very young child learns even in language, they must be structurally equivalent. That, together with the strategic wisdom of taking two mysteries as one (the null hypothesis) commends the conclusion that they are equivalent.

Appendix 1

Diary data on Kieran Macnamara's use of first and second person pronouns before end of 21st month. (See Chapter 3.)

Age in
Months and Days

15:19	*me* of photo of himself, pointing to himself.
15:27	pointed to himself and said *me*.
16:9	game of *mine*.
16:15	*mine/mine; my* paper/*mine*.
16:22	*you* → *me*.
16:26	*mine* (of toes): pointing *me/me*.
16:30	*me/me; mine/mine*.
	Understand *you* and *Kieran*.
17:1	*me/me* → *mine/mine*—similarity.
17:3	*me/me* → *me/*yes *you* → pointed and said Kieran.
17:4	Who's that? pointing—*me*. *Your* and *yours*.
17:10	*me/me/ /me/you; me/Kieran*—delight.
17:12	shadow—*me; mine*.
17:13	Where's Kieran? → *me* pointing.
17:15	pointed to this thigh (not chest) and said *me*.
17:17	called Joyce *me*. Who's Mommy?/points to Joyce.
	Who's me?/points to self.

Age in
Months and Days

17:18	distinguishes between *give me X* and *give Mommy X*. Understand *me*.
17:18	Who's that? of photo → *me;* we said yes *you*.
17:21	*I see you/I see you* (possessives beginning 19 April)
17:22	Who's that?—in mirror—*me*. Real self—*me*.
17:24	Who's that?—pointing to him; *me* and Who's that? pointing to self. *Dad*.
18:8	*Thank you*.
18:17	*He fly*.
18:22	Is it you? *You*. Show me *my* hand—correct Show me *your* hand—correct.
18:25	*See you!*
18:27	*I kick it*.
19:4	Is that you? *You*. Photo. Kieran. Taking over. Joyce: Who do you love? *You* (?)
19:6	Who is that? *Kieran*. Whose is that? *Kieran's*. *Cam* = carry me.
19:13	*Fall Kieran*.
19:15	*I love you/I love Freddie*.
19:17	You did?/*I did*. *See you* (Martha, George, Anne). *I throw it*.
19:18	*I see kitten*.
19:19	*I singing: I Kieran; I see moon*.
19:20	*I coughing; you coughing*. (Razor *shave*—17 June)
19:22	*Thank you Dad; Thank you Mommy*.
19:28	*You're a girl*.
19:29	*My book, my feet; your glasses, your book*.
20:1	*Wear my shoe: my knees, See me*.
20:2	*My glasses; my pencil*.
20:5	*I see Teddy. I going do it*.
20:8	*I give F. cereal*.
20:9	*I like have cheese. Have Kieran*.
20:10	*K's blanket*.
20:11	*Your juice. My juice*.
20:12	*I don't know*.

Appendix 2

Responses given by individual children to the questions: *Is this a toy? Is this an animal?* (see chapter 5).

Note: If one type of response was given on more than one trial by a particular child, the number in parentheses following that reply indicates on how many trials it was given. Replies not followed by numbers were given once by that child.

Subject	Is this a toy?	Is this an animal?
1	Toy. (3) Train. No.	Animal. (2) Duck. Pig. No.
2	Yeah. (5) No, a doll. No, Rupert.	Yeah. (10) No, Fido. Bad wolf.
3	Yeah. (8)	Yeah. No, (*specific*). (5) e.g., No, a pig. No. (2)
4	Yeah. (7) Toy.	Yeah. (5)

Subject	Is this a toy?	Is this an animal?
5	No, (specific). (2) Yes. (2) It's a toy.	No, (specific). (4) No.
6	Specific name only— train, phone, etc. (3)	No, (specific). (5) Monkey.
7	Yeah. (12) No, it's (specific). (3)	Yeah. (5) No. No, that's (specific). (4) Specific name only—kangeroo, etc. (3)
8	No, that's (specific). (7) No. Yep.	No, (specific). (6) Yep.
9	Yeah. (8)	Yeah. (12) Nope, a (specific). (2)
10	Specific name only— shovel, boat, etc. (5)	Animal. Specific name only—dog, etc. (3)
11	Yeah. (7) No.	Yeah. (4) No, that's (specific). (3)
12	Specific name only—boat, etc. (5) No, (specific). (2) No. Yes.	No, (specific). (3) No. Ducks.
13	No. (4) No, (specific). (2) Specific name only—house, etc. (2) Toy. (3)	Specific name only—monkey, etc. (4) Animal. (4)
14	Yeah. (2) No. (2) No, (specific). (3) Toy.	Yeah. (6) No. No, (specific). (4) Big one.
15	Yes. (5) No, it's a spoon.	Yes. (8) No, it's a lion.
16	Toy. (5) Yeah. No.	Animal. (5) Cat, animal. Tiger, animal. Rabbit.

Subject	Is this a toy?	Is this an animal?
17	Yeah. (6) No, (specific). (2)	Yeah. (5)
18	No. (10)	No. (3) No, horsie. That animal. (3) Animal. A pussy cat. (2)
19	No, (specific). (4) No.	Yes. (3) Animal. No, wow-wow. No, horse.
20	Yeah. (3) No, (specific). (5)	Yeah. (3) No, doggie. Amal-horsie. Cow-amal. Amal-alligator.
21	Yeah. (3) No, (specific). (2)	UmHumm. (yes) (3) No, (specific). (5)
22	Yeah. (6)	Yeah. (5)
23	Yeah. (7)	Yeah. (4) No, it's a bunny.
24	No, (specific). (5) Yeah.	No, (specific). (9) It's a horsie. Yeah.
25	No, (specific). (3) Yeah. (5)	Yeah. (4) No, (specific). (2) No.
26	Yeah. (3) No. No, (specific). (7) Truck.	Yeah (or Yep). (6) No, (specific). (3) Nope. (5)
27	No, they're my block. No. Gun-toy. Yeah. (2) That's a fire-engine. That's a snow-plow.	Animal. (4) Yeah. That elephant. Elephant. (Specific)-animal. (2) No, gerbil.

Subject	Is this a toy?	Is this an animal?
28	No, (*specific*). (12) Yeah. (3)	No, (*specific*). (7) No. Yeah. (2)

Appendix 3

Words and word combinations used by Kieran Macnamara before the end of his 21st month (See Chapters 8 and 9).

WORDS LEARNED IN FIRST 19 MONTHS
KIERAN MACNAMARA

Modifiers

all
allgone
big
clean
cold
dirty
dry
gone
good
happy
hot
other
pretty
tight
two
wet

Exclamations

boo!
byebye!
c'est beau!
go way!
hi!
how d'you do!
I see you!
in a minute!
listen!
Oh boy!
Oh gosh!
Oh my!
OK!
pew!
please!
quick!

right back!
see!
see you!
tata!
thank you!

Animal Noises

bow wow
cock-a-doodle-doo
kiki (cat)
moo
oink oink (pig)
oo, oo (owl)

Action Demands

again (repeat)
carry

down

nana (general)

off (clothes)

see

thank you (take)

this (I want)

up

walk

want

Action Descriptions

barking

bel_2 (exp)

cooking

coughing

crying

cut

dancing

eats

fall

fly

flying

kick

mine (I take)?

peepee (?)

playing

rain (?)

raining (?)

run

running

shave (event)

sing

singing

sits

sleep (?)

sleeping (?)

sneezing

tickle

winking

yawn

yawning

Proper Names

Amy

Alex

Betsy

Boo

Dad (da)

Freddie

John

Joyce

Judy

Lisa

Lucas

Mammy

Max

Memere

Niki

Noah

Pepere

Robert

Teddy

Terri

Wonako

Common Names

airplane

alligator

ant

anteater

apple

applejuice

ark

arm

baboon

baby

ball

balloon

ban (exp)

banana

bath

bear

bee

bel_1 (exp)

belly

bell

bicycle

bird

boat

bone

book

boot

bosom

bottle

boy

bread

breakfast

bucket

buckle

buggie

bull

bunny

bus

butterfly

button

cake

cards

carrot

castle

chair

cheek

cheese

chick

chicken

clown

cock

comb

combing (comb)

cone

cookie

cork

cow

crab

cracker

crocodile

deer

dog

door

duck

ear

earring

egg

elbow

elephant

eye

eyebrows

farmer
feet(s)
fence
fish
flower
flute
food(?)
fork
friend
frog
garbage
giraffe
girl
glasses
goat
grape
grapefruit
grass
gun
hair
hand
hat
he
head
hedgehog
hen
him
home (?)
honey
horn
horsie
horses
geese
jacket
juice
key
kids
knife
koala
lady
leaf

leg
light
lion
man
me
medicine
men
mess
mice
milk
mitten
monkey
moose
mother
mouse
mouth
muscle
music
nail
nappy
nest
noise
nose
olive
onion
orange juice
owl
pants
paper
pear
peepee
pepper
phone
picture
pig
pin
plane
plant
puddle
puppy
pupu (feces)

ring
rock
rooster
school
sheep
shirt
shoes
sky (?)
soap
sock
spagetti
spoon
squirrel
stick
stone
sweater
swing
tail
taxi
tea
teeth
thumb
tie
tiger
tire
toe
tomato
tongue
tractor
tree
truck
turtle
vicuna
watch (timepiece)
water
whale
whiskers
window
wine
yak
yogurt

WORDS LEARNED IN 20TH MONTH
KIERAN MACNAMARA

Modifiers

all done
all wet
bad
best
broken
crazy
dead
dry
fat
finished
fresh
my
new
nice
no more
old
open
our

Exclamations

bang bang!
by gum!
careful!
enough!
faker!
goodnight!
great!
messer!
my God!
my goodness me!
Oh dear!
ouch!
sorry!
stink!
stop it!
watch it!
why!

Locatives

here
here's
in there
there
top
up in

Miscellaneous

and
for
has (possession)
how many?
like (resemble)
no (neg. answer)
too (intensive)
too (also)
yes

Action Demands

clean
come
come here
come on
fix it
get down (put me
   down)
hug
kiss
look
more
read
smile
surprise (show)
this one (give me)

Action Descriptions

break
burp
catch
cough
drink
drinking
drip
drying
find
fun
funny } (laughing)?
hugging
jumping
kissing
laughing
like (eats)
lives (?)
made
out (come)?
play (music)
push
pushing
reading
ride
rub
rubbing
sat down
sit down
sneeze
swims
swings
talking
throw
walking
want(s)
washing
wear
whistling
writing

Proper names

Anne
Cara
Catherine
Doug
Eileen
Elise
George
Grammy
I

I feel (name of song)
Jesus
Kieran
Lena
Marianne
Martha
Monique
Moon
Nat
Nini
Peggy Anne
Ray
Robbie
Sarah
Steve
Tom

Common Names

animal
another one (yogurt)
bathroom (tub)
bed
beer
blanket
bobo
bug
bugles
butter
calf
celery
cereal
cherries
coconut
coffee
corn

cover
dandelion
deer
drum
eggplant
elevator
face
fesso (buttocks)
flag(s)
flour
forehead
fox
garbage truck
goof
higher (ramp)
him
hippo (potamus)
hole
house
ice
icecream
iced tea
iron
it
kite(s)
leg(s)
lunch
meat
mellon
mess
mole (on skin)
money
muscle
mushroom
nailbrush
name

noise
nut
one(s) (pronoun)
peaches
peacock
pen
pencil
people
pet
pickles
piece of
plum
rainbow
records
rubber
sailboats
sand
sandal
seat
shave (razor)
shorts (pants)
slide
sloth (animal)
some
tennis (raquet)
thunder
toothbrush
toothpaste
treats
tunnel
umbrella
work (?)
worm
you

21ST MONTH—NEW WORDS
KIERAN MACNAMARA

Modifiers

awful
dangerous
different
empty
his

last
like (resemble)
terrible
three
tiny
tired
warm

Exclamations

be soft!
careful!
goodbye!
hallo!
hate you!

hold tight!
how are you!
I don't know!
Let go!
No thanks!
Oh no!
peekaboo!
right here!
that's it!

Action demands

close
don't touch
get out of
hop in
let me do
like (want)
no like (stop)
put
put on
take off

Action descriptions

bang
biting
bringing
changing
comb
combing
cutting
flush
gave
get
give
going to (?)
got
good time (laughing)?
happened (?)
have
helping

hiding
loves
make
making
open
pulling
rock
shake
sit
shaving
smiling
stretching
touch
write

Locatives

back
down
in
on
outside

Miscellaneous

no + verb (don't)
not me (to me)

Proper names

Barry
Big bird
Carol
Macnamara (?)
Ride-a-cock-horse
Rock-abye baby
RoseMarie

Common names

bagle
belly button

bite (piece)
booger (nasal discharge)
box
breadknife
candles
chocolate milk
clock
cork
corkscrew
dragon
dress
eyelash
helicopter
jam
lamp
leash
lemon
lip
mint
moss
mountain
necklace
nightie
peanut butter
periwinkle
pillow
raincoat
razor
rocking chair
rope
sandwich
seaweed
seashell
shell
spider
stairs
steamshovel
steps
towel
wave(s)

WORD COMBINATIONS UP TO END OF 19TH MONTH
KIERAN MACNAMARA

15:10 *This is X*
16:21 *Pretty baby*
16:26 *See X*
  a X
  allgone, all clean, all dirty.
16:27 *Hot tea*
16:29 *See a car. See a bus.*
17:2 *See crying*
17:5 *Big bus. Big belly. See John.*
17:8 *See tree. See truck.*
17:15 *This is the puppy.*
17:21 *I see you.*

17:24 *The other shoe.*
18:13 *Bad boy.*
18:16 *Mammy's.* General rule—
   proper name + *s*
18:17 *He fly*
18:21 *Judy friend.* General rule—
   proper name + *friend*
   Don't want. I will
8:22 *Kiss him.*
18:25 *Eat the grass*
18:27 *Freddie barking. Him crying.*
   I kick it.

WORD COMBINATIONS IN 20TH MONTH
KIERAN MACNAMARA

Rule 1. Proper name ⎫
    Personal pronoun ⎬ + Action description ± *ing*

    Ko crying   *I singing*   *Seed drop*
    Old Mammy crying *I coughing* *Coconut drop*
    Dad talking   *You coughing* *I did*
    Reverse order of root words: *Washing Dad. Fall K. Fall Freddie*

Rule 2. Action description ± determiner ± object word.

    Kick the ball *Like it*   *Made noise*
    Find a shoe   *Catch you* *Pushing car* (note *ing*)
    Find the shoe *Catch ball* *Hug* (hugging puppy)
    Find the moon *Kick ball*
    Wear my shoe *Saw X*

Rule 3. Proper name ⎫   ⎧object word
    Personal pronoun ⎬ ± Action description ± ⎨pronoun

    I find shoe *I see kitten* *Kieran water* (spilt)
    I find it   *I see moon* *Kieran pen* (take)
    I throw it *He wants it*

Rule 4.   ⎧determiner + object word
    Action demand + ⎨   pronoun

    See the kites *See a moon*
    See the ball   *See me*
    Look the watch *See them*
    Read the book   *Cut it*

Rule 5. Modifier + {Proper name / Object word}

Best dog	*Dead horse*	*Other dog*
Good boy	*Baby sheep?*	*Other George*
Bad boy	*Baby bird?*	*Another cup*
Good cake	*Two boots*	Doubtful:
Good chair	*Two horses*	*Friend Amy*
Old Mammy	*Two balls*	*Friend Robbie*
Old Freddie	*Two lights*	*Catherine friend*
Old puppy	*Three feet*	Reverse order:
New truck	*Other feets*	*Mammy great*
New teeth	*Other bosom*	*Freddie great*
Dry ones	*Other fesso*	*Daddy great*
Fat pig	*(buttocks)*	*Buckle open*
Nice hat	*Other ins*	

Rule 6. Pronoun ± copula + {determiner + proper name / object word}

It's a car	I Kieran
It's a cover	That's Mammy
You're a girl	

Rule 7. Possessive pronoun ± {proper name / object word}

Our car	*My knees*	*My Dad*
Our dog	*Our Mammy*	*My Mammy*
My ball	*Our Freddie*	
My shoe	*Our Kieran*	

Rule 8. Proper name ± 's + {object word / proper name}

Nat's bed	*Dad cake*	*Ko's Mammy*
Freddie's nose	*Dad book*	*Peggy Anne's Daddy*
Dad's sandal	*Freddie hair*	*Peggy Anne Daddy*
Anne's fishies	*Mammy keys*	
Freddie ball	*Freddie ice cream*	

Rule 9. Locatives (no rule suggested)

Spaghetti here	*Here's a boy*	*In there*
More spaghetti here	*Up in sky*	*Water bucket* (on)
Here Freddie	*Out tunnel* (of)	*Raining car* (on)
Come here Freddie	*Honey top* (on)	

Rule 10.   Object word ± *for* + proper name

        Medicine Freddie   *Water Freddie*
        Medicine Mammy   *Kisses for Mammy*

Rule 11.   Negative particle ± object word

      No pencil   *No airplanes*   *Allgone some*
      No book   *Allgone money*   *No more*

PRINCIPLE WORD COMBINATIONS IN 21st MONTH
KIERAN MACNAMARA

Rule 1.   Proper name ⎫
          Object word ⎬ + Action description ± *ing*
          Pronoun   ⎭

		Reverse order:
Freddie coughing	*I shaving*	*Sleeping Mammy*
Freddie crying	*Bee flying*	*Crying Robbie*
Tina singing	*Bird flying*	*Running Kieran*
Baby hiding	*Other blanket*	*Walk Freddie*
Dad coming	*coming*	*Walk Granny*
Mammy walking	*Granny cough*	*Have Kieran*
Dad shaving	*Dad drink*	

Rule 2.   Proper name ⎫
          Pronoun   ⎬ + Action description ± determiner ±
                   ⎭ {object word⎫
                            {pronoun ⎬ ± Indirect object pronoun

		Additional:
I find it	*Mammy get the*	*I like get down*
I get the cereal	*juice*	*I like to get down*
I like have cheese	*Mammy get orange*	*Changing the*
I find it	*juice*	*nappies*
I find the key	*Mammy make the*	*Cutting the hair*
I see the eye	*coffee*	*Pulling the boy*
I see the ear	*Freddie loves you*	*Making noise*
I find the comb	*Dad is reading*	*Making a sand-*
I find the juice	*book*	*wich*
I like it	*Dad fix the music*	*Likes it egg*
I got the ball	*(gramophone)*	*Hate you*
I drink it	*Freddie likes it*	*Cut's Freddies*
I shake it	*Mammy gave me*	*toes*
I write it	*that*	
I find a train	*Mammy gave it you*	
I get a shoe	*Mammy gave*	
I want a bagel	*Kieran that*	
I going do it	*Mémère gave you*	

Rule 3.   Imperative (no rule suggested)

Kiss froggie	*Fix it truck*	*Make Freddie cry*
Close the door	*Clean it jacket*	*Put on on me*
Play the flute	*Clean it thumb*	*Let me do it*
Throw the ball	*Drop it pencil*	*Hop in Rose Marie*
Clear the boogers	*Wants it*	*Hop in Freddie*
Fix this	*Put it back*	*Pants change*
Read the book	*Take it off*	*No sing*
Clean the hand	*Flush it*	

Rule 4.   determiner + modifier $\left.\begin{array}{l} \text{determiner + modifier} \\ \text{numeral} \\ \text{(an)other} \end{array}\right\}$ + object word

a nice hat	*two towel*	*other Mamie*
a dead bee	*two cows*	*other George*
a big garbage truck	*two lips*	*other tiny baby*
terrible flies	*two pedal*	*another booger*
green car	*two wings*	Additional:
tiny baby	*three cows*	*nice and cool*
big dragon	*three candles*	*nice and easy*
dirty boy	*other cereal*	
last bite	*other bee*	

Rule 5. $\left.\begin{array}{l} \text{Proper name} \\ \text{Pronoun} \\ \text{Nominal} \\ \pm \text{ determiner + object word} \\ \pm \text{ modifier + object word} \end{array}\right\}$ $\pm$ copula $\pm$ *not* + modifier

Feet not wet	*That's different*	Additional:
This shell broken	*They're not wet*	*This is Kieran*
Our car gone	*I'm tired*	
Freddie warm	*Biting bad*	

Rule 6. $\left.\begin{array}{l} \text{Proper name} \pm s \\ \text{Pronoun} \end{array}\right\}$ + $\left\{\begin{array}{l} \text{proper name} \\ \text{object word} \end{array}\right.$

My glasses	*Kieran's toothbrush*	*Jesus Mother*
My pencil	*Dad's nightie*	*Granny neck*
My blanket	*Dad's shirt*	*Daddy neck*
My juice	*Mammy's bobo*	Reverse order:
His nose	*Freddie's toes*	*Flute Daddy*
His ball	*Mammy dress*	*Pencil Daddy*
Our car	*Freddie blanket*	*Toothbrush Daddy*
Tom's car	*Mammy iced tea*	*Toothbrush Kieran*
Kieran's blanket	*Dad blanket*	
Puppy's eyebrows	*Peggy Anne Daddy*	

Rule 7.   Locatives

Sleep on bosom	*Mammy in the bath-*	*Sleeping Teddy* (on)
Squirrel on tree	*room*	*On shirt*
Like a boat on	*Peepee in the pot*	*On pants*
water	*Peepee in there*	*Put on on me*
Tooth paste on it	*Running water* (in)	*Freddie outside*
Sand muscle (on)	*Sit up bed* (in/on)	*Put it back*
Egg head (on)	*Get up*	*Peggy Anne bus*
Bee our car (on)	*Sit down bed* (in/	(in)
In the mouth	on)	*Puppy bed* (in)
Nuts in this	*Sit down pants* (on)	*Our car there*
I sit in Pepere's	*Sit down shirt* (on)	*That's one there*
chair	*Downstairs*	*Dad sleep here*

Rule 8.   ± Object word ± *for* + $\begin{cases} \text{proper name} \\ \text{modifier + object word} \end{cases}$

Keys for our car	*Banana Kieran*	Reverse order:
For Kieran	*Breakfast Kieran*	*Freddie medicine*
For Dad	*Truck Kieran*	
Milk Kieran	*Water Kieran*	

Rule 9.   Expressions in which *like* (verb) or *like* (adjective) occur.

Verb	Adjective
No like it	*Like Freddie*
I like have cheese	*Puppy's eyebrows—like you*
I like get down	*Like a crab* (pair of pincers)
Freddie likes it	*Like an airplane* (sound)
Likes it, egg.	*Like an airplane* (wheel)
	Like a boat (piece of iron)
	Like a boat on water (dress)
	Like a garbage truck (wheel)
	Like a helicopter (rotating search light)

References

Ajdukiewicz, K. (1969) Three concepts of definition. In T. O. Olshensky ed., *Problems in the philosophy of language.* New York: Holt, Rinehart, and Winston, 1969, pp. 288–299.

Anderson, J. R. (1976) *Language, memory and thought.* Hillsdale, N.J.: Lawrence Erlbaum, 1976.

Anglin, J. M. (1977). *Word, object, and conceptual development.* New York: Norton, 1977.

Anscombe, G. E. M. (1958). *Intention.* Oxford: Basil Blackwell, 1958.

Aristotle. (1941). *Metaphysics.* In R. McKeon, ed., *Basic works of Aristotle,* New York: Random House, 1941.

Bellugi, U., and Brown, R., eds. (1964). The acquisition of language. *Monographs of the Society for Research in Child Development,* 1964, Serial No. 29.

Berko, J. (1958). The child's learning of English morphology. *Word,* 14, 1958, 150–177.

Bloom, L., Lightbown, P., and Hood, L. (1975). Structure and variation in child language. *Monographs of the Society for Research in Child Development,* 1975, 40, Serial No. 160.

Bowerman, M. (1973a). *Early syntactic development: A cross-linguistic study with special reference to Finnish.* Cambridge University Press, 1973.

Bowerman, M. (1973b). Structural relations in children's utterances. in T. E.

Moore, ed., *Cognitive development and the acquistition of language.* New York: Academic, 1973.

Bowerman, M. (1976). Semantic factors in the acquisition of rules for word use and sentence construction. In D. Morehead and A. Morehead, eds., *Directions in normal and deficient child language.* Baltimore: University Park Press, 1976.

Bowerman, M. (1978a). Semantic and syntactic development: A review of what, when, and how in language acquisition. In R. L. Schiefelbusch, ed., *Bases of language intervention,* Vol. 1. Baltimore: University Park Press, 1978, pp. 97–189.

Bowerman, M. (1978b). The acquisition of word meaning. In N. Waterson and C. Snow, eds., *Development of communication: Social and pragmatic factors in language acquisition.* New York: Wiley, 1978.

Bowerman, M. Reorganizational processes in lexical and syntactic development. In L. Gleitman and E. Wanner, eds., *Language acquisition: The state of the art.* Cambridge University Press, in press.

Braine, M. D. S. (1963). On learning the grammatical order of words. *Psychological Review,* 1963, *70,* 323–348.

Braine, M. D. S. (1976). Children's first word combinations. *Monographs of the Society for Research in Child Development,* 1976, *41,* Serial No. 164.

Braine, M. D. S. (1978). On the relation between the natural logic of reasoning and standard logic. *Psychological Review,* 1978, *85,* 1–21.

Bresnan, J. The representation of grammatical relations in syntactic theory. In J. Bresnan, ed., *The mental representation of grammatical relations.* Cambridge: MIT Press, in press, a.

Bresnan, J. A theory of lexical rules and representations. In J. Bresnan, ed., *The mental representation of grammatical relations.* Cambridge: MIT Press, in press, b.

Brown, R. (1957). Linguistic determinism and the part of speech. *Journal of Abnormal and Social Psychology,* 1957, *55,* 1–5.

Brown, R. (1958a). *Words and things.* New York: Free Press of Glencoe, 1958.

Brown, R. (1958b). How shall a thing be called? *Psychological Review,* 1958, *65,* 14–21.

Brown, R. (1973). *A first language: The early stages.* Cambridge: Harvard University Press, 1973.

Brown, R., Fraser, C., and Bellugi, U. (1964). Explorations in grammar evaluation. In U. Bellugi and R. Brown, eds., *The acquisition of language.* Monograph of the Society for Research in Child Development, 1964, Serial No. 29, pp. 79–92.

Carey, S. (1978). Productive thinking in preschool children. Unpublished paper, M.I.T., Department of Psychology, 1978.

Carnap, R. (1959). Psychology in physical language. *Erkenntnis,* 1932/33, *3.* English translation by Max Black in A. J. Ayer, ed., *Logical Positivism.* New York: Free Press, 1959.

Carnap, R. (1932/33). Über Protokollsätze. *Erkenntnis*, 1932/33, *3*.

Carroll, J. B., Davies, P., and Richman, B. (1971). *The American Heritage word frequency book*. Boston: Houghton Mifflin, 1971.

Cassirer, E. (1953). *Substance and function*. New York: Dover, 1953.

Clark, E. V. (1973). What's in a word? On the child's acquisition of semantics in his first language. In T. E. Moore, ed., *Cognitive development and the acquisition of language*. New York: Academic, 1973, pp. 65–110.

Clark, E. V. (1974). Some aspects of the conceptual basis for first language acquisition. In R. L. Schiefelbusch and L. L. Lloyd, eds., *Language perspectives—Acquisition, retardation and intervention*. Baltimore, Md.: University Park Press, 1974, pp. 105–128.

Clark, E. V. (1975). Knowledge, context, and strategy in the acquisition of meaning. In D. Plato, ed., *Georgetown University round table on languages and linguistics, 1975*. Washington, D.C.: Georgetown University Press, 1975.

Clark, E. V. (1977). Strategies and the mapping problem in first language acquisition. In J. Macnamara, ed., *Language learning and thought*. New York: Academic, 1977.

Cole, R. A., and Jakimik, J. (1978). Understanding speech: How words are heard. In G. Underwood, ed., *Strategies of information processing*. New York: Academic, 1978.

Corballis, M. C., and Beale, I. L. (1976). *The psychology of left and right*. Hillsdale, N.J.: Lawrence Erlbaum, 1976.

Denny, J. P. (1976). What are noun classifiers good for? Paper from the Twelfth Regional Meeting of the Chicago Linguistic Society, Chicago: Chicago Linguistic Society, 1976.

Denny, J. P. (1979). The "extendedness" variable in classifier semantics. In M. Mathiot, ed., *Boas, Sapir and Whorf revisited*. An issue of the *International Journal of the Sociology of Language*. The Hague: Mouton, 1979, 97–119.

Denny, N. W. (1972). Free classification in preschool children. *Child Development*, 1972, *43*, 1161–1170.

Derwing, B. L. and Baker, W. J. (1977). The psychological basis for morphological rules. In J. Macnamara, ed., *Language learning and thought*. New York: Academic, 1977, pp. 85–110.

deVilliers, P. A., and deVilliers, J. G. (1974). On this, that, and the other: Nonegocentrism in very young children. *Journal of Experimental Child Psychology*, 1974, *18*, 438–447.

Donaldson, M. (1977). *Children's minds*. London: Fontana, 1977.

Donaldson, M., and Wales, R. (1970). On the acquisition of some relational terms. In J. R. Hayes, ed., *Cognition and the development of language*. New York: Wiley, 1970, pp. 235–268.

Dummett, M. A. E. (1973). *Frege: Philosophy of language*. London: Duckworth, 1973.

Dummett, M. A. E. (1978). What is a theory of meaning? (11). In G. Evans and J. McDowell, eds., *Essays in semantics*. Oxford: Clarendon, 1978.

258   REFERENCES

Eilers, R., and Minifie, F. (1975). Fricative discrimination in early infancy. *Journal of Speech and Hearing Research*, 1975, *18*, 158-167.
Eimas, P. D., Siqueland, E. R., Jusczyk, P., and Vigorito, J. (1971). Speech perception in infants. *Science*, 1971, *171*, 302-306.

Ferguson, C. A. (1977). Words and sounds in early language acquisition. Papers and Reports on Child Language Development, Department of Linguistics, Stanford University, 1977.
Field, H. (1972). Tarski's theory of truth. *Journal of Philosophy*, 1972, *69*, 347-375.
Fishman, J. A. (1960). A systematization of the Whorfian hypothesis. *Behavioral Science*, 1960, *5*, 232-239.
Fodor, J. A. (1975). *The language of thought*. New York: Crowell, 1975.
Fodor, J. A., Fodor, J. D., and Garrett, M. (1975). The psychological unreality of semantic representations. *Linguistic Inquiry*, 1975, *6*, 515-531.
Fodor, J. D. (1977). *Semantics: Theories of meaning in generative grammar*. New York: Crowell, 1977.
Ford, W. G. (1976). *The language of disjunction*. Unpublished Ph.D. thesis, Department of education Theory, University of Toronto, 1976.
Fraiberg, S., and Adelson, E. (1973). Self-representation in language and play: Observations of blind children. *Psychoanalytic Quarterly*, 1973, *42*, 539-562.
Franks, J. J., and Bransford, J. D. (1971). Abstraction of visual patterns. *Journal of Experimental Psychology*, 1971, *90*, 65-74.
Frege, G. (1960). On sense and reference. First published in 1892—published in English translation in P. Geach and M. Black, *Philosophical writings of Gottlob Frege*. Oxford: Blackwell, 1960.
Frege, G. (1960). *Grundgesetze der Arithmetik, begriffsschiftlich abgeleitet*. Jena, 1893, Vol. 1. Partial translation in P. Geach and M. Black, translators, *Translations from the philosophical writings of Gottlob Frege* (2nd edition). Oxford: Blackwell, 1960.
Frege, G. (1968). The thought. First published in 1918—published in translation in G. Iseminger, ed., *Logic and philosophy: Selected readings.* New York: Appleton–Century–Crofts, 1968.
Friedrick, P. (1970). Shape in grammar. *Language*, 1970, *46*, 379-407.

Gardner, B. T., and Gardner, R. A. (1971). Two-way communication with an infant chimpanzee. In A. M. Schrier and F. Stollnitz, eds., *Behavior of non-human patients*. New York: Academic, 1971, pp. 117-184.
Gazdar, G. (1979). *Pragmatics: Implicature, presupposition, and logical form*. New York: Academic, 1979.
Geach, P. T. (1962). *Reference and generality*. Ithaca, N.Y.: Cornell University Press, 1962.
Geach, P. T. (1972). *Logic matters*. University of California Press, 1972.
Gibson, J. J. (1979). *The ecological approach to visual perception*. Boston: Houghton Mifflin, 1979.

Gleason, H. A. (1965). *Linguistics and English grammar.* New York: Holt, Rinehart, and Winston, 1965.

Glucksberg, S., Hay, A., and Danks, J. H. (1976). Words in utterance contexts: Young children do not confuse the meanings of *same* and *different.* *Child Development,* 1976, *47,* 734-741.

Goodman, N. (1951). *The structure of appearance.* Cambridge: Harvard University Press, 1951.

Goodman, N. (1972). *Problems and projects.* New York: Bobbs-Merrill, 1972.

Gruber, J. S. (1973). Correlations between the syntactic constraints on the child and the adult. In C. A. Ferguson and D. I. Slobin eds., *Studies of child language development.* New York: Holt, Rinehart, and Winston, 1973, pp. 440-444.

Gupta, A. K. (1980). *The logic of common nouns.* New Haven: Yale University Press, 1980.

Harris, Z. S. (1955). From phoneme to morpheme. *Language,* 1955, *31,* 190-222.

Hayes, J. R., and Clark, H. H. (1970). Experiments on the segmentation of an artificial speech analogue. In J. R. Hayes, ed., *Cognition and the development of language.* New York: Wiley, 1970, pp. 221-234.

Hintikka, J. (1975). Behavioral criteria of radical translation. In D. Davidson and J. Hintikka, eds., *Words and objections* (Revised edition). Dordrecht: D. Reidel, 1975, pp. 69-81.

Hockett, C. F. (1958). *A course in modern linguistics.* New York: Macmillan, 1958.

Hockett, C. F. (1963). The problem of universals in language. In J. H. Greenberg, ed., *Universals of language.* Cambridge: MIT Press, 1963.

Hoffman, M. (1968). Child language. Master's thesis, Department of Psychology, Mcgill University, 1968.

Hurford, J. T. (1974). Exclusive or inclusive disjunction. *Foundations of Language,* 1974, *11,* 409-411.

Huttenlocher, J. (1974). The origins of language comprehension. In R. L. Solso, ed., *Theories in cognitive psychology.* Potomac, Md.: Earlbaum, 1974.

Huxley, R. (1970). The development of the correct use of subject personal pronouns in two children. In G. Flores d'Arcais and W. J. M. Levelt, eds., *Advances in Psycholinguistics.* Amsterdam: North Holland, 1970.

Inhelder, B., and Piaget, J. (1958). *The growth of logical thinking from childhood to adolescence.* New York: Basic Books, 1958.

Inhelder, B., and Piaget, J. (1964). *The early growth of logic in the child.* London: Routledge and Kegan Paul, 1964.

Jackendoff, R. (1977). $\bar{X}$ *Syntax: A study of phrase structure.* Linguistic Inquiry Monograph No. 2, 1977.

Jusczyk, P. W. (1980). Infant speech perception. In P. D. Eimas and J. L

Miller, eds., *Perspectives on the study of speech.* Hillsdale, N.J.: Lawrence Erlbaum, 1980.

Kanner, L. (1943). Autistic disturbances of affective control. *Nervous Child,* 1943, *2,* 217-250.

Katz, N., Baker, E., and Macnamara, J. (1974). What's in a name? A study of how children learn common and proper names. *Child Development,* 1974, *45,* 469-473.

Kintsch, W. (1977). *Memory and cognition* (2nd edition). New York: Wiley, 1977.

Kiparsky, P. and Menn, L. (1977). On the acquisition of phonology. In J. Macnamara, ed., *Language learning and thought.* New York: Academic, 1977. pp. 47-78.

Kripke, S. (1977). Speaker's reference and semantic reference. *Midwest Studies in Philosophy,* 1977, *11,* 255-276.

Kučera, H., and Francis, W. N. (1967). *Computational analysis of present-day American English.* Providence, R.I.: Brown University Press, 1967.

Kuczaj, S. A. (1978). Why do children fail to overgeneralize the progressive inflection? *Journal of Child Language,* 1978, *5,* 167-171.

Labov, W., and Labov, T. (1974). The grammar of *cat* and *mamma.* Paper presented at the 49th Annual Meeting of the Linguistic Society of America, New York, N.Y., 1974.

Laurendeau, M., and Pinard, A. (1962). *Causal thinking in the child.* New York: International Universities Press, 1962.

Lindsay, P. H., and Norman, D. A. (1972). *Human information processing.* New York: Academic, 1972.

Luria, A. R. and Yudovich, F. *Speech and the development of mental processes in the child.* London: Staples, 1959.

Macnamara, J. (1976). Stomachs assimilate and accommodate, don't they? *Canadian Psychological Review,* 1976, *17,* 167-173.

Macnamara, J. (1977a). From sign to language. In J. Macnamara, ed., *Language learning and thought.* New York: Academic, 1977, pp. 11-35.

Macnamara, J. (1977b). Children's command of the logic of conversation. In J. Macnamara, ed., *Language learning and thought.* New York: Academic, 1977, pp. 261-288.

Macnamara, J. (1978). Another unaccommodating look at Piaget. *Canadian Psychological Review,* 1978, *19,* 78-81.

Macnamara, J. (1981). Physical objects: The relation between philosophy and psychology. *Canadian Psychologist,* 1981, *22,* 271-281.

Macnamara, J., Baker, E. and Olson, C. L. (1976). Four-year-old's understanding of *pretend, forget* and *know:* Evidence for propositional operations. *Child Development,* 1976, *47,* 62-70.

Macnamara, J., and Niall, K. *Visual perception.* Unpublished manuscript, Department of Psychology, McGill University.

Maratsos, M. P. (1976). *The use of definite and indefinite reference in young children.* Cambridge University Press, 1976.

Maratsos, M. (1979). How to get from words to sentences. In D. Aaronson and R. W. Rieber, eds. *Psycholinguistic research: Implications and applications.* Hillsdale, N.J.: Lawrence Erlbaum, 1979, pp. 285-353.

Maratsos, M. and Chalkley, M. A. (1980). The internal language of children's syntax: The ontogenesis and representation of syntactic categories. In K. Nelson, ed., *Children's language* Vol. 2. New York: Gardner, 1980.

Markman, E. M. (1979). Classes and collections: Conceptual organization and numerical ability. *Cognitive Psychology,* 1979, *11,* 395-411.

Markman, E. M., and Seibert, J. (1976). Classes and collections: Internal organization and resulting holistic properties. *Cognitive Psychology,* 1976, *8,* 561-577.

McCarthy, D. A. (1954). Language development in children. In L. Carmichael, ed., *Manual of child psychology.* New York: Wiley, 1954, pp. 492-630.

McNeill, D. (1963). The psychology of *you* and *I.* Paper presented at the American Psychological Association Symposium on Child Language, 1963.

Menn, L. (1976). Pattern, control, and contrast in beginning speech: A case study in the development of word form and word function. Unpublished Ph.D. thesis, Department of Linguistics, University of Illinois at Urbana-Champaign, 1976.

Merleau-Ponty, M. (1963). *The structure of behavior.* Boston: Beacon, 1963.

Miller, G. A. (1977). *Spontaneous apprentices.* New York: Seabury, 1977.

Miller, G. A. and Johnson-Laird, P. N. (1976). *Language and perception.* Cambridge: Harvard University Press, 1976.

Miller, W., and Ervin, S. (1964). The development of grammar in child language. In U. Bellugi and R. Brown, eds., The acquisition of language. *Monographs of the Society for Research in Child Development,* 1964, No. 29, pp. 9-34.

Morris, C. *Signs, language and behavior.* (1946). Englewood Cliffs, N.J.: Prentice-Hall, 1946.

Neisser, U. (1976). *Cognition and reality.* San Francisco: W. H. Freeman, 1976.

Nelson, K. (1972). Semantic structures of the earliest lexicons. Paper delivered to the Eastern Psychological Association, Boston, 1972.

Nelson, K. (1973a). Some evidence for the cognitive primacy of categorization and its functional primacy. *Merrill-Palmer Quarterly,* 1973, *19,* 21-39.

Nelson, K. (1973b). Structure and strategy in learning to talk. *Monographs of the Society for Research in Child Development,* 1973, *38,* (1-2, serial number 149).

Nelson, K. (1974). Concept, word and sentence: Interrelations in acquisition and development. *Psychological Review,* 1974, *81,* 267-285.

Nelson, K. (1976). Some attributes of adjectives used by young children. *Cognition,* 1976, *4,* 13-30.

Nelson, K. (1977). The conceptual basis for naming. In J. Macnamara, ed., *Language learning and thought.* New York: Academic, 1977.

Olson, D. R. (1970). Language and thought: Aspects of a cognitive theory of semantics. *Psychological Review,* 1970, *77,* 257–273.

O'Mahony, B. (1965). The medieval treatise on modes of meaning. *Philosophical Studies* (Ireland), 1965, *14,* 117–138.

Osgood, C. E. (1953). *Method and theory in experimental psychology.* New York: Oxford University Press, 1953.

Perry, J. (1977). Frege on demonstratives. *Philosophical Review,* 1977, *86,* 474–497.

Piaget, J. (1926). *La représentation du monde chez l'enfant.* Paris: Alcan, 1926.

Piaget, J. (1929) *The child's conception of the world.* London: Routledge and Kegan Paul, 1929.

Piaget, J. (1964). *La formation du symbole chez l'enfant: Imitation, jeu et rêve, image et représentation* (3rd edition). Neuchâtel: Delachaux et Niestlé, 1964.

Posner, M. I. (1973). *Cognition: An introduction.* Glenview, Ill.: Scott, Foresman, 1973.

Premack, D. (1976). *Intelligence in ape and man.* Hillsdale, N.J.: Lawrence Erlbaum, 1976.

Putnam, H. (1975a). The meaning of "meaning." In K. Gunderson, ed., *Language, mind and knowledge.* Minnesota studies in the philosophy of science. Minneapolis: University of Minnesota Press, 1975.

Putnam, H. (1975b). Language and reality. Reprinted in H. Putnam, ed., *Mind, language and reality.* Cambridge University Press, 1975.

Putnam. H. (1978). *Meaning and the moral sciences.* London: Routledge and Kegan Paul, 1978.

Quillian, R. M. (1967). Word concepts: A theory and simulation of some basic semantic capabilities. *Behavioural Science,* 1967, *12,* 410–430.

Quillian, R. M. (1968). Semantic memory. In M. Minsky, ed., *Semantic information processing.* Cambridge: MIT Press, 1968, pp. 216–270.

Quillian, R. M. (1969) The teachable language comprehender: A simulation program and theory of language. *Communications of the ACH,* 1969, *12,* 459–476.

Quine, W. V. (1960). *Word and object.* New York: Wiley, 1960.

Quine, W. V. (1969). *Ontological relativity and other essays.* New York: Columbia University Press, 1969.

Quine, W. V. (1975). Replies. In D. Davidson and J. Hintikka, eds., *Words and objections.* (Revised edition). Dordrecht: D. Reidel, 1975, pp. 292–352.

Ricciuti, H. N. (1965). Object grouping and selective ordering behavior in infants 12-24 months old. *Merrill Palmer Quarterly*, 1965, *11*, 129-148.

Rinsland, H. D. (1945). *A basic vocabulary of elementary school children.* New York: Macmillan, 1945.

Rosch, E. (1973). On the internal structure of perceptual and semantic categories. In T. E. Moore, ed,. *Cognitive development and the acquisition of language.* New York: Academic, 1973, pp. 112-144.

Rosch, E. (1975). Universals and cultural specifics in human categorization. In R. Breslin, S. Bochner, and W. Lonner, eds., *Cross-cultural perspectives on learning.* New York: Sage/Halsted, 1975.

Rosch, E. (1977). Human Categorization. In N. Warren, ed., *Advances in cross-cultural psychology.* London: Academic, 1977.

Rosch, E,. Mervis, C. B., Gray, W. D., Johnson, D. H., and Boyes-Braem, P. (1976). Basic objects in natural categories. *Cognitive Psychology*, 1976, *8*, 382-439.

Saltz, E. (1971). *The cognitive basis of human learning.* Homewood, Ill.: Dorsey, 1971.

Sankoff, D. (1978). *Linguistic variation: Models and methods.* New York: Academic, 1978.

Schlesinger, H. S., and Meadow, K. P. (1972). *Sound and sign.* Berkeley, University of California Press, 1972.

Schlesinger, I. M. (1974). Relational concepts underlying language. In R. L. Schiefelbusch and L. L. Lloyd, eds., *Language perspectives: Acquistion, retardation, and invention.* Baltimore: University Park Press, 1974.

Schlesinger, I. M. (1977). *Production and comprehension of utterances.* Hillsdale, N.J.: Lawrence Erlbaum, 1977.

Searle, J. R. (1969). *Speech acts: An essay in the philosophy of language.* Cambridge University Press, 1969.

Skinner, B. F. (1957). *Verbal behavior.* New York: Appleton-Century-Crofts, 1957.

Smith, E. E., Shoben, E. J., and Rips, L. J. (1974). Structure and process in semantic memory: A featural model of semantic decisions. *Pyschological Review*, 1974, *81*, 214-241.

Snow, C. E. (1976). Mothers' speech to children. In W. von Raddler-Engel and Y. LeBrun, eds., *Baby talk and infant speech.* Amsterdam: Swets and Zeitlinger, 1976.

Stevenson, C. L. (1944). *Ethics and language.* New Haven: Yale University Press, 1944.

Strawson, P. F. (1959). *Individuals.* London: Methuen, 1959.

Strayer, J. (1977). The development of personal reference in the language of two-year-olds. Unpublished Ph.D. thesis, Department of Psychology, Simon Fraser University, 1977.

Streeter, L. (1976). Language perception of 2-month-old infants show effects of both innate mechanisms and experience. *Nature*, 1976, *259*, 39-41.

Stross, B. (1969). Language acquisition by Tenejopa Tzeltal children. Unpublished Ph. D. Thesis, University of California, Berkeley, Language-Behavior Research Laboratory, 1969.

Talmy, L. (1978). The relation of grammars to cognition: A synopsis. In D. Waitz, ed., *Theoretical issues in natural language processing*, 1978, Vol. 2.

Tarski, A. (1956). *Logic, semantics and mathematics.* Oxford University Press, 1956.

Taylor, C. (1964). *The explanation of behaviour.* London: Routledge and Kegan Paul, 1964.

Thorndike, E. L., and Lorge, I. (1944) *The teacher's word book of 30,000 words.* New York: Bureau of Publications, Teachers College, Columbia University, 1944.

Trehub, S. E. (1976). The discrimination of foreign speech contrasts by infants and adults. *Child Development,* 1976, *47,* 466–472.

Trehub, S. E., and Rabinovitch, M. S. (1972). Auditory-linguistic sensitivity in early infancy. *Developmental Psychology,* 1972, *6,* 74–77.

Trentman, J. A. (1973). Speculative grammar and transformational grammar: A comparison of philosophical presuppositions. In H. Parret, ed., *History of linguistic thought and contemporary linguistics.* The Hague: Mouton, 1973.

Tucker, G. R., Lambert, W. E., and Rigault, A. A. (1977). *The French speaker's skill with grammatical gender: An example of rule governed behavior.* The Hague: Mouton, 1977.

Vygotsky, L. S. (1962). *Thought and language.* Cambridge: MIT Press, 1962.

Wargny, N. (1976). Cognitive aspects of language learning in infants: What two-year-olds understand of proper, common and superordinate nouns. Unpublished Ph.D. thesis, Department of Psychology, McGill University, 1976.

White, N. P. (1976). *Plato on knowledge and reality.* Indianapolis: Hackett, 1976.

Wiggins, D. *Identity and spatio-temporal continuity.* Oxford: Basil Blackwell, 1967.

Winner, E. New names for old things. Unpublished paper, Department of Psychology and Social Relations, Harvard, 1978.

Wright, G. Von. (1971). *The logic of preference.* Ithaca, N.Y., Cornell University Press, 1971.

Notes

CHAPTER 4. THINGS HAVE MORE THAN ONE NAME

1. It is interesting that several linguists mark such expressions as *John is an American or a Californian* as badly formed, precisely because Californians are Americans (see Hurford, 1974, and Gazdar, 1979, p. 81). Gazdar formulates a rule that has the general effect of saying that two predicates can be conjoined by *or* only if they are potentially exclusive of one another.

CHAPTER 5. WHAT IS A GORGON?

1. The hypothesis was suggested to us by Anne Entus.

CHAPTER 7. NOUNS AS NAMES

1. One might consider the alternative, of a (small) proper subset of syntactic properties that is common to nouns in all languages that have nouns. It is difficult to imagine what such a subset might be, and I have not seen detailed proposals. Among the problems of working out such a subset would be that of determining, in some principled fashion, which languages have nouns. Even if that problem were surmounted, there would remain the difficulty of stating the subset in terms that are neutral with respect to particular languages. Suppose, for example, someone were to propose as a universal feature

that a noun could always be the grammatical subject of the main verb. How do we define grammatical subject of the main verb? If we were to follow one standard move, we might try defining it as the syntactic head of the noun phrase immediately dominated by S (the initial symbol). But now we have begged one question, by introducing the term noun phrase, and it includes the word we are attempting to define. And we have introduced a second problem: how do we define head of a noun phrase and how do we decide that the syntactic notion of head is the same for all languages?

I do not say that this alternative could not work; only that it needs a vast amount of investigation before one could begin to judge its plausibility. The stance taken in the text is that the notion, noun, varies from language to language; what is innate is mainly a set of semantic rules that enables the child to learn the notion for his language. Implicit in this way of thinking is the idea that while grammatical categories may show family resemblances across languages, the number of possible categories is infinite. That does not preclude the existence of strong linguistic constraints on what can be a grammatical category (and that, I think, despite her terminology, is all that Bresnan (in press, a and b) is proposing. There are very strong constraints on what can be an ordinal number, strong enough to exclude everything that is not an ordinal number. Yet there are infinitely many ordinals.

The alternative mentioned in this note does not remove the necessity of endowing the child with the capacity for infinite learning related to grammatical categories. A small defining subset of syntactic features for the notion noun might be either innate or learned without recourse to infinite capacity. Clearly, however, the child cannot make do with just such a defining subset. He needs to know the entire set of syntactic properties belonging to the notion noun in his language. In general that will not be equal to the defining subset. And while there are probably strong constraints on what these additional syntactic properties might be, there is no reason to doubt that their number is infinite.

CHAPTER 8. NAMES AS NOUNS

1. Although the account in the text seems attractive, the distinction between mass and count nouns, insofar as it rests on semantic grounds, probably demands a more basic analysis. Before one can count things, they must be discriminable one from another and they must retain their identity over time, at least until the count is finished.

But such identity is not enough to differentiate mass from count, because both are associated with a principle of identity. It makes just as good sense to speak of the same gold as of the same dog. It looks as if the difference between the two types of words must attach to discriminability.

Discriminability itself, I believe, presupposes the notion of differentiation among objects; and if the objects are to be counted, there must be a basic similarity among those objects. We make a single count of sheep and goats only when we note some such similarity as that they are all animals. To capture this complex notion of differentiation of things that are similar, we talk of token and type. It seems that counting presupposes the individuation of a type in such a way as to result in several tokens or exemplars of the type.

Consider now water—impurities aside. The relevant fact about water is that when a body of water is divided into two smaller bodies, each is water, in a way that the division of a cat does not lead to two cats. Moreover, each body of water, to untutored experience, divides innumerably into smaller bodies, each of which is water. It seems unlikely that only a single token is involved, since each subdivision exemplifies the type water. But where does token begin and end in such stuff? The refusal to apply quantifiers to water as such seems to reflect the failure of untutored experience to answer that question satisfactorily. It reflects the stance that one can count only tokens that one can discriminate. The molecular theory of water is, I believe, profoundly satisfying to the human mind. It explains why subdivisions of water are water, until one reaches the level of the molecule. It also tells us that the tokens of the type, water, are molecules.

Obviously much more needs to be said about this topic, extending the discussion to attributes, to invisible objects like electrons, to possible objects like the children one might have had, and the like. But I believe the foregoing will provide the basis for the extension. It will not, of course, help with the distinction between mass and count insofar as it is basically linguistic. It will not help to explain why *furniture* in English is mass while *meuble*, its nearest French equivalent, is count. Perhaps what we have in mass nouns, after all, is something similar to nouns. Noun is a linguistic category with semantic induction conditions. Perhaps the mass/count distinction is likewise linguistic. But even if it is, it retains a closer affinity than noun does with its semantic induction rules.

CHAPTER 11. REFERENCE, NAMES, AND OBJECTS

1. Issues and problems related to how reference works have a knack of leaping on one unexpectedly. The theory of reference sketched here is far from complete and will no doubt have to be revised, but it is the best I know of at present. It derives, with some extensions, from the writings of Peter Geach. A better theory is almost certain to be more subtle and more complicated, rather than less. At all events, the theory I present enables us to raise questions of what the child must learn in connection with reference and what he must bring to the learning. The study of reference should go hand-in-hand with the study of how children come to master it. Hitherto they have proceeded as though they had nothing to do with one another. This has been detrimental to both.

2. Standard logical notation seems to muffle the business of reference. The standard reading of *dogs are carnivorous* is $(\forall x)(Dx \rightarrow Cx)$, where $D = is\ a$ *dog* and $C = is\ carnivorous$. That places *dog* in logically the same position as *carnivorous;* neither is in referring position. So the entire expression fails to refer. It would refer if proper names were substituted for x. It follows that

the logical expression is only potentially referring. I have a strong intuition that *dogs* in the original sentence refers to each and every dog. The sentence says in effect that *is carnivorous* is true of each and every dog.

Note that Frege's suggestion to take predicates as referring to concepts does nothing for us. The concept DOG is certainly not carnivorous.

3. More formally, Tarski's hints about defining reference come to this. We set up a criterion of the adequacy of our definition as follows.

Criterion R: $(\forall x)$ (Refers $(\alpha, x) \longleftrightarrow a$ is x)

where for α we must supply a structural description of a name—say a name in quotation marks; and for a we supply the same name without quotation marks. We also form a sequence of the objects to be named, and x_i will designate an object uniquely through the object's position in the sequence. We can now give the definition itself.

Definition: Refers $(\alpha, x_i) \longleftrightarrow (\exists S)$ (Sequence S & satisfies $(\ulcorner x_i = a \urcorner, S)$ & the value of S at i is x_i).

As explained in the text, satisfies is interpreted as: in accord with the semantics that have been specified. It is important to note that the expression in Quine's corner quotes, $\ulcorner x_i = a \urcorner$, is not itself a sentential function (or schema), but the structural description of one. The nearest I can come in ordinary English to the function it specifies is: the ith object and α are identical, just as Samuel Clemens and Mark Twain are identical.

I have been greatly aided in my understanding of these issues by Anil Gupta, though the formulation of them is my own.

4. Wiggins (1967) discusses many hard cases that arise in connection with the individuation of objects and their identity through time. Such difficulties include the fact that the set of molecules that make up a man's body (or a dog's for that matter) may be different from the set that made it up ten years ago. Yet he is the same man (or same dog). Such problems are notoriously troublesome, yet they do not destroy our common-sense faith in the existence of such things as men which do retain their identity through all sorts of changes. Moreover, few such problems arise in the child's acceptance and employment of the belief.

CHAPTER 12. MEANING

1. Praise the young and they will improve.

2. This point is by way of comment on an interesting suggestion made by Fodor (1975) and Fodor, Fodor, and Garrett (1975) to the effect that a word's meaning is an unanalyzed monad. The suggestion comes from a discussion of semantic feature accounts of word meaning. I agree with the rejection of such accounts. Nevertheless, meanings may still be seen as complex at a far more abstract level. Meaning, as we now conceive it, is the manner in which a concept is designated. Then, since the phenomena to be explained by a concept are usually complex, the meaning which connects the two will naturally represent the complexity of the phenomena.

3. One problem in the individuation of meaning that may occur to readers

of Nelson Goodman (1949, 1972) relates to mythological creatures like centaur and unicorn. The basis for the query is that since these creatures do not
exist, one may scruple to allow that we have sensory tests that distinguish
them. On the account of meaning that is being offered, absence of sensory
tests would be an embarrassment. No sensory tests, no individuation of the
meanings of subordinate terms, like *centaur* and *unicorn*! Goodman, however,
shows the way out. Centaur and unicorn phenomena are quite distinct, whether as shown in pictures or in stories. They differ in appearance and behavior.
To tell them apart we need sensory tests. So if one is otherwise disposed to
accept meaning as here presented, one need have no qualms occasioned by
mythological beasts.

Index

DATE DUE